Writing Black Panther

BLACK LITERARY AND CULTURAL EXPRESSIONS

Bloomsbury's **Black Literary and Cultural Expressions** series provides a much-needed space for exploring dimensions of Black creativity as its local expressions in literature, music, film, art, and so on, interface with the global circulation of culture. From contemporary and historical perspectives, and through a multidisciplinary lens, works in this series critically analyze the provenance, genres, aesthetics, intersections, and modes of circulation of works of Black cultural expression and production.

Series Editors

Toyin Falola and Abimbola A. Adelakun, University of Texas at Austin, USA

Advisory Board

Nadia Anwar, University of Management and Technology, Lahore, Pakistan

Adriaan van Klinken, University of Leeds, UK

Alain Lawo-Sukam, Texas A&M University, USA

Nathaniel S. Murrell, University of North Carolina, Wilmington, USA

Mukoma wa Ngugi, Cornell University, USA

Bode Omojola, Mount Holyoke and the Five College Consortium, USA

Nduka Otiono, Carleton University, Canada

Bola Sotunsa, Babcock University, Nigeria

Nathan Suhr-Sytsma, Emory University, USA

Volumes in the Series:

Wole Soyinka: Literature, Activism, and African Transformation
by Bola Dauda and Toyin Falola

Social Ethics and Governance in Contemporary African Writing: Literature, Philosophy, and the Nigerian World by Nimi Wariboko

The Birth of Breaking: Hip Hop History from the Floor Up
by Serouj "Midus" Aprahamian

Literature of the Somali Diaspora: Space, Language and Resistance in Somali Anglophone and Italian Novels by Marco Medugno

The Decolonizing Work of Jessica Huntley: The Political Roots of a Radical Black Activist by Claudia Tomlinson

Afro-Centered Futurisms in Our Speculative Fiction edited by Eugen Bacon

Chinua Achebe: Narrating Africa in Fictions and History by Toyin Falola

Writing Black Panther: Ta-Nehisi Coates and Representation Struggles
by Howard Rambsy II

Writing Black Panther

Ta-Nehisi Coates and Representation Struggles

Howard Rambsy II

BLOOMSBURY ACADEMIC
NEW YORK · LONDON · OXFORD · NEW DELHI · SYDNEY

BLOOMSBURY ACADEMIC
Bloomsbury Publishing Inc, 1359 Broadway, New York, NY 10018, USA
Bloomsbury Publishing Plc, 50 Bedford Square, London, WC1B 3DP, UK
Bloomsbury Publishing Ireland, 29 Earlsfort Terrace, Dublin 2, D02 AY28, Ireland

BLOOMSBURY, BLOOMSBURY ACADEMIC and the Diana logo are trademarks of
Bloomsbury Publishing Plc

First published in the United States of America 2026

For legal purposes the Acknowledgments on p. 141 constitute
an extension of this copyright page.

Cover design by Eleanor Rose
Cover illustration © George Grey | www.royalstondesign.com

A catalog record for this book is available from the Library of Congress.

ISBN: HB: 979-8-7651-5096-2
         PB: 979-8-7651-5095-5
       ePDF: 979-8-7651-5098-6
      eBook: 979-8-7651-5097-9

Series: Black Literary and Cultural Expressions

Typeset by Integra Software Services Pvt. Ltd.
Printed and bound in the United States of America

For product safety related questions contact productsafety@bloomsbury.com.

To find out more about our authors and books visit www.bloomsbury.com
and sign up for our newsletters.

For Psyche Southwell

Contents

Introduction

On May 20, 2015, Ta-Nehisi Coates interviewed Sana Amanat, an editor for Marvel Comics, widely known for co-creating Kamala Khan (Ms. Marvel), for an event sponsored by the Aspen Institute and *The Atlantic*. "I've been a comic book fan," Coates said at the start of the conversation, "since I was about 10 years old." He and Amanat went on to discuss her projects at Marvel, as well as the overarching significance of comics. As the session concluded, Coates reaffirmed his admiration for Marvel and how its foundational fictional universe shaped him. "As a writer," he said, "I don't know where I would be without, you know, Marvel particularly. That is not an advertisement. It is literally true."[1]

That flattering, non-advertisement reached employees at Marvel. The next morning, Tom Brevoort, a senior editor at the company, wrote Coates on Twitter: "Heard that you had an interest in writing something for Marvel. Let's talk!"[2] The subsequent conversation between Brevoort and Coates apparently went well. Just eleven months after Brevoort's tweet, Marvel released *Black Panther* #1, written by Coates and drawn by veteran comic book artist Brian Stelfreeze. Coates's debut as a comic book writer was widely praised, and in December 2016, commentators cited *Black Panther* #1 as one of the best-selling titles of the year.

The tremendous reception of Coates and *Black Panther* marked a series of pivotal occurrences in the history of African American artistic writing and comics. Here was one of the rare occasions when a Black comic book writer received widespread validation apart from the field of comics. The publicity increased Coates's profile and inadvertently made such a route to success more challenging for other Black writers. The reporting on Coates as the new writer for *Black Panther* seemingly attested to Marvel's commitment to diversity, simultaneously overshadowing its problems employing women, African Americans, and queer creators. These concurrent dilemmas of progress and setbacks, these multifaceted contests over inclusion and debates about diversity, are what I refer to as representation struggles.[3]

To view diversity or representation as struggle, rather than simply a goal, is imperative. Single acts of inclusion hardly resolve legacies of exclusion, and such acts, though vital, create new open-ended results. An achievement in diverse representation can, in tandem, serve as a regression or hindrance. From one vantage point, hiring a well-known Black journalist and memoirist to write a title character for an influential comic book company was an unexpected and critical step forward, but such a hire also meant that Marvel bypassed more experienced African American comic book writers. Or, consider that by prioritizing Coates, media professionals often ignored his African American peers, thus continuing an enduring, troubling practice of elevating one Black writer at a time.[4] When we think of struggle as fundamental to diversity and representation, we acknowledge multidirectional processes and outcomes associated with Black writers in comics as well as in fields external to comics. More importantly, there's the humbling recognition that any and all representation is, by definition, underrepresentation.

Representation struggles can occur at the levels of decision-making, production, narrative, and reception. Enthusiasts and cultural workers advocate for more diverse hires and depictions in comics. Executives at comic book companies make strategic hiring decisions and can shape representation struggles when, for instance, they hire women and creators of color—groups historically underrepresented in the mainstream comic book industry. Comic creators participate in representation struggles when they perpetuate or disrupt stereotypical depictions. Storylines that champion underrepresented characters contest the status quo. Journalists and commentators engage in representation struggles when they urge comic book companies to hire diverse creators. Fans participate in representation struggles when they celebrate the emergence of diverse characters or when they urge companies to diversify their hiring practices.

Black Panther, with its emphasis on a fictive African country and Africans, and a sprawling cast of diverse creators and characters, stands out as a generative site for representation struggles. Stan Lee and Jack Kirby created a counterpoint to centuries-long racist depictions of Africans and Africa when they introduced the highly intelligent T'Challa and the technologically superior Wakanda. Still, as Todd Steven Burroughs noted, "for the first thirty-two years of his existence—from 1966 to 1998—[T'Challa's] writers were all White."[5] For quite some time, *Black Panther* continued a familiar practice of presenting Africans in exotic and undeveloped settings. Today, part of the appeal of the imagined Wakanda as a powerful, thriving nation rests on its contrast with pervasive views of downtrodden African countries that depend on international assistance and charity. Representation struggles emerge in *Black Panther*'s varied depictions of Africa and Africans.

This project, *Writing Black Panther: Ta-Nehisi Coates and Representation Struggles*, charts a contemporary history of African American artistic production and reception, demonstrating how Coates, a newcomer to the comic book industry as a writer, quickly became a consequential creator. His noteworthy creativity was supported by a highly skilled group of collaborators who transformed his narratives into visually stunning works of art. What's more, Marvel leveraged its promotional resources to make hundreds of thousands of readers and viewers aware of Coates's involvement in comics. Additionally, dozens of journalists and commentators actively covered Coates and his comic books. This study situates Coates's contributions within the broader contexts of Black writing and sequential art, positioning his work at the intersection of African American literary studies and comic book studies.

A reading of the relationship between Coates's work and a continuum of Black literary art makes a distinctive contribution to the study of comic books. Coates's narrative, starring a Black protagonist navigating challenging circumstances, parallels the themes found in autobiographies and novels by African American authors. T'Challa's quest for answers and his reckoning with his past echo the character development in fiction by Ralph Ellison, Toni Morrison, Octavia Butler, and Charles Johnson. Moreover, Coates's references to a broad spectrum of African American ideas and issues, along with his incorporation of Black cultural criticism in *Black Panther*, resemble approaches seen in novels by Ishmael Reed, Colson Whitehead, Paul Beatty, and Percival Everett, to name a few. Coates, by the way, hardly stands as the first and only creator whose comic book writing parallels Black literature. In *Icon* #1 from 1993, one of Dwayne McDuffie's characters observes, "I always wanted to be a writer, like Toni Morrison."[6] McDuffie, Reginald Hudlin, Eve Ewing, John Jennings, and N. K. Jemisin engaged with African American literary and cultural references in their works. Nonetheless, Coates's stature as a Black author creates special opportunities. By tracing how his creativity and cultural imperatives complement Black literature, I make the case for using African American literary studies as a lens for illuminating the work of Black comic book writers.

At the same time, this book raises the possibility that some Black comic writing deserves a place in African American literary studies. Coates's depiction of Black characters, his exploration of intra-racial and interracial conflicts, his excavations of Black histories, and his interest in cultural geography overlap with prevalent themes and topics in the creative domain of African American literature. For decades now, literature teachers and scholars have privileged novels, short stories, and poems. We delivered conference presentations and published articles and books on cultural figures, literary trends, and Black authors. As a field, we have shown relatively little interest in Black comic books and creators. Nevertheless, in light of the evolving landscape of Black creative expression as well as the increased availability of genres for readers, it's essential that we expand our frameworks to include comics as a form of African American literature.

Those of us who have covered comics for years in our classes realize the educational and cultural value of this mode of storytelling. We also find that students show considerable enthusiasm for reading and learning about comics.[7] Similar to African American literary works, comic books by African American writers explore topics such as identity, cultural heritage, Black history, social justice, and intricacies of community dynamics. Unfortunately, though, comics are dismissed as low art or only for children and thus rarely show up on syllabi for African American literature courses. The lack of institutional regard for comics makes it all the more significant when a principal Black writer contributes to the art form.

As an essayist, best-selling author, and successful comic book writer, Coates acts as a notable gateway figure who bridges genres. He actively contributed to the comic book industry from September 2015, when he was first announced as the writer for *Black Panther* through July 2021, when he ended his run on *Captain America*. This relatively short span of time constituted an important, defining phase of Coates's professional career. During this period, separate from the field of comics, he became one of the most widely discussed contemporary African American writers in the country based largely on the overwhelming responses to his article "The Case for Reparations" (2014), his memoir *Between the World and Me* (2015), his collection of articles *We Were Eight Years in Power: An American Tragedy* (2017), and his novel *The Water Dancer* (2019). He was a best-selling, widely read and cited author outside of comics during this time when he wrote fifty issues of *Black Panther* and thirty issues of *Captain America*, which further extended his reach.

Coates's entry into comics coincided with a rising presence of Black creators and characters in the field. For one, experienced Black comic creators like David F. Walker and Bryan Hill began receiving more visibility. The field also welcomed new African American writers, and Coates facilitated the entries of writers such as Roxane Gay, Yona Harvey, Evan Narcisse, and Rembert Browne. A growing number of Black superheroes headlined solo titles or within ongoing storylines. Less than a month after its release in February 2018, the *Black Panther* movie earned over $1 billion at the worldwide box office.[8] The film gave Wakanda and Afrofuturist concepts prime real estate in the public imagination, and thus paved the way for *Black Panther* comic book spinoffs, novels, resource guides, and merchandise.

Somewhat overlooked or taken for granted was the rise of a discourse on diversity or representation struggles during this period. Journalists, commentators, and general online commenters spoke out about cultural appropriation and the lack of diversity at comic book companies, which motivated them to address these issues. Commentators and cultural critics performed advocacy work on behalf of Black writers. Karama Horne pointed out that Marvel took concerted efforts to employ a Korean American to write a Korean protagonist, a Muslim woman to write a Muslim girl protagonist, and Black men to write Black men characters, "but they couldn't find a single black woman to write Moongirl, Nova, and now Iron Man," whose lead character at the time was taken on by a Black girl, Riri Williams.[9] Horne, Jamie Broadnax, Evan Narcisse, David Betancourt, along with additional popular culture journalists, published reviews and opinions on comics, making cases for more diverse representation. Their collective news articles, blog entries, tweet threads, podcasts, and convention panels ultimately raised the value and visibility of works produced by Black creators.

Coates was undoubtedly a beneficiary of this widespread advocacy. In addition to websites such as *Comic Book Resources (CBR)*, *Bleeding Cool News*, *Black Nerd Problems*, *Comics Alliance*, and *Vox* covering his work, publications like *The New York Times*, *The Washington Post*, *Business Insider*, and *The Hollywood Reporter* produced articles on Coates's *Black Panther* run. This media visibility significantly boosted his profile within the comic book industry and in cultural conversations. Interest in Coates as a comic book writer was heightened in part because cultural critics and fans previously advocated for increased racial diversity among creators. A host of commentators therefore expressed excitement when, as one journalist put it, "the best living writer on race in America" was announced as the upcoming writer for Marvel.[10] Coates's entry into comics was the result of long-standing representation struggles.

Like other media empires, Marvel fits what Tim Wu described as an "attention merchant"—a company deeply invested in "the game of harvesting human attention and reselling it to advertisers."[11] Beyond promoting diversity, Marvel stayed focused on the bottom line: profits. In hiring Coates, they did more than recruit a best-selling Black writer; they secured someone with immense attention power. Even though Coates is not as famous as Denzel Washington or LeBron James, he holds some celebrity status. His level of name and face recognition exceeds that of numerous best-selling authors. Prior to his debut in comics, he had already been covered in newspapers, magazines, and television appearances, all of which contributed to his substantial attention power, a form of virtual capital that Marvel could harness and leverage.

Scholarship on comics expanded over the last two decades as increasing numbers of researchers produced articles and book-length treatments on an array of topics related to sequential art, superheroes, comics and pedagogy, and so forth. Within the field, Sean Howe, Douglas Wolk, Paul Young, and Carolyn Cocca produced substantive studies.[12] We still await plentiful studies on developments in contemporary African Americans comics. Scholars produced a growing body of work in this regard: Jeffrey A. Brown's *Black Superheroes, Milestone Comics, and Their Fans* (2001) and *Panthers, Hulks, and Ironhearts: Marvel, Diversity, and the 21st Century Superhero* (2021), Adilifu Nama's *Super Black: American Pop Culture and Black Superheroes* (2011), Sheena C. Howard and Ronald L. Jackson II's edited collection *Black Comics Politics of Race and Representation* (2013), Tim Jackson's *Pioneering Cartoonists of Color* (2016), Qiana Whitted's *EC Comics: Race, Shock, and Social Protest* (2019), and Rebecca Wanzo's *The Content of Our Caricature: African American Comic Art and Political Belonging* (2020). We need more projects like these in order to gain deeper and nuanced views of African American contributions to comics. Furthermore, we do not yet have enough studies documenting the changes taking place involving Black creators and characters since 2015.

Scholars of African American literature have produced an expansive body of writings on authors, fiction, artistic modes, and literary history. This collective scholarship, along with wide-ranging conversations about literary art and pedagogy, has created and honed frameworks for examining the creativity of Black writers.[13] African American literary studies provides useful possibilities for appreciating the contributions of Black creators when applied to the analysis of Black comics. Literary scholars and cultural critics have examined Coates's *Between the World and Me* and his novel *The Water Dancer*.[14] In contrast, the field of African American literary studies has paid comparatively little consideration to Coates's work in comics, as well as to the contributions of other Black comic creators. My proposition to merge African American literary studies and comic book studies proposes a promising avenue to bridge this gap, fostering a more comprehensive understanding of Black creativity spanning diverse mediums.

When editors at Marvel first approached Coates and asked him for a list of preferences for the superhero he would like to write, he did not immediately choose the King of Wakanda. "When I was a kid," explained Coates in an NPR interview, "Spider-Man was a star. Spider-Man was right under Malcolm X for me in terms of heroes."[15] The question of what hero he wanted to write, therefore, was hardly a question. If given the choice, he wanted to write a comic book starring the much-adored web-slinger. Coates was also a fan of the X-Men. So, if Spidey was not available, mutants would make a good consolation prize. Similarly, when Christopher Priest was first approached about writing *Black Panther* during the late 1990s, he was uninterested, preferring instead to write *Daredevil*.[16] Marvel had other plans. They wanted Coates to write *Black Panther*, and although the book was not his first choice, the assignment ended up presenting him and ultimately his readers with renewed views of T'Challa, his ensemble cast, and Wakanda.

Coates's take on T'Challa followed a long line of creators—white and Black—including Stan Lee, Jack Kirby, Don McGregor, Christopher Priest, Reginald Hudlin, and Jonathan Maberry. In an interview with Evan Narcisse, Coates conceded that T'Challa had not been a central figure to him during his "strong formative period" as a young, active comic book reader. Only after receiving the Marvel assignment to write the series did Coates go back to "research and read more Panther-related titles." Narcisse made the point that not previously reading the series informed Coates's approach. "You don't have a nostalgic, fannish attachment to T'Challa from the '70s or '80s or even the '90s incarnations," said Narcisse. "And you're subverting a lot of the stuff that reinvigorated him, which is an interesting place for you to be."[17] Part of the subversion that Narcisse may have had in mind included characters questioning T'Challa's authority and decisions and having T'Challa question himself. Presenting the king as flawed may have seemed strange if not disappointing for fans who longed to see an all-powerful Black superhero.

A deep exploration of a Black man central figure corresponded to Coates's writing as a journalist. He devoted his most thoroughly researched articles to formidable Black men, including Louis Farrakhan, Bill Cosby, Malcolm X, and Barack Obama. His first memoir *The Beautiful Struggle* examined his sometimes overly stern father, Paul Coates. He published dozens of blog entries about Black men athletes and rappers, and he shared examinations of his own experiences as a Black man. Coates was primed to express a complex rendering of a lead Black man character, who he once described as "a superhero who happens to be a king."[18]

Coates delved into the inner thoughts of his protagonist, positioning T'Challa within a rich tradition of introspective Black men characters. Writers such as James Weldon Johnson, Richard Wright, Ralph Ellison, Ishmael Reed, Charles Johnson, Walter Mosley, Paul Beatty, and Colson Whitehead have portrayed intelligent brooding Black men. In *Looking for Leroy: Illegible Black Masculinities* (2013), scholar Mark Anthony Neal described factors that have historically obscured the complexity of Black men in popular culture. Media depicted Black men as criminals, brash, impulsive, and uneducated. By contrast, African American literary artists countered these reductive narratives by crafting narratives of Black men protagonists navigating challenging circumstances and thoughtfully addressing complex problems.

While his depictions of T'Challa are notable, Coates further distinguished his *Black Panther* run by showcasing women characters such as Shuri and the Dora Milaje, whom he repurposed as the Midnight Angels. Coates's contributions in increasing the presence of Black women characters in *Black Panther* and its spinoffs deserve more acknowledgment. Some commentators criticized the absence of women in Coates's *Between the World and Me*.[19] The prevalence of Black women throughout *Black Panther*, though, may have been taken for granted. The Midnight Angels of Coates's writing anticipated the appearances of the Dora Milaje in the two *Black Panther* films.

Coates also expanded visions of Wakanda, mapping out distinct zones throughout the nation for the first time. By identifying specific regions and presenting characters in diverse settings, Coates enriched the depictions of the African country. The varied locales and spectacular artwork challenged long-held stereotypes of Africa as static and primitive. Later, Coates's narratives of Wakandans exploring the outer reaches of space typified his commitment to broadening the geospatial possibilities of *Black Panther*. These creative expansions redefined Wakanda as a dynamic and complex world and universe.

The reconfiguration of Wakanda and the in-depth depictions of an African king and African women reflect aspects of representation struggles—a long-standing concern for African American creators and thinkers. In an 1872 speech, the ex-slave and revered abolitionist Frederick Douglass recounted that "I was once advertised in a very respectable newspaper under a little figure, bent over and apparently in a hurry, with a pack on his shoulder, going North."[20] He was referring derisively to an oft-published illustration of a Black man, fugitive slave carrying a knapsack on a stick, as he walks forward. The illustration opposed the symbol of strength and power that Douglass sought to represent in photographic images of himself. As early as the nineteenth century, he and others expressed their concerns about representation.

In 1926, in *The Crisis* magazine, W. E. B. Du Bois published "The Negro in Art: How Shall He Be Portrayed." The questions he asked included these: "When the artist, black or white, portrays Negro characters is he under any obligations or limitations as to the sort of character he will portray?" "Can any author be criticized for painting the worst or the best characters of a group?" "What are Negroes to do when they are continually painted at their worst and judged by the public as they are painted?"[21] Those questions reflect sentiments and concerns that have preoccupied African Americans before and long after Du Bois posed them in *The Crisis*. Discussions and debates about the depiction of Black people in novels, music, paintings, film, television, and more have persisted. Analyses regarding race and representation in comic art thus correspond to the enduring imperative of determining how Black people shall be portrayed.

The terms "diversity" and "diverse representation" overlap and are sometimes used interchangeably. In any case, people often deploy diversity to sanitize, or even downplay, the tougher and messier processes involved in disrupting historically white institutions and cultural productions. A correlated concern is that the notion of diversity does not go far enough in addressing the concerns that artists, cultural critics, educators, and activists have about how people and ideas are depicted. The term "representation struggles" is more fitting when describing efforts to hire Black creators and analyze the implications of those creators presenting ideas, characters, and locales in their compositions. Coates's run on *Black Panther*, the responses to his work, and developments in the field concerning Black comic book creators and characters since 2015, exemplify the multiplicity of representation struggles.

The terms "struggle" and "struggles" reflect the push and pull of concerns and debates about representation and even progress. In a 2021 interview with Ezra Klein, Coates recalled that there was considerable praise when it was announced that Nikole Hannah-Jones and he would join the faculty at Howard University, though soon after people quickly began raising questions about unresolved challenges at the institution. "I'll be honest with you and say at first I was annoyed," said Coates. "But as I thought about it, I think the conversation reflects something true about life, that this is what it is, it's constant struggle. Question after question after question. There is no place where you reside and you get to feel like you are the good guy in the story."[22] Two acclaimed Black writers chose to work at a historically Black university, yet there was still criticism that they could and should do more. Indeed, struggles over representation are like that—question after question, with new challenges continuously emerging.

Black representation sometimes spurs more Black representation. Lee and Kirby's creation of T'Challa was generative. Comics scholar Jeffrey A. Brown commented that, "Black Panther helped clear the way for several other early black superheroes, including Marvel's Falcon in 1969, Luke Cage in 1972, Brother Voodoo in 1973, Black Goliath in 1975, and Storm (in *The X-Men*) in 1975, as well as DC Comics' Tyroc (in *Legion of Superheroes*) in 1976 and Black Lightning in 1977."[23] Select characters from that group have fared well. Yet, challenges emerged. Interest in those figures was uneven. The creation of Black superheroes did not immediately lead to ventures for Black creators. The success of Black heroes was tied to whether predominantly white audiences embraced them, which influenced sales and decisions by publishers. All of this is to say, that despite gains, representation remains a constant struggle.

Even as white audiences have their interests, Black superheroes hold profound importance for African American audiences, including countless young fans. When scholar Adilifu Nama first encountered superhero toy action figures as a child, he was captivated by Aquaman, Captain America, and Spider-Man, but he had a favorite: Falcon. "Why? He was a black man that could fly," Nama explained. He added, "With Falcon, I was able to imagine myself as a superhero, rising above my socioeconomic environment, beating the neighborhood bullies," and gaining respect and popularity with peers.[24] During the early 1970s, the Black Owned Communication Alliance (BOCA), reported Brown, called "for greater racial diversity in the media" through a series of public service advertisements.

One of these ads included a Black boy striking a heroic pose as he gazed at an image of a white superhero. The ad emphasized the problem of representation of a Black child who "can't even *imagine* a hero the same color he or she is."[25] Before and after the 2018 release of the Black Panther film, countless African American children proudly appeared in images cosplaying as Black Panther and the Dora Milaje, as well as playing with action figures inspired by the film.

The inclusion of underrepresented superheroes matters. In her study *Superwomen: Gender, Power, and Representation* (2016), Carolyn Cocca observed that "While you do not have to have a perfect demographic match with a fictional character to identify with her or him, seeing someone who looks like you can have a positive impact on self-esteem and seeing no one who looks like can have a negative impact on self-esteem." These observations confirmed the influence representation had on how individuals perceived themselves. As Cocca added, "You are more likely to imagine yourself as a hero if you see yourself represented as a hero."[26] The expansion of diverse representation in superhero narratives ensures that more people can see themselves as empowered and valued. However, representation alone does not suffice, as the visibility and engagement these characters generate are critical.

In some cases, fans and commentators complain when they feel a central Black figure receives too little spotlight. A recurring critique of Coates's run on *Black Panther* was that supporting characters too often overshadowed T'Challa. As Osvaldo Oyola pointed out, readers of Coates's work "might be disappointed to find the Wakandan king displaced and decentered in his own book."[27] Conversely, there are instances when observers understandably perceive a central Black figure as receiving too much exposure. *The New York Times*, *The Washington Post*, *Time* magazine, *The Hollywood Reporter*, *The Guardian*, *Vulture*, and *Entertainment Weekly* collectively produced writings about Coates, leaving comparatively less room for other Black comics creators. A similar imbalance exists in African American literary studies, where canonical figures such as Frederick Douglass and Toni Morrison receive significantly more scholarly attention than lesser-known authors. Striking the right balance with representation—what constitutes too little or too much emphasis on a central Black figure—persists as a challenge.

The issues surrounding representation struggles that emerged or intensified during Coates's run made this period in contemporary comic book history decidedly compelling. A convergence of developments linked to diversity occurred, and these developments deserve greater study. This moment was also pivotal in the cinematic imaginings of T'Challa, Wakanda, and Wakandans, which, as we will see, Coates influenced in subtle yet salient ways. Crucially, his breakthroughs are exemplary in the context of African American literary studies, where notable authors rarely achieve crossover acclaim as comics creators.

The intersections of cultural and artistic significance affirm the importance of examining Coates's contributions as an inflection point in both comics and the history of Black writing.

Chapter Descriptions

The first three chapters explore how representation struggles and calls for more Black writers in comics set the stage for Marvel's decision to hire Coates in 2015. The announcement that he would write *Black Panther*, along with the lead-up to his debut, generated media write-ups, pointedly boosting Coates's cultural capital in the field of comics. This examination articulates the importance of considering a theory of buzz—the humming, persistent public attention directed toward creators and cultural productions. Buzz made Coates one of the most talked-about Black comic book creators and turned *Black Panther* #1 into a phenomenal bestseller. A clear grasp of the dynamic of buzz proves essential to appreciating the impact of Coates's entry into the world of comics.

The next three chapters examine Coates's first story arc, "A Nation Under Our Feet," which introduces internal conflicts in Wakanda that lead to restructuring the country's system of government. Coates exhibits inventive narrative capabilities, drawing on the artistic talents of Brian Stelfreeze, Chris Sprouse, and Laura Martin to produce a visually stunning series. By pushing *Black Panther* in new directions, Coates interrogates T'Challa's authority as king and repositions Black women characters within the comic. Additionally, he delivers an expanded geospatial perspective of Wakanda, including the creation of a new map of the country. Coates's storytelling ultimately reconfigured aspects of *Black Panther*, reshaping the character's legacy and world.

Chapters 7, 8, and 9 delve into developments associated with Black comic creators and popular culture. Coates was part of a wave of Black writers, including David F. Walker, Bryan Hill, Roxane Gay, Kwanza Osajyefo, Eve Ewing, and John Ridley who either entered the comics industry or gained increased visibility during this period. Challenges awaited as well, including the debates in early 2017 over whether "diversity sells" in comics. Soon after, the tremendous financial success and cultural impact of the film *Black Panther* had profound effects on Coates's career and the broader participation of Black creators in the field. These developments validated the shifting landscape of the comic industry and representation struggles.

The closing chapter explores Coates's "The Intergalactic Empire" story arc where he envisions Wakanda in an interstellar setting. The narrative and illustrations suggest a kind of African American version of *Star Wars*, representing a bold and imaginative expansion of the *Black Panther* universe. The arc showcases Coates's impressive capabilities as a fiction writer. The onset of a global pandemic momentarily paused the release of the closing issues, which appeared after a months-long delay. Nonetheless, what Coates produced was a genre-pushing Black comic book. His work leaves a lasting imprint on *Black Panther* and Marvel.

Biographical sketches of Coates understandably cite his award-winning memoir, *Between the World and Me*, his essay collection *We Were Eight Years in Power*, and his novel *The Water Dancer*. Meanwhile, commentators treated his identity as a comic book creator as an afterthought, if mentioned at all. Yet, his contributions to comics proved far from minor. Writing *Black Panther* revealed the incredible expanse of his creativity and deep examination of representation struggles. From this viewpoint, Coates emerges as an outstanding and imaginative comic book writer who also happens to have authored best-selling books.

Throughout this study, I mention more than two dozen Black literary artists and their works in relation to Coates's *Black Panther* writing. To maintain narrative flow, I forgo in-depth analyses of these texts by African American authors. Instead, I establish a catalog of literary works that complement Coates's approach to comics and amounts to lists of complementary readings. This catalog opens a pathway for exploring thematic and stylistic continuums, elucidating the rich interplay between novels, short stories, poems, and comics by Black writers. Expanding African American literary curricula to include comics depends on our ability to recognize the interconnectivity of Black storytelling across modes of composition.

Notes on Keywords

Along with my recurring use of *representation struggles*, I employ keywords throughout the chapters in this book. *Visibility disparity* refers to the uneven spotlighting of select prominent writers compared to countless others in a field. *Representational redemption* connotes instances when creators revise or rework past depictions of Black characters or storylines that they found troubling. *Representation grievances* involve audiences critiquing how groups are depicted, underrepresented, or excluded. These terms collectively assisted in illuminating the complexities of representation in comic books and the field.

In discussions of media coverage, I introduce *attention power*, a phrase I developed to describe a figure or product's ability to attract notice based on prominence in distinct fields or broader popular culture. Unlike most African American authors and comic book creators, Coates achieved fame as a writer. Though he did not seek celebrity—acknowledging he was "in a place that I didn't really ask to be"—his reputation outside of comics was essential to the widespread notice he received. In a world where the ability to draw audience interest is a valuable commodity, Coates's substantial attention power made him a cultural force in comics.[28] The comparatively lower levels of attention power held by others contribute to explaining why they struggled to attain similar recognition.

Black aesthetics encompass distinct terminology, language practices, visual styles, character types, people, and cultural signifiers rooted in African American and Black diasporic histories and cultures. I derive my use of Black aesthetics from "the Black aesthetic," a widely discussed and debated concept that emerged during the late 1960s.[29] As a component of Black aesthetics, I employ *Afrofuturist aesthetics* to distinguish representations at the intersection of science fiction, technology, and Black people and histories. The term *Afrofuturism* was coined by Mark Dery in 1993, and in the late 1990s, scholar Alondra Nelson expanded its scope by organizing a discussion group and repurposing the term "to describe analysis, criticism and cultural production that addresses the intersections between race and technology."[30] As the term gained traction and usage in the 2010s, Afrofuturism and Afrofuturist became common labels for diverse cultural productions. I prefer the term *Afrofuturist aesthetics* to distinguish it from popularized uses of Afrofuturism and to connect it more directly to Black aesthetics.

Chapter 1
Representation Struggles in Comics

On February 4, 2013, Joseph Hughes published "Outrage Deferred: On the Lack of Black Writers in the Comic Book Industry" for *Comics Alliance*. Black History Month, noted Hughes, was a good time to "reflect on where we've been, as a people and as a nation, and to contemplate exactly where it is we're going." But thinking about the comic book industry in the context of Black history and progress raised concerns. "There is currently not a single black writer," observed Hughes, "working on a monthly series for either of the two biggest comic book publishers in the United States, and precious few working for any of the others." According to Hughes, despite the fact that people had previously expressed interest in diversity in comics, the inclusion of Black writers in the field had waned. "Why is it that we no longer seem to care about this as much as we once did?" asked Hughes. "Where has our outrage gone?"[1]

Hughes went on to point out that Marvel and DC as well as Dark Horse, Image, IDW, and Valiant had only a couple or no Black writers at the time. Despite the glaring omission of Black writers, he felt there was hardly any acknowledgment of the issue. "The focus on bringing more black writers into the industry has been largely ignored, both by publishers and," wrote Hughes, "it needs to be said, by the comic book press." One reason that "the dearth of female writers" was discussed, he concluded, was because "many passionate, intelligent" women comics professionals and media professionals were at the "forefront of this discussion." Quite a few of those professionals consisted of white women, and their discussions about industry representation may have placed greater emphasis on gender diversity over racial diversity. But according to Hughes, Black representation in comics suffered in part because of the loss of Dwayne McDuffie in 2011. "Since the untimely passing of McDuffie, there has been a very obvious void in terms of recognizable and established figures speaking out on behalf of black creators," explained Hughes. Despite circumstances, Hughes showed some optimism. "Maybe this will be the year we see significant change," he wrote. "It is incumbent upon all of us—publishers, editors, fans, and members of the comic industry media—to keep this conversation going."[2]

Hearing Hughes's plea, comics journalist Heidi MacDonald sought to extend the conversation. The next day, she published "Why aren't there more black writers in the comics industry?" for the Beat.[3] "The lack of black writers is especially odd given that comics have a huge minority readership," lamented MacDonald. She also pointed out that "while the issues of sexism in nerd culture are aired every five minutes, racial roles are rarely given the same examination." At the close of the article, she invited people to identify the names of Black comics writers in the comments. Her readers responded by mentioning writers who would be good candidates to write books for the Big Two—Marvel and DC.

The writings by Hughes, MacDonald, and MacDonald's commenters affirmed that reporting on representation struggles could facilitate various developments. For one, such observations could make visible the absences of Black creators. At the same time, the articles and postings from commenters captured an outpouring of concern about those absences. These individuals called out or critiqued the inaction of powerful nominally white institutions, in this case, Marvel and DC, for their neglect of Black writers and audiences. Finally, the articles created occasions for identifying and raising awareness about potential Black comic book writers.

Commenters on MacDonald's article collectively put forward African American creators as strong candidates to write future titles for the Big Two such as Brandon Thomas, Vincent Moore, Gerimi Burleigh, Geoffrey Thorne, Brandon Easton, and David Walker. The commenters identified a small number of Black women creators—Tammy Taylor, Rachel Renèe Russell, Dani Dixon, and Marguerite Abouet. Not surprisingly, no one recommended Ta-Nehisi Coates, who was primarily known for his blogging and journalism in 2013. MacDonald did identify John Ridley, who had previously worked on a series, *The American Way* in 2006. In 2021, Ridley succeeded Coates as the writer for *Black Panther*. The listing of Black creators was a critical component of cultural criticism surrounding representation struggles. Black writers existed, but they had not been given adequate opportunities, such listing suggested.

Comic book fans compiled lists and joined campaigns to identify women and people of color companies should look to hire. Articles like those by Hughes and MacDonald have brought to the forefront the collective representation grievances of fans. According to Jeffrey A. Brown, "Comic book fandom is one of the most popular and best organized of media fan cultures."[4] The interests and demographics of fan communities vary greatly: some fans enthusiastically discuss storylines and celebrate their favorite heroes; others engage in these activities and also work to call attention to barriers and shortcomings regarding diversity in the industry. Conversely, some groups of fans bemoan the increasing representation of women and people of color in comics, castigating the inclusion of apparent liberal or progressive subjects in comics as the work of "social justice warriors." The disparaging term "social justice warrior" (or SJW), which first emerged in gaming culture, quickly migrated to comic book fandom.[5] As an example of the activism and multiplicity within fan culture, in 2014 and 2015, at the moment when some fans called for more diversity in comics, others lamented what they perceived as the unwelcome rise of social justice warriors.

In February 2014, a year after the publication of Hughes's article, Joseph Illidge launched "The Color Barrier: A Message of Comics, Diversity, and Hope" for *Comic Book Resources*, and in his opening entry pointed out that "there are less writers of color in the combined creative pool of the top two publishers of comic books [today] than there were at Milestone in 1993." Illidge disclosed that "many creators of color have discussed the matter, in secret and in public, online and in print, with either discretion or righteous frustration." The rising popularity of comics made the issue of representation more important than ever. The move from fringe culture to popular culture, stated Illidge, meant that "it is more imperative for the full range of heroes to be shown in the comic books and graphic novels serving as the source material for Hollywood films and small-screen shows."[6]

In retrospect, the 2013 and 2014 appearances of Hughes's and Illidge's articles, respectively, in February carried resonance. After all, Black History Month was created in part to address representation struggles. In February 1926, historian Carter G. Woodson and the Association for the Study of Negro Life and History introduced Negro History Week to raise awareness about and acknowledge Black people's contributions, which official histories and mainstream coverage overlooked or underrepresented. Over the course of decades, African Americans transformed Negro History Week into Black History Month and included a wider array of subjects. Hughes and Illidge demonstrated that Black History Month was an appropriate time to single out African American contributions as well as exclusions. February was an opportune occasion to celebrate achievements and also to lodge representation grievances about the lack of Black writers. Black history comprised a record of accomplishments, yes, but such history also consisted of a series of advances and reversals.

Individual articles like those by Hughes, MacDonald, and Illidge could usefully address underrepresentation, but more comprehensive efforts could ensure the issues received examinations. Five months after the publication of Illidge's article, Omar Holmon and William Evans launched *Black Nerd Problems*, a site issuing African American positions on comic books. The site resulted from Holmon and Evans "complaining about the lack of minority representation" in comics.[7] Complaining or articulating grievances about the absence of Black writers and a dearth of Black superheroes proved foundational for the establishment of their site.

There is no evidence that the founders of *Black Nerd Problems* directly referenced the previously cited articles, but they clearly engaged in struggles over the depiction of Black people in comics and assorted mediums. These efforts contributed to a long history of people seeking to address the lack of Black creators and characters in media and popular culture realms.

Keep in mind that before they created *Black Nerd Problems* Holmon and Evans identified as comic book fans. They transformed their seeming casual interests into a platform that could, along with other tasks, showcase Black comic book creators and characters. Aldo Regalado detailed in his book *Bending Steel: Modernity and the American Superhero* (2015) that comic book fandom has a long history, stretching back decades. For fans, reading, collecting, discussing, and responding to superhero comics "became a locus of intellectual pursuit, a rallying point for civic awareness, a medium for personal expression, a tool for building identity, a forum for organizing community, a road to professional development."[8] Accordingly, Holmon and Evans, like countless comic book fans interested in diversity, channeled their interests in intellectual and community-building pursuits. Fan advocacy was instrumental in intensifying complaints about the absence of Black writers in comics.

Taken together, the articles by Hughes and MacDonald, the series by Illidge, and the site by Holmon and Evans, to name just a few contributions, signaled the increased development of commentary about representation struggles in popular culture. This expanding cultural criticism addressed issues of diverse representation in comics, gaming, movies, television, streaming services, and adjacent media spheres. For decades, people criticized comic book companies like Marvel and DC for their lack of diverse creators, but during the 2010s, the increased use of online platforms and social media "amplified the voices of minority creators and critics," maintained journalist Laura Hudson.[9] The intensified representation grievances about a lack of Black comic book creators urged Marvel to continually address diversity, which, along with other developments, influenced the company's decision to eventually hire Coates to write *Black Panther*. Without steady streams of analyses about underrepresentation, the public and comic book executives would have been less mindful about the need to increase the numbers of Black people as creators and characters.

Although Marvel was on the receiving end of critiques, the company also managed to garner favorable assessments for perceived improvements with respect to diversity. In early 2014, Kamala Khan, a Pakistani American girl from Jersey City, who took on the mantel as the new Ms. Marvel, began appearing in comics.[10] On July 15, 2014, on ABC's *The View*, Marvel announced that Thor would be replaced by a woman. The next evening, Joe Quesada, chief creative officer for Marvel, appeared on *The Colbert Report* and announced that the new Captain America would be Sam Wilson, also known as the Falcon. By July 17, news organizations had actively covered this pertinent development. Anna Silman and Abraham Riesman, writing for *Vulture*, relayed that the announcements of a woman Thor and a Black Captain America appeared "to indicate a concerted effort on Marvel's part to include more diverse faces within the top-tier superhero landscape."[11] Jess Denham reported for *The Independent* that "Marvel is aiming for greater diversity in its big titles, hence these important changes to major characters."[12] *ABC News*, *The Guardian*, NPR, *The Today Show*, *E! News*, *The New York Post*, *Screen Crush*, and *Polygon* covered the news that Sam Wilson would become the new Captain America. The elevation of Falcon to the mantle of Captain America and the rise of Kamala Khan as a popular, well-received character indicated progress with respect to diversity, but some commentators expressed reservations.

Writing for *Wired*, Graeme McMillan asserted, "As genuine attempts to diversify the Marvel universe, both the Thor and Captain America announcements are significantly flawed, and are likely doomed to fail." For one, he noted, these new heroes would serve as "replacements—forced to live up to legacies established by white male characters," and the changes are "guaranteed to be temporary." McMillan added that Marvel's efforts appeared sincere, and the comics starring the new heroes might be enjoyable. Yet, temporarily including a woman and Black man in leading positions usually held by white men would not be enough. "*Thor* and *Captain America* may get all the headlines," wrote McMillan, "but living up to their promise of these announcements may require more meaningful measures."[13] The uneasiness expressed by McMillan, along with the mixed news, some optimistic, some skeptical, confirmed the complexity of representation. The promotion of Falcon was progress with limits.

The announcements about Thor and Captain America on *The View* and *The Colbert Report* revealed Marvel's ability to gain access to venues with large audiences to promote developments with comic books and diversity. The subsequent media appearances kept Marvel in the mass-media news cycle and extended its reach past the realm of comics. The coverage gave Marvel an edge in exposure, at least with respect to diversity, over its rival DC Comics. In the constant struggle to capture audience interest and engage potential customers, diverse representation proved vital. Looking back, hardly anyone would have guessed that just four years after the introduction of Sam Wilson as Captain America, the white Captain America, Steve Rogers, would be penned by a Black writer, Ta-Nehisi Coates.

Largely absent from discussions of Sam Wilson as Captain America was who was writing and drawing the character. A lack of criticism about white creators writing a renowned Black character suggested that conversations about cultural appropriation in particular had not become pronounced in the writing about comics in 2014. On July 23, Marvel released *Storm* #1, and reviewers scarcely complained that the creative team for the book did not include any Black women. In the months that followed, discussions of cultural appropriation in relation to white men creators producing titles built around Black characters, would become pervasive. Additional oversights would occur, and greater scrutiny would emerge involving who writes whom, that is, which creators are granted the opportunity to produce stories about which characters, before discussions about the absence of Black writers became a more prevalent and recurring aspect of comics discourse.

On January 16, 2015, in an article in *Rolling Stone*, Marvel announced a future April release of two comic book covers for *Deadpool* and *Howard the Duck* that would be based on the logo for the rap group Run the Jewels.[14] The logo includes one hand mimicking the shape of a gun alluding to a stick-up gesture toward another hand holding jewels. Rocket Raccoon and Howard the Duck represent the gesture on the cover of *Howard the Duck* #2. The cover of *Deadpool* #45 shows two hands, reproducing the Run the Jewels hand symbol as well. Those two covers formed the basis of Marvel's Hip Hop Variants project, which would launch with several covers that coming October.

On July 14, 2015, the Hip Hop Variants received an encouraging response, when outlets announced the project. "Marvel Comics recently invoked Run the Jewels for a series of variant comic book covers," wrote Evan Minsker for *Pitchfork*. "Now, they're paying homage to even more hip-hop greats with a series of variant covers inspired by classic and contemporary hip-hop albums."[15] *The Verge*, *Comic Book Resources*, and *BuzzFeed*, to name a few, published stories about the announcement. The inclusion of hip hop also gave music magazines such as *Spin* and *Complex* reason to cover this development in comics. "It's no secret that the hip-hop and comic book cultures have always had a symbiotic relationship," wrote Paul Thompson for the hip hop magazine *XXL*. "This fall, Marvel Comics plans to give fans physical evidence of that phenomenon by reissuing five of its seminal works with covers that invoke classic hip-hop albums."[16]

Eventually though, some commentators questioned aspects of Marvel's project. Writing for *The Guardian*, Noah Berlatsky complained that "Marvel comics have historically been created almost exclusively by white men; the major super-properties are almost entirely white guys." He went on to observe that despite some efforts to change, "Marvel remains largely complacent in its whiteness," and in Berlatsky's view, not enough Black creators participated in the project. Berlatsky mistakenly thought Sanford Greene was white, and cited his contribution to the variant covers as evidence of Marvel's exclusionary practices.[17] Berlatsky later apologized, noting that he should have credited Marvel with "making an effort to address the legacy of hip hop."[18]

Laura Hudson, writing for *Wired* magazine, informed that the variant covers raised concerns about "whether mainstream comics has done enough to bring minority creators themselves into the fold."[19] In an article for *Business Insider*, Joshua Rivera reported that critics claimed that the Hip Hop Variants represented "a classic case of cultural appropriation, yet another instance where a company capitalizes on the art and ethos of a marginalized culture it doesn't engage with in order to drive profits."[20] Allegations of cultural appropriation became a fixture in conversations about popular culture and representation.

Apart from criticizing the Marvel Hip Hop Variants project, observers pointed out the problem of two white men, J. G. Jones and Mark Waid, producing the comic book *Strange Fruit*, a Boom! Studios miniseries about racism in the South in 1927. J. A. Micheline published a strongly worded and widely cited critique of *Strange Fruit* #1 that closed by dissuading comic book readers from purchasing the publication: "giving money to this project and contributing to its success signifies to the industry (and your peers) that you are absolutely fine with oppressors continuing to control the narrative of the oppressed."[21] Prevalent critiques about white writers and artists producing books headlined Black characters brought into focus the limited number of Black creators given the opportunity to write those stories.

Conversations had moved from only pointing out an absence of Black writers to discussing the problem of white creators controlling narratives about underrepresented people. The discourse on representation struggles involves considerations of Black exclusion, yes, and also white power. J. A. Micheline, Laura Hudson, Joshua Rivera, and David Brothers took the comics industry to task for its diversity troubles. "You can't celebrate and profit off something without also including the group that you're profiting off the back of," remarked Brothers in reference to the Hip Hop Variants. "Marvel has made a lot of money off brown faces."[22]

The critiques about cultural appropriation and assorted problems with diversity or lack thereof prompted some companies and creators to rethink their plans. Marvel had initially announced the upcoming release of an updated version of *Blade*, following the titular African American vampire hunter alongside his daughter. Marvel announced two white men, Tim Seeley and artist Logan Faerbe, as the creative team for the book. In the aftermath of criticisms about the absence of Black comic creators with the Hip Hop Variants and *Strange Fruit*, Seeley chose to quit the *Blade* project. "I couldn't help but feel like a black woman might write this stuff better than me," he said a year later in an interview with *CBR*.[23] Here was a case when representation grievances from fans and commentators influenced white creators to abandon a project showcasing Black characters.

Similarly, Waid showed openness listening to and learning from critiques about cultural appropriation and *Strange Fruit*. "We're in a social media era where there are so many people who didn't have a voice for a long, long time, and suddenly they have a voice… and this is awesome," he said. "What I say about this is not what's important. What's important is what other people, who don't have the privilege that I have, want to say."[24] Waid's reference to social media spoke to the growing influence of online appraisals and critiques in shaping conversations about representation in comics. When Jeffrey A. Brown published his study book on Milestone Comics in 2001, he observed that "over the last two or three years comic book readers have begun to rely on electronic bulletin boards (BBSs) as a new form of communication." Readers he interviewed said they used comics BBSs at least once a week.[25] Since then, readers and fans have become far more engaged in online discussions about comics. Today, their compliments and critiques more readily reach creators and publishers.

Scholars produced thorough examinations of artistic creators and superheroes and extended analyses and histories of comic books. While less credited in public conversations, fans and commentators—journalists, bloggers, and general commenters on social media platforms—have also been at the forefront addressing issues such as the absence of Black creators, the harmful implications of cultural appropriation, and the tendency of comic book companies to maintain exclusive and exclusionary creative practices. "Comics—you have a race problem," wrote J. A. Micheline.[26] The intensity of select critiques made clear the seriousness with which commentators approached this field of entertainment. Their efforts to analyze and respond to announcements of upcoming comic book projects validated the importance of evaluating works long before the release of products. Prepublication critiques put companies and creators on notice, encouraging them to be more mindful of oversight and neglect and to be more responsive to audience interests. What's more, these critiques contributed to raising public awareness about the comic book industry's shortcomings regarding Black people and additional underrepresented groups.

Meanwhile, amid the critiques, Marvel was quietly working on a plan to hire a high-profile African American writer. The public conversation Coates conducted with Sana Amanat in May 2015 had set the process in motion.[27] As a journalist and blogger for *The Atlantic*, which hosted the event with the interview, Coates was well-placed to converse with an accomplished Marvel executive. He jumped at the opportunity to facilitate a discussion with a professional in the industry. Just as importantly, the interview gave Coates an outlet to express his enthusiasm for comics and Marvel. In other words, he could tell a representative from the comic book company that he admired since childhood that he was a big fan.[28]

In his book *Speculative Blackness*, André M. Carrington wrote about the need to take fans and fan culture seriously and reimagine how audiences interpret and contribute to cultural production.[29] In writings for *The Atlantic* and elsewhere, Coates expressed his interests and revealed that he belonged to fan communities. "In my lifetime," he wrote in early 2010, "I have floated through all manner of geekdom—comic books, sci-fi, sports, medieval history, video games."[30] Coates regularly wrote about comics. In December 2010, he wrote about Marvel's *Secret Wars* and remarked that "comics are so often seen as the province of white geeky nerds. But, more broadly, comics are the literature of outcasts, of pariahs, of Jews, of gays, of blacks. It's really no mistake that we saw ourselves in Doom, Magneto or Rogue."[31] In a guest op-ed for *The New York Times* in 2011, Coates wrote about viewing *X-Men: First Class* with his son and observed that "in 1962, the quintessential mutants of America were black."[32] These and additional writings referencing comics and attesting to Coates's identity as a fan anticipated the excitement he showed during his public meeting with Amanat. In retrospect, the discussion functioned as a preliminary interview with Marvel.

Discussions involving Coates and Marvel personnel continued to move forward. In late July 2015, in an interview with *CBR*, Marvel editor in chief Axel Alonso spoke about the company's upcoming releases. "We have incredibly exciting stuff to announce in the next few months—titles, artists and writers—building to a crescendo for Black History Month," said Alonso. He conceded the lack of Black creators. "We are experiencing a lull in African-American writers at this moment, but it is temporary," he said, and assured that Marvel would address that problem with its actions. "We will be announcing new series very soon that will prove that. I'm talking about new voices, familiar voices and one writer whose voice is heard round the world. [Laughs]."[33] Alonso's statement and laugh foreshadowed his confidence that Marvel would soon make an announcement that would counter the criticisms about its commitments to diversity.

On July 14, Spiegel & Grau, an imprint of Penguin Random House, published *Between the World and Me*, and by the end of the month, the overwhelming media recognition surrounding the book had significantly expanded Coates's attention power. Placing his name and image in dozens of major publications, including *The New York Times*, *The Wall Street Journal*, *The New Yorker*, the *Los Angeles Times*, *USA Today*, *The New Republic*, *The Washington Post*, and *The Boston Globe*, made him more widely known and recognizable.[34] He made guest appearances on news television programs, and *Between the World and Me* was discussed, celebrated, and critiqued on social media platforms. Arguably, no other book by an African American published in the twenty-first century received such extensive exposure. Though rigorously debated, Coates and his writing became central to national conversations on race and racism in America. His presence in public discourse was pervasive.

No wonder Alonso was optimistic about the upcoming announcement of this new contributor. Brevoort had reached out to Coates months before he achieved widespread fame. His blogging and journalism for *The Atlantic*, most notably his article "The Case for Reparations" in 2014, had made him somewhat well known, and the release of *Between the World and Me* vaulted him to new heights. By securing Coates as a writer, Marvel positioned itself to benefit from adding an esteemed Black writer on its roster. Fans and commentators had been vocal in their critiques of the company's shortcomings with respect to diversity. Executives at the publisher expressed confidence that they now had a compelling response to those criticisms. To convey its commitment to diverse representation, Marvel had hired someone rare and special: a famous Black writer.

Chapter 2
Announcing a Leading Writer on Race

On July 31, 2015, a Twitter user, Charles, sent a message to Rich Johnston, founder of the comics news site *Bleeding Cool*, showing a screenshot of Axel Alonso's comment about a then yet-to-be-named new writer. The screenshot also showed Brevoort's May 21, 2015 tweet to Coates requesting a conversation about writing for Marvel. "Can we go ahead & call this 'mystery' solved?" tweeted Charles.[1] The next morning on *Bleeding Cool*, Johnston published an article "Is Ta-Nehisi Coates Writing a New Comic Book for Marvel?" that supplied examples from writings by Coates demonstrating his interest in comic books. Johnston closed the article by thanking Charles and providing a link to the original tweet.[2]

Johnston's speculation and subsequent confirmation about Coates writing for Marvel might seem inconsequential to some. Nevertheless, informed conjectures hold value within the realm of comic book discourse. The interplay between publisher executives, journalists, and comic book fans constitutes an ecosystem of ideas and transactions. "To amass cultural capital within the comic community," Jeffrey Brown noted, "the fan must build an extensive knowledge of the industry."[3] Communities of fans and industry professionals assist in facilitating the growth of audiences' knowledge. Comic news sites such as *Bleeding Cool*, *CBR*, *ComicBook.Com*, and *Comics Alliance* gain symbolic or cultural capital by correctly predicting and producing early reports on developments in the field and conducting interviews with executives and creators who confer hints on privileged information. Johnston's interest in exclusive or secret information encourages his readers, like Charles, to share scoops and discoveries, which strengthens *Bleeding Cool*'s abilities and reputation as a leader in comic news reporting. Nearly two months after Charles and Johnston first predicted that Coates would write for Marvel, the news was publicly announced.[4]

On the morning of September 22, 2015, *The New York Times* released an article titled "Ta-Nehisi Coates to Write Black Panther Comic for Marvel."[5] This big reveal sparked immediate, substantial buzz. A range of publications and websites—*Essence*, *Forbes*, *The Hollywood Reporter*, *Vox*, *CNN Money*, *Tech Insider*, *HuffPost Black Voices*, *The Guardian*, and more—magnified the announcement of the Coates hire.[6] "We just got the most significant superhero-comics news of the year," wrote Abraham Riesman for *Vulture*.[7] "He may have sat atop *The New York Times* bestseller list for most of the summer with a well-received book about race in America," commented Lanre Bakare in *The Guardian*, "but now Ta-Nehisi Coates is venturing into the world of comics after Marvel confirmed he will author new Black Panther editions."[8] Jason Concepcion, writing for *Grantland*, assessed that "To pair a writer and thinker of Mr. Coates's particular talents and interests with the Black Panther is, well, perfect."[9]

The enthusiasm for Coates's run on *Black Panther* was phenomenal. Few, if any, comic book writers had received this level of appraisals in Black and white publications before the release of their debut. Then again, few possessed as much attention power with such widespread cultural saturation stretching over multiple platforms. Dwayne McDuffie and Christopher Priest spent years steadily building followings, but they did not attract much attention outside of comics. They had not yet gained recognition in other mediums, though McDuffie participated in the production of the animated series *Static Shock*. Coates, by contrast, had already earned distinction as a journalist and book author, bringing a large following with him. As Concepcion explained, "Coates is, for those who may be unfamiliar, one of the most important and wide-reaching voices on the subject of race in America."[10]

Compositions that receive favorable acclaim can positively influence the reception of subsequent works by the author. Consider the growing interest in successive works by Coates. Buzz for "The Case for Reparations" begot buzz for *Between the World and Me*, which begot buzz for *Black Panther* #1, which begot variant editions and three *Black Panther* spinoffs. Buzz accumulates, and that accumulation bestows additional market value onto focal products, authors, and publishers.

A theory of buzz assists us in accounting for why some books become bestsellers and more discussed than other publications. Successful books are the beneficiaries of promotional resources issued long before official release dates. Prepublication coverage matters. Hence, news about Coates writing *Black Panther* circulated eight months before the release of issue 1. Keep in mind that at this moment in late September 2015, the Black Panther franchise was not yet the cultural touchstone and financial juggernaut that it would become in 2018 with the release of the film. Interest in the upcoming *Black Panther* comic book was largely linked to the appeal of Coates.

"The buzz that surrounds a bestselling title can feel organic and mysterious. All of a sudden, a book seems to be 'in the air,' everywhere and nowhere," wrote Beth Driscoll and Claire Squires. "But the creation of book buzz takes concerted effort."[11] Marvel, like other resourceful publishers, possessed wide-ranging experience positioning and promoting its products and creators across platforms. Moreover, the company benefited from connections to media outlets that can generate buzz. Marvel first announced its introduction of a woman Thor on ABC's *The View* and a Black Captain America on *The Colbert Report*. Accordingly, *The New York Times* was chosen as the venue for announcing the Coates hire.

The act of generating buzz registers as essential for capturing attention, a precious resource in a society inundated with competing demands. Tim Wu identifies the original attention merchants in the United States as ambitious, fiercely competitive newspaper publishers operating out of New York City, who, in the 1830s, discovered that "newsstand earnings were trivial; advertising revenue could make it all happen." Over the course of nearly two centuries, these early innovators of attention harvesting "would spawn generations of imitators, from radio networks and broad television to Google and Facebook."[12] Today, attention merchants, professionals seeking to drum up interest in their products, span industries—comic books, film, television and streaming services, video games, publishing, podcasting, and social media. Companies invest massive resources to gain an edge in the high-stakes races to attract and hold audiences, cultivating attention power along the way. Without buzz, a critical component of attention-grabbing, cultural products encounter diminished chances of gaining interest from critics, distributors, and consumers. For Marvel, securing a buzz-generating, attention-commanding African American writer presented a unique opportunity in a field long criticized for its lack of diversity.

The story of a bestselling Black author becoming the writer for *Black Panther* created a swarm of news activity and commentary, and, importantly, the pieces exuded a positive mood. The development of excitement for upcoming titles was integral to success. Driscoll and Squires stated that "creating buzz requires not only commercial activity and cultivated networks, but also enthusiasm." The emergence of a favorable, enthusiastic mood in response to a product or author "leads directly to economic profit."[13] Marvel reasoned that the company could facilitate an optimal mood among audiences by announcing the Coates hire during the extraordinary popularity he was experiencing shortly after the publication of *Between the World and Me*.

Spiegel & Grau, an imprint of Penguin Random House, along with editor Chris Jackson, made dedicated efforts to ensure the peak performance of Coates's book. For one, Jackson secured a blurb from novelist Toni Morrison for Coates's manuscript. A ringing endorsement from the Nobel Prize in Literature recipient designating Coates as the heir of James Baldwin and promoting *Between the World and Me* as "required reading" gave the book and author added credibility.[14] Second, on June 17, 2015, a white supremacist shot and killed nine African Americans at Emanuel African Methodist Episcopal Church in Charleston, South Carolina. London King, a publicity executive at Penguin Random House observed that the South Carolina massacre led the company "to drastically accelerate the schedule so we could publish on July 14," as opposed to a previously agreed upon publication in September.[15] In the aftermath of national tragedies involving race or racism, large numbers of white readers increase purchases for seemingly relevant Black books in part to gain an understanding of pertinent topics.[16] *Between the World and Me* was met with intensified interest, partly because the publication of the book occurred shortly after a white supremacist killed Black people in Charleston.

The response to Coates's book was incredible. Within a week of publication, his publisher announced "175,000 copies in print after five printings."[17] In the months following the July publication, dozens of media outlets, journalists, and commentators reported on *Between the World and Me*. The reception to the book made Coates one of the most widely discussed Black writers in the country. "In an America consumed by debates over racism, police violence and domestic terror," wrote Carlos Lozada for *The Washington Post*, "it is Coates to whom so many of us turn to affirm, challenge or, more often, to mold our views from the clay."[18] Jennifer Schuessler, writing for *The New York Times*, mentioned that "Ta-Nehisi Coates's meditation on being a black man in America, has had an almost frictionless glide straight to the heart of the national conversation."[19] Dozens of publications reviewed the book and ran stories on Coates. He was invited to speak on television and radio programs, and he gradually achieved celebrity status as an author.

The ascent of Coates undoubtedly pleased Marvel executives. The tremendous visibility he gained after the release of *Between the World and Me* proved invaluable to the fanfare surrounding his entry into comics. Headlines such as "Marvel Was Smart to Hire Coates to Write Black Panther," "Marvel Wises Up, Hires Ta-Nehisi Coates to Write Black Panther Comic," and "Ta-Nehisi Coates' Black Panther Comic Is a Dream Come True" served as excellent PR for a company recently criticized for its lack of representation.[20] The publisher had faced backlash for failing to employ Black writers and for alleged cultural appropriation. Hiring a major Black writer was a commendable step toward addressing those representation grievances.

On the one hand, some people deride diversity hires or hiring practices that take race into account, even though the routine hiring of white employees often goes unremarked. In January 2025, a presidential executive order from the Donald Trump administration referred to diversity, equity, and inclusion (DEI) efforts as "radical and wasteful" and "illegal and immoral."[21] These characterizations reflect long-held sentiments that accuse women, Black people, and other people of color of unfairly taking jobs from ostensibly more deserving white candidates. On the other hand, a multiplicity of people recognized the inherent value of disrupting industries that overwhelmingly employ white men. A report by the management firm McKinsey & Company declared, "Companies that are diverse, equitable, and inclusive are better able to respond to challenges, win top talent, and meet the needs of different customer bases."[22] A comic book company willing to make a diverse hire took steps toward improving its reputation and performance.

The swarm of articles published on September 22, announcing Coates as an upcoming writer placed Marvel in a favorable position with respect to representation struggles. Even though the inclusion of one Black writer could hardly close the decades-long racial gap, Coates's widespread acclaim allowed Marvel to project the image of making a serious effort to counter allegations of inadequately addressing diversity. The company benefited from positive news items, with articles lauding the decision to hire Coates. In *The New York Times* article announcing that he would write *Black Panther*, Coates said that Marvel was "an intimate part of my childhood and, at this point, part of my adulthood."[23] Statements like this confirmed Marvel's enduring appeal to readers like Coates and positioned him as a longtime fan of comics.

Above all, the Coates announcement gave Marvel an advantage in surpassing its main competitor, DC Comics, in making a high-profile, diverse hire. The two companies have long competed for dominance in market share, top talent, and eye-catching products. This rivalry extends beyond sales, influencing the perception of each company's cultural relevance. Commentators outline distinctions between the two companies.[24] Diehard fans for DC and Marvel engage in debates about which company outshines the other. Marvel's decision to employ a famed Black writer certainly gave it an edge over DC in certain respects.

Marvel, so the writings about its recent hire indicated, diversified its roster of creators with one of the most highly regarded commentators on race in the country. Graeme McMillan emphasized that "Coates is known as one of the leading American writers on race."[25] Evan Narcisse relayed that Coates is "widely regarded as one of the most important chroniclers of the modern black experience."[26] Joshua Rivera, writing for *GQ* magazine, stated that Coates is "one of our foremost cultural critics and quite possibly the best living writer on race in America."[27] What a buzzy news item: the foremost commentator on race in America was taking his talents to Marvel.

Now look, no individual writer can or should hold the title of best race writer. Such a designation emerges from a long, troubling racialized history whereby decision-makers select a single principal African American as the spokesperson, unelected representative, or H.N.I.C.[28] To his credit, even Coates routinely spoke out against reporters praising him at the expense of other Black writers and thinkers.[29] Despite the problems associated with labeling someone the "best living writer on race," as Rivera had put it, doing so made the idea of such a writer all the more appealing and provocative for audiences. Who wouldn't be intrigued that a supposed principal chronicler of Black experience was hired to write *Black Panther*?

Marvel initiated buzz by coordinating with *The New York Times*, and a chorus of reporters and commentators enhanced the narrative by describing Coates's importance as a commentator on race. The participation of media outlets and cultural critics in swarming around an author and product and thus building buzz to shape reception and purchases are vital for success in a competitive marketplace. "One of the nation's brightest and most influential writers will be writing a comic book for Marvel," wrote Alex Abad-Santos for *Vox*.[30] Writing for *Forbes* magazine, Rob Salkowitz observed that comic book companies like Marvel faced mounting pressure to increase the diversity of their creative talent and to employ creators whose identities reflected the identities of lead characters. "Hiring Coates to write Black Panther," concluded Salkowitz, "hits that target with a shoulder-launched missile."[31] According to Joseph Illidge, "The fusion of Black creator to Black character is quite unique to monthly American superhero comic books," thus making Marvel's selection of Coates to write T'Challa a "brilliant" and "perfect" choice.[32] The appraisals by Illidge, Salkowitz, and Abad-Santos contributed to spreading the word about Coates and clarified the overall significance of his upcoming authorship of *Black Panther*.

The announcements about Coates's writing for Marvel included criticisms and hopefulness concerning diversity in the comics industry. "That fans and non-fans alike are already excited to see Ta-Nehisi Coates writing a Black Panther series for Marvel Comics," noted Arturo Garcia for *The Guardian*, "tells us a lot about the resurgent appetite for inclusiveness within comics communities." Garcia then reminded readers that Marvel had been critiqued for hiring only a small number of creators of color, and he took the occasion of the Coates announcement to express representation grievances. For instance, Garcia noted that *The Ultimates* comic book series brings together T'Challa and other characters of color but was written by "a white Englishman, Al Ewing." Garcia wonders about the benefits for readers and creators of color, "if Coates's signing is not accompanied by more black talent signings on other books in the Marvel line?"[33]

According to Scott Woods in an article for *Black Nerd Problems*, "Putting Coates on Black Panther is practically a superhero team-up in and of itself." People greatly admired Coates, viewing him as a talented thinker and writer, and comic book fans T'Challa in high regard. Woods determined that "a steadfast grassroots movement like #BlackLivesMatter has literally forced the hand of long-entrenched institutions and typically indifferent political candidates to address the very value of Blackness on its own terms." Woods predicted that Coates's writing for the series "has the potential to be real political theater, to bring some earnest observations about Black life into a notoriously (in every sense of the word) White space. And the field could use 1000% more of that."[34] Woods, Garcia, David Betancourt, Yanan Wang, Joshua Rivera, Hugh Armitage, and Illidge, to name a few, addressed diversity challenges and prospects in their articles about the announcement of Marvel hiring Coates to write *Black Panther*.[35]

These articles, addressing criticisms leveled at Marvel and comic book companies in general about the lack of diverse creators, revealed that reporters and commentators could actively address the representation struggles of Black writers in comics while announcing an upcoming publication. Even in the midst of expressing excitement about an exalted Black writer entering the field, cultural critics leveled direct and implicit critiques. Marvel "has been suffering from a well-documented representation problem (and it's not alone in the comics industry)," noted Armitage, "so the news comes as a welcome surprise."[36] The writers influenced and contributed to the content of buzz focusing on Coates and *Black Panther* by reminding audiences about the recent struggles of Marvel to adequately address diverse representation.

In an interview, J. A. Micheline, described as "a vocal critic of Marvel and their struggles with diversity," shared her point of view on the Coates hire. "I think it's a bittersweet announcement," she said. On the positive side, Coates is "an amazing writer who really understands the semiotics of race, of how black people have been depicted in media, and really understands the nuances of history." She anticipated that Coates would have "so much to bring to the table, and it's amazing to have someone like that writing comics." That said, she also spoke to the "bitter" aspect: the incredibly high bar set for Black writers to gain opportunities on major titles. "Is this what it takes for Marvel to hire a black writer? Do you have to have two books out? Do you have to be a household name and a writer for *The Atlantic* in order to be considered for a role?" Micheline wondered.[37]

In the case of Micheline and additional cultural critics, the announcement about Coates writing for Marvel, well ahead of the release of *Black Panther* #1, proved to be an opportune time to address diversity challenges. Marvel's announcement about Coates constituted a big news event that guaranteed large numbers of people with varying degrees of knowledge and experience tuned in. For years, commentators critiqued cultural appropriation and the lack of Black writers in comics, but there had rarely been moments where dozens of comic book news sites and mainstream media chose to reference those issues over the course of a few days. From September 22 to 24, 2015, however, more than fifty reporters and commentators wrote about Marvel hiring Coates to write *Black*

Panther, and a mix of the articles addressed diversity issues in comics. Oliver Sava pointed out that the selection of Coates to write *Black Panther* was "a surprising but very welcome decision," given Marvel's "ongoing problems with creator representation."[38]

The articles did more than address diversity; they also sparked anticipation for the eventual release. The quantity of publicity signaled potential consumer interest, which is critically relevant in comics since store owners determine the size of orders based on their predictions of what and how much customers will purchase.[39] A book being discussed across media gave store owners confidence to place large orders, reducing their risk. This journalism ensured broader exposure and fueled anticipation for fans. In short, prepublication fanfare fueled preorders.

If abundant, positive reporting for an upcoming author and book led to rewarding returns, then what about authors and books that received minimal notice? As it turns out, indifference defines the standard for most books. The relative lack of analyses for Black comic book writers makes it less likely for store owners to take a chance on preordering issues of the titles that they produce. Indeed, John Ridley and then Eve Ewing, both of whom followed Coates as writers on *Black Panther*, received nowhere near the notice prior to publication that he did. In fact, Marvel, DC Comics, Image, and Boom! Studios have not yet managed to recreate *Black Panther*-level buzz for titles by other Black comic book writers, including Bryan Hill, David F. Walker, N. K. Jemisin, Victor LaValle, Brandon Thomas, and Roxane Gay. Accordingly, those writers and their titles have received relatively little public notice outside of the domain of comics.

The considerable news items devoted to Coates were a grand achievement and a confirmation of his attention power, but in some respects, they raised issues. For one, Coates's pathway to comics, as Micheline had observed, was exceptional. What a rarity for Marvel to recruit a Black journalist who worked for a venerated publication, *The Atlantic*, became a bestselling book author, and hailed by critics as a respected commentator on race. If Coates's possession of numerous accolades and attributes gave him advantages, would the lack of similar attributes count against aspiring Black writers in comics? If Coates's route to success as a Black comic book writer was unlikely, then what odds did other Black writers have in the field?

The dispatches following Coates's entry into comics brought to light another challenge. The imbalance in media for one Black writer as opposed to others was on full display. The profuse stories on the Coates announcement set a high standard for the visibility and reception of a Black writer that would be difficult to replicate. Aside from Coates, most other Black writers received diminished acknowledgment and enthusiasm, resulting in less comprehensive promotion.

With limited attention power, the likelihood of works by most Black writers receiving recognition and achieving profitable sales stayed low.

The visibility disparity in the ranks of Black writers indicates a critical component of representation struggles, namely, intra-racial competition. Black writers must ultimately compete with each other for limited, coveted available positions. The competition takes on an indirect and nonhostile form at times, but a contest of sorts persists. Because publishers and media platforms devote limited resources to promoting Black authors, those writers ultimately compete for a few available opportunities. Bryan Hill, N. K. Jemisin, David F. Walker, and Roxane Gay received significantly more discussion than other Black writers, yet their appraisals paled in comparison to that of Coates. Comparisons of reviews for books by Black writers in comics expose differences in visibility and reception.[40] Unlike most of his peers in the field, Coates's debut and career encompassed much more than comics, which contributed to the disproportionate publicity he received, even prior to the release of his first comic book.

Similar to the situation in comics, visibility disparity exists throughout African American literary studies. Novelists Zora Neale Hurston, Richard Wright, Ralph Ellison, and Toni Morrison pervade scholarly discourse, as dozens of other authors receive far fewer examinations. Likewise, studies of poems by Langston Hughes, Gwendolyn Brooks, and Amiri Baraka far outnumber examinations of hundreds of other Black poets. These uneven patterns of visibility leave innumerable Black writers in obscurity with a select few receiving intensive attention. Whereas observers critique the underrepresentation of Black writers compared to white writers, we must also recognize that most Black writers are underrepresented even in relation to the small group of widely acclaimed Black writers. Put another way, with underrepresented writers, a few are overrepresented, and plenty remain overlooked. This uneven distribution of acknowledgment restricts views of Black writing and writers, limiting options to fully appreciate their vast and diverse contributions.

Despite the challenges of visibility, the emergence of major figures in a field can bring benefits. Such figures served as catalysts for field-defining conversations and the convergence of cultural critics on landmark texts. The copious commentary and scholarship on Hurston, Wright, Ellison, and Morrison enriched American literary studies and contributed to the growth and formation of African American literary studies as a field. Their works sparked engaged analyses and drew broad audiences to the field. Similarly, the crossover appeal of Coates and the wide-ranging analysis of his work contributed to the growth of Black comic studies as a field. Additionally, Coates's status as a major Black writer might raise the likelihood that literature scholars incorporate aspects of his comic book writing into African American literary studies.

Although comic book commentators and fans lodged critiques about widespread underrepresentation in the industry, the euphoria that accompanied the Coates hire seemed to undermine interest in the equitable distribution of analysis for other creators. The call for Marvel to hire more Black writers was one matter. The effort to persuade media outlets to cover a variety of creators with comparable enthusiasm was a different, challenging undertaking. The imbalances in news accounts perpetuated existing disparity among Black writers. Furthermore, the disproportionate valuation of one Black writer, like in the case of Coates, implied to publishers that employing and elevating a singular African American creator was an adequate response to diversity demands.

Finally, the precedent set by Marvel's decision to hire Coates suggested that comic book companies could address their diversity problems by prioritizing Black writers from domains outside of comics over experienced Black comic book writers. Coates, Roxane Gay, Eve Ewing, Yona Harvey, N. K. Jemisin, Evan Narcisse, and Rembert Browne, none of whom had prior comic book writing experiences, received assignments to write titles without following the conventional extended path traveled by other Black comic book writers such as Dwayne McDuffie, Christopher Priest, Brandon Thomas, David F. Walker, and Bryan Hill. The introduction of Black comic writers with no prior comic book experience came with mixed results. On the one hand, the emergence of a figure like Coates raised the visibility of comics for audiences outside the field and those interested in underrepresented creators. On the other hand, the decision to bypass or under-invest in Black writers already working within comics implied a disregard for their talents and contributions as well as the typical processes of professional advancement in the field.

Still, the inability of Marvel, DC, and Image Comics to inspire high levels of interest in Black creators did not necessarily reflect a failure on their parts. Instead, it clarified the factors that must be in place for an author to garner significant buzz. Marvel's announcement of Coates as a comic book writer drew immediate recognition from journalists, commentators, comics enthusiasts, and even casual cultural observers, who recognized the makings of a game-changing development. They engaged in steady, humming conversations—buzz—about this renowned Black writer and his forthcoming comic book work. The abundant treatments of Coates, characterized by a hopeful and excited tone, built anticipation and assigned value to his Marvel writing long before his comic books appeared. This keen interest in Coates's yet-to-be-published work foreshadowed the tremendous reception his debut ultimately received.

Chapter 3
The Buzziest of Books

The buzz for Coates's debut paid off in a big way. On March 18, 2016, *CBR* reported that retailers had already placed three thousand preorders for *Black Panther* #1 in anticipation that the book would be in high demand upon its April 6 release. "When fans see what Ta-Nehisi and Brian [Stelfreeze] have planned for the first—and best—Black super hero, it's going to be the buzz book of the industry," said Alonso.[1] On March 31, *The New York Times*, an incredibly far-reaching buzz generator, published an article about the soon-to-be-released *Black Panther* #1: "Most comics don't generate that much buzz, but then again, most comics aren't written by Ta-Nehisi Coates, a national correspondent for *The Atlantic* and the best-selling author of 'Between the World and Me,' which won the National Book Award last year."[2] With so much news and anticipation, *Black Panther* #1 stood out as the buzziest of books.

A three-day span in April amounted to an extraordinary response to a comic book by a Black creator. On April 4 and 5, approximately twenty publications and online platforms, including *Ebony*, *IGN*, *Black Girl Nerds*, *Newsarama*, *The New Republic*, *The Baltimore Sun*, and *Nerdist*, published reviews of *Black Panther* #1. On April 6, the official release date of *Black Panther* #1, journalists and cultural critics published another twenty-five assessments of the comic book. The reviews appeared in *The Boston Globe*, *Comics Bulletin*, *Vox*, *BuzzFeed*, *Comicosity*, *Vulture*, and *Time*. This exposure—unprecedented for a debut by a Black comic book writer—resulted from—and extended—the buzz initiated back in September 2015, when Marvel announced Coates as a new hire.

The appearance of scores of reviews for *Black Panther* #1 across diverse publications leading up to and on the comic's official release date reflected a publisher actively shaping the book's reception. Marvel distributed early copies of Coates's debut issue to the press, shaping the scope of venues that reviewed *Black Panther* #1. Prerelease issues function as a standard feature of both the book publishing and comics industries. Coates's *Between the World and*

Me had previously benefited from robust promotional efforts spearheaded by Spiegel & Grau, a Penguin Random House imprint. *Black Panther* #1 received similar promotional resources through Marvel's marketing apparatus.

Over the last two decades, dozens of reviewers covered book releases by African American authors such as Colson Whitehead, Jesmyn Ward, James McBride, and the late Toni Morrison. In comics, hardly any Black writers receive that level of publicity. Reviewers from *The New Republic*, *Ebony*, *The Baltimore Sun*, *The Boston Globe*, *The Hollywood Reporter*, and *Vox* rarely converged on a single comic book by a Black writer. The treatment of Coates's *Black Panther* #1 stood out as an atypical case within comics, which resembled the receptions of well-known Black novelists. For instance, just months after the release of *Black Panther* #1, Whitehead's *The Underground Railroad* (2016) garnered extraordinary notice and acclaim.[3]

Dozens of reviewers responded positively to Coates's first issue. "The new *Black Panther* comic book series, written by Ta-Nehisi Coates and drawn by Brian Stelfreeze, is the most anticipated comic debut of the past decade," wrote Alex Abad-Santos. "And let's get one thing squared away up front: It's excellent."[4] Toussaint Egan reviewed the book and concluded that "*Black Panther* #1 is just a damn good read that will appeal to both die-hard enthusiasts and curious literati looking to see what all the fuss is about. Coates and Stelfreeze's first issue captures the reader's attention and leaves a deep impression."[5] In a direct appeal to comic book fans, Jesse Schedeen asserted that "[w]hether you're a hardcore fan of the character or Captain America: Civil War has you interested in learning more about T'Challa, this comic has plenty to offer."[6] According to Robert Reed, "*Black Panther* #1 is a stellar debut that delivers an intriguing premise, backed by interesting characters and beautiful artwork." He closed by noting that "It is a testament to the creators that *Black Panther* #1 is able to impress in spite of heightened expectations."[7]

The debut did not impress all reviewers. "As someone who isn't up on all the latest drama in the life of T'Challa these past several years," wrote Eric Diaz, "I kept finding myself a bit lost." He observed that referencing so much prior history made Coates's opening "feel like issue #50, not issue #1."[8] Troy Powell, too, expressed disappointment: "If I am to be honest, I was expecting a bit more from this story." He went on to note, "Coates needs to punctuate why this new status quo is different from instances past in order to sustain reader investment."[9] Douglas Ernst, in a review on his blog, praised certain aspects of *Black Panther* #1 but determined that "Coates' desire to write a cerebral superhero may cause him to needlessly sacrifice the kind of action and adventure that translates into return customers."[10] Brett Schenker issued a comparable critique, noting that "[i]deas are presented in an almost poetic staccato way without much of a flow to bring it together. It's a disjointed beginning."[11] Thus, even though *Black Panther* #1 received largely positive reception, some cultural critics expressed reservations and critiques.

The celebration of *Black Panther* #1 constituted a win for Coates and Marvel, but it also made evident a disparity compared to other Black writers who debuted first issues in 2016. While critics favorably evaluated David F. Walker's *Nighthawk* #1 and *Occupy Avengers* #1, Kwanza Osajyefo's *Black* #1, and Geoffrey Thorne's *Mosaic* #1, these titles received far fewer reviews than *Black Panther* #1. John Semper Jr.'s *Cyborg: Rebirth* #1 and Christopher Priest's *Deathstroke* #1, amassed total review counts closer to Coates's, but they lacked the accompanying interviews and author profiles. On top of that, unlike Coates, Semper and Priest received little discussion of their works on African American sites, and their titles failed to attract reviews outside comics-specific publications. These disparities in reporting revealed the struggles of Black comic book creators who may lack the attention power necessary to secure prolonged, high-quality visibility for their works. That power included securing necessary promotional backing from publishers.

Even when an artistic work by a Black creator receives public notice, the limited representation of Black cultural critics results in white critics serving as the primary evaluators. "Those who have for decades been given the biggest platforms to interpret culture are white men," specified Elizabeth Méndez Berry and Chi-hui Yang. "This means that the spaces in media where national mythologies are articulated, debated and affirmed are still largely segregated."[12] Berry and Yang raised concerns about the overwhelming participation of white cultural critics and the paucity of Black critics. The racial imbalance, they suggested, distorted interpretations of Black art and restricted the diversity of perspectives shaping conversations about artistic productions. Berry and Yang's article dealt with art, film, and music, yet the racial imbalance of cultural critics was just as evident in comics journalism. The underrepresentation of African American critics in comics exposes cultural criticism as a site of representation struggles.

Although white journalists and commentators provided the most reviews for *Black Panther* #1, an unusually high number of Black writers contributed segments as well. Jamie Broadnax, Alanna Bennett, Allen Thomas, Shawn Taylor, David Betancourt, William E. Ketchum III, Darryl Holliday, and Egan all published assessments of Coates's first issue. J. A. Micheline, Audie Cornish, Kwame Opam, Jonathan Gray, and Evan Narcisse published interviews and profiles dedicated to Coates. Just so we're clear, in any given year, seldom do ten or more Black culture journalists working for established venues produce write-ups on one issue of a comic book by an African American writer. The plethora of Black reviewers on *Black Panther* #1 testified to the fact that Coates's debut was momentous.

Observers across the comics industry have increasingly acknowledged the lack of diversity among Black creators. But what about the scarcity of Black comic journalists? Commentators hardly mention diversity in comics journalism, yet African American interpretations, or lack thereof, in this realm carry significance. White assessments of cultural productions usually dominate the field. Recall that Joseph Hughes and Joseph Illidge had raised concerns about an absence of Black writers in the industry. J. A. Micheline propelled a conversation about cultural appropriation. Jamie Broadnax's *Black Girl Nerds*, launched in 2012, and Omar Holmon and William Evans's *Black Nerd Problems*, filled voids in African American-run venues with an emphasis on comic books and popular culture. These and other Black cultural critics contributed to the discourse on comics, though their efforts have received relatively little notice.

More than a few Black reviewers responded to Coates's work with enthusiasm. "This is a moment to celebrate," opened David Betancourt in his review for *The Washington Post*. "It's finally time to read and rejoice."[13] In his review for *Black Nerd Problems*, William Evans wrote that "*Black Panther* #1 is basically what many of us anticipated or hoped for, a fresh and ambitious take on the beloved King of our favorite fictional nation."[14] J. A. Micheline linked the timing of Coates's work on *Black Panther* with developments "when marginalized groups are pushing back with visible strength and anger, from Black Lives Matter to #OscarsSoWhite." For her opening question in an interview, Micheline asked Coates about his audience: "Is this Black Panther for us? Or has it been made with whiteness in mind?"[15] Questions about "us" (presumably Black people) and white audiences reflected a line of inquiry about race that abundant white commentators avoid addressing. That did not hold true for Micheline and some other Black fans, critics, and journalists.

On March 20, at 2 a.m., Evan Narcisse held an extended conversation with Coates, who was living in France at the time. On April 6, the release day for *Black Panther* #1, Narcisse published an article on *Kotaku* based on his interview with Coates, and on the same day, Narcisse published the full interview.[16] Rather than read like a standard question and answer interview between a journalist and author, the exchange between Narcisse and Coates read as an extended discussion between two friends discussing their memories and views on comic books. They shared ideas about diversity in comics, Miles Morales, and Coates's greater cultural visibility after the publication of *Between the World and Me*, to identify a few topics, before Narcisse began with his official *Black Panther*-related interview questions. "I know it's two in the morning there but buckle up," Narcisse announced before launching into some of his formal questions. "I'm wide awake, Evan," Coates responded.[17]

The Narcisse-Coates interview delivered something rarely seen: an expansive published conversation between two Black men journalists discussing the history of *Black Panther*, comic books, comic creators, and writing. Nowhere else, in the interviews that he did during his time writing comic books, did Coates show such a willingness to share such a range of his ideas, influences, and interests. Narcisse, a seasoned comics writer with a prior acquaintance with Coates, brought deep knowledge of Black Panther and comic book history, which enabled him to prompt Coates to engage with a wide array of topics. The rich dialogue that emerged attested to the importance of diverse journalists in comics.

Interviews with Coates and reviews of *Black Panther* #1 by Narcisse, J. A. Micheline, Jonathan Gray, Toussaint Egan, L. E. H. Light, and William Evans ensured the inclusion of Black points of view. At the same time, the widespread interest in *Black Panther* raised the likelihood that readers would encounter works by these Black journalists. In at least one case, thoughtful writing on Coates led to a publishing opportunity for a journalist. Wil Moss, Coates's editor at Marvel, read Narcisse's article and interview and recognized Narcisse's strong command of comics knowledge. Moss asked Coates whether Narcisse might be interested in writing comics. Coates introduced Moss and Narcisse, which led to Narcisse becoming the writer for *The Rise of Black Panther*, released in 2018.[18]

Black journalists contributed to the larger body of pieces examining *Black Panther* #1 and Coates. Cultural critics, serving as first responders to texts, stimulate interest and set the mood for how and, crucially, whether audiences will engage in a recent or upcoming comic book, novel, volume of poetry, collection of essays, or memoir. Not long after the release of Coates's first issue, *GQ* magazine published an article titled, "Black Panther, Marvel's First Black Superhero, Is Now the Star of the Year's Most Important Comic."[19] This headline echoed the enthusiastic mood about Coates that journalists expressed when Marvel initially announced hiring him in September 2015. The early promotion and swarm of articles had effectively paved the way for the book's success. In other words, *Black Panther* #1 thrived as a beneficiary of buzz.

Indeed, audiences took notice of the profuse and favorable praise for Coates and his work. On April 8, Rich Johnston reported that retailers sold out of the initial print run of three hundred thousand for *Black Panther* #1.[20] That figure—300,000—is a phenomenal sales performance. "To put that number into context," clarified Eliana Dockterman in *Time* magazine, "Marvel's best-selling 'event series' usually sell around 100,000, and its controversial female *Thor* first issues sold 200,000."[21] *Black Panther* #1 outperformed previous top performers. Marvel soon announced the production of a second printing, which they released on May 11. The company released a third printing on July 20. Those printings accounted for only two of the assorted versions of *Black Panther* #1.

The existence of variant covers for the first book in Coates's run pointed to an additional way that Marvel capitalized on the interest in the book. Comic book companies produced a few variant covers for milestone issues expected to draw the interest of collectors. For *Black Panther* #1, Marvel coordinated the release of more than twenty variant covers, along with those additional second and third printings.[22] That marked an unusually high number of variants for a title by a debut Black writer. The production of those variants represented a substantial investment aimed at confirming *Black Panther* #1 as a pivotal publishing event. The variants also associated Coates's writing with artwork by Alex Ross, Sanford Greene, Scottie Young, Larry Stroman, and Gabriele Dell'Otto.

The large number of visual artists who contributed to the *Black Panther* #1 variants, consequently transformed one comic book into a production by multiple illustrators. Besides the main cover, Stelfreeze drew two additional variants, and Marvel reused his initial cover for the second and third printings of the comic book. One of his covers shows black-and-white sketches of T'Challa. One image shows the hero holding a beaker, a reminder that Black Panther is a man of science. Another Stelfreeze variant overlaps with Marvel's Hip Hop Variants, where the cover images channel hip hop album covers. Stelfreeze draws T'Challa pulling a mask over his head, a direct reference to the cover of *The Black Album* (2003), where Jay-Z adjusts a black baseball cap, covering his eyes.

Alex Ross drew an image showing T'Challa leaping into the air with a white police officer behind him aiming his gun. Outside of Stelfreeze, who drew the images for Coates's script, Ross and the other illustrators likely had no access to the contents of Coates's script, so they could only speculate about the series. Ross's image of T'Challa targeted by a police officer suggests that Coates would address racial conflict in the United States. Gabriele Dell'Otto produced a variant that showed T'Challa battling Doctor Doom. Artist Skottie Young, known for his signature covers showing infant versions of superheroes, presents an image of a kitten playing with a ball of yarn for his *Black Panther* variant.

Felipe Smith's variant appears as part of Marvel's *Black Panther* fiftieth anniversary issue. The cover shows an image of Black Panther joined by the Fantastic Four—The Thing, Mister Fantastic, Invisible Woman, and the Human Torch. The assemblage of heroes recalls T'Challa's first appearance from *Fantastic Four* #52 in July 1966. Sanford Greene's variant shows a Black father and mother adoring their newborn child, presumably a young T'Challa. Because of the demographics of comics, viewers rarely see Black parents on the cover of a general-audience comic book. Greene's image functions as part of what's known as a "connecting cover." When his variants for #1–#4 are placed together they form a single artistic composition.

Exclusive agreements led to the production of certain *Black Panther* #1 variants with comic book stores, organizations, and special events. Midtown Comics exclusively released a Mark Brooks variant, available only in-store and on its website. Neal Adams produced a *Black Panther* #1 variant for Newbury Comics, an independent retailer. The Comic Book Legal Defense Fund (CBLDF), a nonprofit organization that supports the First Amendment rights of comics creators and publishers, sponsored Todd Nauck's variant. Dale Keown's image for GameStop exudes Afrofuturist aesthetics as Black Panther rides a flying motorcycle-like vehicle. Greg Horn produced a *Black Panther* #1 variant for the Middle East Film and Comic Convention (MEFCC) held April 7–9, 2016, in Dubai, United Arab Emirates. Horn's cover image shows an illustration of Stan Lee and T'Challa standing back-to-back.

After purchasing exclusive *Black Panther* #1 variants, countless sellers would resell the items. Retailers use online platforms to display and resell rare and hard-to-find issues, while private sellers utilize eBay. The first edition *Black Panther* #1, its two additional printings, and variants now circulate alongside thousands of other comic books online, at comic book stores, and at conventions. The prices of those *Black Panther* #1 issues change, losing and gaining value based on factors such as whether the book contains blemishes, stays in pristine condition, or includes author and artist signatures. In some cases, variants reach exorbitant prices.

The MEFCC Greg Horn *Black Panther* #1 variant with an illustration of Stan Lee and T'Challa standing back to back provides a case in point. One of those issues, encased in a Comics Guaranty Company (CGC) holder with a 9.8 rating, contains autographs from director Ryan Coogler, the late Stan Lee, and the late actor Chadwick Boseman. When the MEFCC released Horn's *Black Panther* #1 variant in early April 2016, Coogler and Boseman had not yet been officially linked to T'Challa, but later, after February 2018, with the release of the *Black Panther* film, those two men became closely connected to the franchise. After the passing of Lee and Boseman in November 2018 and August 2020, respectively, their signatures on that variant significantly increased the symbolic capital of the comic book, which was, at one point, priced at $25,000.[23] Early on, those variants sold for relatively low prices, but the increases reflected the rising popularity and value of *Black Panther* #1.

In February 2023, years after Coates's debut, the online limited edition consumer goods store StockX partnered with Marvel to release yet another variant of *Black Panther* #1. This cover image, drawn by Sanford Greene, depicts Black Panther with his claws extended as he crouches on a statue of a roaring panther. StockX promoted the variant issue as a collector's item tied to *Black Panther: Wakanda Forever*, which premiered in November 2022. "A collectible comic for the ages, the book tells the classic Black Panther #1 story (originally published in 2016)," wrote a StockX press release about the variant, "written by award-winning American author Ta-Nehesi Coates, and features custom cover art by Sanford Greene that punctuates his signature rugged and unfiltered style."[24] The release of this variant attested to the enduring cultural and commercial significance of Coates's *Black Panther* run, as well as its ability to generate new waves of interest years after its initial publication.

The artists involved with covers for *Black Panther* #1 foreshadowed the stellar artistic production that would persist throughout Coates's run on the series. Nearly a hundred artists produced main and variant covers for issues of *Black Panther* between 2016 and 2021. The variant covers became collectors' items and served the ends of a marketing strategy by building interest in a product. The diverse covers equally exemplified creativity and artistic prowess. The variants collectively enriched depictions of T'Challa, providing talented artists with avenues to converge and showcase their skills rendering a common focal subject.

Although white visual artists drew several of the *Black Panther* variants, accusations of cultural appropriation did not gain traction. The bulk of such criticism fell on white writers depicting Black characters and the companies that published their work. Observers either did not determine that white artists drawing Black characters posed an issue, or they implicitly decided to prioritize critiques about writers and publishers. Charges of cultural appropriation had previously surfaced in the context of the Hip Hop Variants when some critics initially assumed the underrepresentation of artists of color. Conversely, few seemed concerned with the demographics of the variant artists for *Black Panther* #1 and later issues.

In the news segments for *Black Panther* #1, Stelfreeze received considerable praise for his artwork. Jesse Schedeen wrote, "Stelfreeze's striking figures and general sense of design made him a natural fit for this series, and this first issue doesn't disappoint," adding "There's both a power and weariness to the way T'Challa is drawn here which suits the story well."[25] In *The Washington Post*, David Betancourt noted that Coates's writing was "aided by the beautiful African vibes of Stelfreeze's artistry."[26] Stelfreeze received equal billing in the headline of a *Vox* article titled, "Black Panther by Ta-Nehisi Coates and Brian Stelfreeze is brilliant, political, and human." Alex Abad-Santos praised Stelfreeze's art as "crisp and expressive," emphasizing his ability to create "a sleek space opera of sorts, since Wakanda's technology is so advanced" and then deftly shifting "into solemn drama, conveying weighty moments and relationships with the same precision."[27] Stelfreeze, who began his career in the 1980s, had already built a reputation as a talented and respected artist within the industry. Collaborating with Coates, though, introduced his work to a much broader audience, ensuring that audiences appreciated his artistry beyond the world of comics.

Wired magazine enlisted Stelfreeze's talents to create a custom image for an interview with Coates. Stelfreeze painted a profile of Coates wearing a Wakandan technological headpiece, with designs superimposed on him that suggest a fusion with T'Challa and Wakandans. As the illustration merges technology and an African American subject, the article's title, "Ta-Nehisi Coates Fights the Power—Literally—With Black Panther" invokes the popular rap song, "Fight the Power" by Public Enemy and frames Coates's work as a serious struggle rather than mere child's play that some might associate with comics.[28] The title and illustration converge to present a compelling vision of Black and Afrofuturist aesthetics. This vision subtly yet significantly strengthened Coates's attention power, captivating audiences by positioning him as a Black Panther figure in his own right.

The highly competitive and densely populated field of comics makes it difficult for most creators to achieve tremendous success. One hurdle comes with the opening issue of a series. "First issues often make or break a series," observed Sean Bartley. "Unfortunately, comics that fail to hook readers with their first offering aren't typically given a second chance by readers."[29] But before even hooking readers, the books must first reach readers. Highly successful first issues are recipients of copious prepublication publicity *and* preorders—rare commodities for most titles—and dispatches immediately following the release. Titles and creators that do not receive backing struggle to gain and maintain interests from sizable audiences.

As noted throughout this book, the visibility disparity between Coates and his peer African American creators constituted a telling but underdiscussed element of representation struggles in comics. Select creators (i.e., superstars) receive a disproportionately high amount of documentation in comparison to the majority of their contemporaries. Disparity in treatments can appear pronounced with underrepresented creators, in view of their already limited participation. The acclaim and fanfare bestowed on Coates stood as an accomplishment, while the absence of commentary on additional Black comic writers was worrisome. The accumulated body of *Black Panther* #1 announcements, reviews, interviews, and visual productions amounted to sizable and valuable information. We lacked comparable information about other Black titles and ended up with an insufficient record of African American creative production at this pivotal juncture in comics.

Marvel published *Nighthawk* #1, written by David F. Walker in May 2016, a month after the release of *Black Panther* #1. Walker's book received little prepublication discussion, and a small number of media sources reviewed the first issue. Those sources consisted of comics publications, which meant Walker's book gained no crossover, mainstream notice. After four issues, Marvel canceled the book. "Marvel is making a reasonable decision given the sales," Walker tweeted. "We made a great book, but sales didn't warrant a longer run."[30]

In an article for *The Washington Post*, Betancourt discussed the cancelation: "*Nighthawk* should have been a slam dunk in terms of satisfying the demands for diversity in comics that have sprang up on social media," he wrote. "Black hero, black writer (David F. Walker), black issues on the black side of a major metropolitan city."[31] Nonetheless, Walker's book did not generate sufficient interest and sales. News in a venue like *The Washington Post* came only after the cancelation as part of the postmortem reflections. Joseph Illidge wrote about a number of factors that explained why comic books fail. Those factors included, noted Illidge, "brand recognition, projected profit and loss, target audience, overall annual promotions budget in relation to the number of titles a publisher puts out in a year." He went on to state that "we have to look at the level of promotional push *Nighthawk* was given, pre-launch, out the gate, and afterwards." What's more, Illidge contended that DC Comics and Marvel released titles, which "mercilessly pushed" *Nighthawk* out of the top-50 slot of sales.[32]

The observations from Betancourt and Illidge suggested that employing a Black writer to produce a story with a Black protagonist does not guarantee success, even as people expressed interest in diversity. To succeed, a comic book by a Black writer or any author needed promotional support, friendly market forces, prelaunch dispatches, and more, all of which link to attention power. Unlike Coates and *Black Panther*, Walker and *Nighthawk* failed to gain wide recognition across media platforms. Though Walker commands respect as an experienced writer and highly respected figure in the realm of comics, having published titles since 2014, including *Shaft*, *Cyborg*, *Power Man and Iron Fist*, and *Bitter Root*, he and *Nighthawk* did not receive timely or robust treatments. By contrast, Coates, whose preexisting fame made him a highly visible figure, entered the comics field well positioned to attract acclaim.

The success of *Black Panther* #1 created opportunities for Coates to lead additional series and secure employment prospects for other Black writers at Marvel. First, on July 22, Marvel announced a spinoff, *Black Panther: World of Wakanda*, which would be written by Roxane Gay and Yona Harvey. The series would follow former Dora Milaje members, Ayo and Aneka, who had figured prominently in *Black Panther* #1. Coates recruited both Gay and Harvey, thinking their contributions could enhance the presentation of women characters who appeared in his ongoing series.[33] Marvel had previously failed to hire Black women writers. But within a year of Coates's hiring, he had leveraged his influence to employ Gay and Harvey.

Second, in January 2017, Marvel announced another Coates-led spinoff, *Black Panther and the Crew*. Cowritten with Harvey, the series introduced a team comprised of T'Challa, Luke Cage, Storm, and Misty Knight. A headline for *The Hollywood Reporter* proclaimed that the spinoff gave Marvel "its first all-black superteam."[34] A version of the comic book had previously been published in 2003 as *The Crew*, written by Christopher Priest. This new version, like *World of Wakanda*, included *Black Panther* in the title, a reflection of Marvel capitalizing on the popularity of the comic and character. The involvement of Coates in two spinoffs showed his decision-making power at Marvel as well as the company's willingness to invest in him for new titles. Marvel executives viewed *Black Panther: World of Wakanda* and *Black Panther and the Crew* as viable projects based on the profitability of Coates's debut.

Within a short span of time, from September 2015 to April 2016, Coates became one of the most widely discussed comic book writers. Some envisioned him as a counterpoint, if not solution, to the field's diversity woes. The headline of an article in *The New Republic* proclaimed, "Superhero Comics Have a Race Problem. Can Ta-Nehisi Coates Fix It?"[35] The extensive reporting on one distinguished African American writer did not necessarily mean ample support for African American creators in comics. Nonetheless, the news, reviews, interviews, and perspectives on Coates and his works technically indicated a stirring development in representation struggles for Black creators. The tremendous appraisals of Coates made his first issue quite bankable.

Black Panther #1 ranked as one of the best-selling comic books of 2016.[36] Brian Cronin identified Coates's opening installment as one of the more consequential #1 issues of the decade. "*Black Panther* #1 changed things for both Black Panther and Marvel Comics," he enthused, "the degree of which continues to unfold."[37] By the end of 2019, sales figures revealed that *Black Panther* #1 ranked within the top-30 best-selling comic books of the 2010s.[38] Coates's issue held the top spot for comic books written by Black authors. And maybe that's no surprise, as Coates's attention power facilitated the swarm of publicity that made *Black Panther* #1 the buzziest of books.

Chapter 4
No One Man

On the afternoon of April 26, 1957, near 125th Street and Lenox Avenue in Harlem, New York, police officers used excessive force on a group of African American men. They then made arrests and took them to the 28th Precinct. The incident may have otherwise become part of the long catalog of troubling yet underreported interactions between police officers and African Americans, but a subset of the men arrested belonged to Mosque No. 7, led by a young minister named Malcolm X. When he heard what happened, he took action. Malcolm assembled a group of fellow Muslims to go to the station house.

When they arrived, the police officers eventually permitted Malcolm inside the precinct, and he discovered that one of the men needed immediate medical assistance. The police eventually relented and allowed medical personnel to transport the man to Harlem Hospital. A hundred Muslims "who walked in formation north up Lenox Avenue" followed the ambulance transporting the man. After receiving treatment, the officers returned the Muslim man to the police station house. Malcolm and an auxiliary unit of the Nation of Islam, known as the Fruit of Islam (FOI) followed. At approximately 2:30 a.m., as angry Harlem citizens stood outside of the jail and watched, they witnessed something remarkable. Malcolm, "gave a hand signal to his FOI," and they "silently and immediately" marched away. The sight of this Black man followed by a large disciplined group of Black men stunned the policemen. One officer, who observed what happened, commented to a journalist from the *Amsterdam News* that "[n]o one man should have that much power."[1]

Those events unfolded in 1957 and gained popularity in 1992, when Spike Lee recreated the scene in his movie Malcolm X, introducing the charismatic Muslim leader on the big screen to a generation of viewers. In the film, Malcolm, played by Denzel Washington, holds his hand up, and the dozens of gathered FOI facing him turn in unison to their left. The large crowd of protestors falls silent.

When Malcolm points his finger, the FOI turn and silently walk off. A white police captain observes and then says, "That's too much power for one man to have."

In 2010, the comment about an individual Black man with too much power gained popularity yet again. In his song "Power," Ye, then known as Kanye West, utters a chorus that includes the line "No one man should have all that power." Here, a famous performer repurposed the line for the braggadocio of rap discourse. With the line, West restated what critics said about him or what he hoped that they might say. From the *Amsterdam News* to a Spike Lee movie to a rap song, the line about a Black man with an apparent excess of power eventually made its way to comics.

In the closing pages of *Black Panther* #1, Aneka expresses her frustration to her fellow Dora Miljae and lover Ayo: "I am tired of living and dying on the blood-right of one man." Ayo responds, "No one man should have that much power." In the next issue, Aneka and Ayo vow to begin taking matters into their own hands. Their supporters use fire to burn a message in the ground, which blazes "NO ONE MAN." Here, in the first two issues, we witness what would become a critical development in the history of *Black Panther*: a reconfiguration of monarchical rule in Wakanda.

Adilifu Nama made the case that T'Challa was "an idealized composite of third-world" African leaders such as Jomo Kenyatta, Patrice Lumumba, and Kwame Nkrumah.[2] By adding "no one man" to the storyline, Coates extended this T'Challa lineage to include Malcolm X. In fact, given the roots and routes of the phrase, the line now calls to mind Spike Lee, Denzel Washington, and Kanye West. From this angle, "no one man" resonates with Black aesthetics, invoking African American figures by presenting a single phrase. Coates also repurposed the utterance. Unlike in previous instances, he presented Black women raising concerns about a Black man holding too much solitary power.

The opening series titled "A Nation Under Our Feet," appeared each month from April 2016 to March 2017 and ultimately formed three trade paperback editions. Taking the title and inspiration from Steven Hahn's Pulitzer Prize winning book *A Nation Under Our Feet: Black Political Struggles in the Rural South from Slavery to the Great Migration* (2003), Coates seeks to present a narrative showing a people organizing to occupy a new status in their country, which may have previously taken them for granted. When asked why he chose *A Nation Under Our Feet* as the title of his series, Coates said that "Hahn's book is all about the grassroots," which is a contrast from much of "Great Man theory," on figures like Abraham Lincoln, Frederick Douglass, and others. Hahn is "interested in the little movements of the people who are underneath, of the slaves whose stories haven't been told." Coates took a similar approach with *Black Panther*: "As much as this is the story of T'Challa, you're going to see him grappling with the nation underneath."[3]

The twelve-issue series weaves together a few different threads. For one, an insurgent group seeks to overthrow T'Challa's rule on the basis of his prior alleged neglect of the country. In addition, the Dora Milaje, led by Midnight Angels, Ayo and Aneka, determine that they will no longer serve as the protection service of their king. Finally, T'Challa agonizes that his sister Shuri is trapped in a coma-like state, and he works to revive her. Shuri, meanwhile, travels along a plane of Wakanda's collective past known as the Djalia. The exploration of these narrative threads, drawn first by Brian Stelfreeze and then Chris Sprouse and colored by Laura Martin, pushed comic book depictions of Black characters in new directions.

The critiques raised about monarchy in *Black Panther* promised to redefine T'Challa's ruling status in his country. Despite abundant reviews of issues 1 and 2, the significance of the changes with Wakanda's system of government that Coates initiated may have been underreported. Granted, two issues did not provide reviewers with enough material to fully recognize what was unfolding. The story needed more time to develop. In comic books, moreover, new developments perpetually occur, and *Black Panther* storylines regularly involve T'Challa fighting to protect his place on the throne. Still, Coates proposed a new direction for Wakanda. The statement "no one man should have that much power" in the context of *Black Panther* amounted to interrogating the very idea of whether a nation of people should be represented by a king. Furthermore, Dora Miljae's articulation of the phrase "no one man" evoked a Black feminist critique.

In an article for *The Atlantic*, Coates outlined his approach to writing a comic book. He disclosed that he approaches journalistic projects with a question in mind. He took a similar query approach writing *Black Panther*, where he wondered, "Would an advanced society tolerate a monarch?"[4] Coates did not apparently think so. He figured that some Wakandans would find the idea of being led and represented by a king limited, if not troubling.

By the way, a version of Coates's words from the article later appears in Coogler's *Black Panther* film. Coates wrote that a simple question at the heart of his comic book narrative was "Can a good man be a king?" In the movie, T'Chaka informs his son T'Challa at one point, "You're a good man, with a good heart, and it's hard for a good man to be king." The questions and struggles that Coates conceived of for T'Challa became components of later narratives created by other creators. The reappearance of Coates's ideas in the works of others indicated the resonance of his formulations.

Black Panther #1 opens with T'Challa visiting the Vibranium mines and finding himself under attack. To the king's surprise, his own people look at him angrily and attempt to overpower him. T'Challa comes to realize that his citizens are possessed by Zenzi, a woman who acts as a revealer. That means, T'Challa explains, "she brings out of us all the awful feelings that we have hidden away."[5] She incites groups of Wakandans to use violence to act on their previously suppressed anger with their king. Their anger had been there, but social norms and the power of the monarchy previously kept them passive. With Zenzi's provoking, the miners had angrily come to realize that no one man should control them. It is worth noting here that Zenzi is not affiliated with Ayo and Aneka, who had their own reasons for questioning T'Challa's power.

Zenzi instead joins forces with Tetu, a villain who plans to overthrow T'Challa and rule Wakanda. "Fall, betrayers!" shouts T'Challa when he first encounters and attacks Tetu, Zenzi, and their army of supporters. Tetu rebukes the charges. "You dare accuse us of treachery," he says, and begins cataloging instances of when T'Challa had seemingly abandoned Wakanda. While speaking, Tetu employs his magical powers to control natural elements and causes tree roots to subdue T'Challa and the War Dogs, a group of Wakandan fighters and secret service.

Trapped, Black Panther must listen as Tetu lists grievances. Tetu references storylines from *The Avengers* and *New Avengers* written by Jonathan Hickman, which involved T'Challa teaming with other superheroes to address a litany of challenges and threats to humanity, sometimes apparently placing the world above specific problems in Wakanda. "Some of us remember the old ways," Tetu says in closing his criticism of T'Challa becoming involved in the affairs of outsiders and thus going against Wakanda's long-standing policy of isolation. He then continues noting that "some of us are more than our birthright," indicating that T'Challa's advantages in life derived from his blood lineage. "Know that a day is coming when Wakanda will be ruled by Wakandans, and the worms of the earth shall devour all wolves, lions, and leopards," says Tetu. "And the era of kings shall end," yet another iteration of the notion that no one man should possess all the power.[6]

Yet another figure, Changamire, emerges who questions the monarchy system of government in Wakanda. Created by Coates as a new character in the *Black Panther* storyline, Changamire emerges as a dissident philosopher who teaches at Hekima Shulē, a learning academy. The inclusion of John Locke quotes and philosophical musings means the character operates as a vehicle for Coates to instill a sense of intellectualism in *Black Panther*. In his debut scene, Changamire lectures to a room full of students.[7] In his next scene, when Ramonda visits him, Changamire appears standing on a library ladder near a bookcase, further indicating his identity as a man of learning.[8]

Images of Black characters reading or surrounded by books recur throughout African American literature. In their respective autobiographies, Frederick Douglass, Richard Wright, and Malcolm X include scenes describing their processes of expanding their reading skills and knowledge growth. Over the decades, scholars of African American referenced these reading scenes. Similarly,

Maya Angelou's *I Know Why the Cage Bird Sings* (1969), charts her childhood encounters with literature that contribute to her developing her voice and self-confidence. Celie, the protagonist of Alice Walker's *The Color Purple* (1982), learns to read as she exchanges letters with her sister. In Ernest J. Gaines's *A Lesson Before Dying* (1993), a local schoolteacher takes the time to instruct a young Black man sentenced to death how to read. The Black woman protagonist of Colson Whitehead's *The Intuitionist* (1999) re-reads an author's books with a new lens when she learns his identity as a Black man. Coates invokes histories of Black people learning and reading, portrayed in African American literature, by showing Changamire surrounded by and engaging with books.

Shortly after Changamire and Ramonda meet and begin speaking, Changamire says, "I won't enroll in your national lie." The words echo a sentiment initially expressed by Coates. On the evening of November 18, 2015, in his acceptance speech for the National Book Award, Coates stated that "you won't enroll me in this lie"—the American narrative stating that all people, regardless of race, had the same rights to freedom and safety.[9] Coates had repurposed his statement as dialogue for Changamire. Whereas Coates interrogated American ideas at the National Book Award event, Changamire questioned the principles of his African country.

"Wakanda has all the intelligence any advanced society would want," states Changamire, "and none of the wisdom that any free society needs."[10] Despite its reputation for technological superiority, Wakanda lacks democratic maturity. With just one man as the leader, the country's citizens are inadequately represented. Through Changamire, Coates further gives voice to the question of whether a forward-thinking country would tolerate a monarch. The inclusion of a philosopher, who was not an enemy of T'Challa and Wakanda but merely a thinker interested in exploring serious concerns, creates space to challenge the status quo without turning to the familiar comic book narrative formula of good versus evil. Changamire primarily urges Wakanda to live up to its professed ideals.

Throughout "A Nation Under Our Feet Series," T'Challa exposes the problems of ruling over a nation and inevitably neglecting the citizenry. At one point, he recalls wisdom about kings passed along to him from his uncle, S'yan, a former ruler of Wakanda. S'yan had shared how "the majesty of kings lay in their mystique." In retrospect, T'Challa wishes his uncle had told him about more than just kings. Instead, he regrets that he lacked more substantial knowledge about everyday people in his nation: "They, too, hold mysteries. They, too, possess, a power all their own."[11]

Later, T'Challa further considers the difficulty of projecting the regal stature of a king while internally holding a desire to raise questions and explore possibilities. "Two men are forever warring within me," T'Challa says to himself, "the man I am called to be, and the man I truly am."[12] Whereas his status as a king requires him to exude strength and an all-knowing demeanor, his identity as a scientist compels him to embrace curiosity. The two warring men within T'Challa resemble W. E. B. Du Bois's famous concept of double consciousness where Black Americans come to feel two-ness: "two souls, two thoughts, two un-reconciled strivings; two warring ideals in one dark body."[13] If T'Challa articulates and recognizes a sense of twoness, then he too believes that no one man can hold sole authority.

The interrogation of Black leadership within majority Black locales amounts to pinpointing intra-racial dimensions of representation struggle. It's one thing for Black citizens to address inadequate representation by white leaders and white-controlled systems. Observers identify the problem as racism or racial prejudice. But what happens when the leaders navigate a Black system? The issue requires a multifaceted approach, one that Coates takes by introducing a flood of characters to affirm various viewpoints.

Depictions of intra-racial tension seldom surface within the majority white context of mainstream comics. Stan Lee and Jack Kirby created a king who first appears based on his interaction with the Fantastic Four. Even later storylines that showed Killmonger challenging the throne did not involve a dissection of monarchy in general. Opponents like Killmonger wanted to replace T'Challa not the Wakandan system of government. By examining and critiquing one-man rule, Coates formulated new possibilities for *Black Panther*. He also updated Wakanda to surpass the antiquated notion of kings and queens in Africa. Put differently, he was decolonizing *Black Panther*—a process that had been taking place over the decades for writers interested in presenting views of Wakanda beyond *jungle action* stereotypes of Africa and Africans. As Rebecca Wanzo noted with attempts to shift directions and depictions about the character and comic, "This slow decolonization of the Black Panther is the effort to decenter the white perspective from the construction of the character."[14]

Late in the "A Nation Under Our Feet" series as he sits in Changamire's library, T'Challa and the philosopher have a discussion about monarchy and the future of Wakanda. "What if I told you I never wanted to be king?" asks T'Challa. Changamire responds that it would not surprise him because "men who wish to be kings have almost never considered their request," and then asks rhetorically, "who, in full sanity, would try to hold a nation under their feet?" Changamire informs T'Challa that others have considered the dilemma of who might rule a nation. The philosopher references the US Civil War as one example where people fought and killed each other "all for the right to live as kings."[15]

The two men's exchange directly confronts the problem of a single man ruling Wakanda. During the conversation, T'Challa admits that "Wakanda must change," even though he acknowledges that he is not yet sure how. A Black king and a Black philosopher sitting down to debate the limits of monarchial rule, and agreeing on the need for change, makes for an astonishing episode. The discussion stands out in part because in the context of *Black Panther* and the Marvel universe in general, since T'Challa's status as a king has long been central to his identity. Here, in this instance, we see T'Challa fully acknowledging that he too thinks that monarchy should not carry forth in Wakanda. He apparently agrees that "no one man should have that much power."

The exchange also presents an opportunity to reflect on why a nation like Wakanda needs practical approaches, like those embodied by T'Challa's government, and the ideals conveyed by a philosopher like Changamire. During their discussion, Changamire asks T'Challa if he recognizes the book in his hand. T'Challa replies that he is unfamiliar with it. "A pity," says Changamire. "Your father did a lot for Wakanda's educational system. But he did not have much use for the humanities."[16] On one level, this comment affirms the value of studying history, literature, and culture—the humanities. Simultaneously, Coates, through Changamire, delivers an incisive critique of Wakanda, a nation renowned for its technological innovation whose citizens rarely show a deep interest in engaging with the history of ideas and the profound questions emerging from global discourse.

By critiquing the absence of humanities and humanists, Coates further decolonizes *Black Panther*. He raises the idea that Wakanda's leaders may have failed them in some ways. Despite the country's reputation for technological innovation and achievement, little effort went toward exploring or foregrounding intellectualism. Coates exposes potential weaknesses of Wakanda. People celebrated the country for giving rise to heroic warriors and scientists, but not philosophers like Changamire. Coates challenges the notion that the earlier technological and practical conceptions of Wakanda sufficed. This tension between ideals and reality emerges again when the Midnight Angels face difficult decisions about who they can trust in the fight for Wakanda's future.

The Midnight Angels briefly considered an alliance with Tetu and Zenzi in the effort to overthrow Wakanda. However, reports emerged that Tetu's army, in the wake of liberating the country had abused and sexually assaulted women. When the Midnight Angels confronted Tetu about the behavior of his men, he responded dismissively. "We are at war," he said, "and war is not a context of chivalry and manners." When pressed, Tetu says that "there will be a process of re-education for my men." The mother elder of the Midnight Angels informs him that "No, Tetu, it must stop *now*. Not after. We will not submit to tyranny under a different name."[17]

Ayo and Aneka ultimately decide against supporting Tetu. They hold fast to their idea that no one man should represent Wakanda, and certainly a troubling man like Tetu should not hold the throne. When Aneka informs Tetu that she and the Midnight Angels will not stand with him against T'Challa, she says that "it was always an alliance of interests, Tetu. You knew that."[18] She makes him aware that his means and the actions of his men no longer make the alliance acceptable for her group, especially girls and women. Their interests remained unmet, and in fact, they sensed that they would be treated much worse than with T'Challa as the leader.

In the end, during the final battle with the army of Tetu and Zenzi for Wakanda, T'Challa wins. To achieve victory, he receives support. For one, Shuri returns to aid him and fight by his side. In addition, Changamire agrees to broadcast a message to all of Wakandans. The philosopher says that "no one man can have all the power, but the path to our new country cannot be written in blood and fire."[19] He essentially encourages those who had taken up arms against T'Challa to find an alternative peaceful solution to express their differences. Finally, bygone Wakandans—leaders and everyday citizens—return to support for T'Challa and his forces as they combat and defeat Tetu and Zenzi. "We are a Nation," they announce as they combat Tetu's army. Although they emerged victorious, Shuri explains that "we can never go back."[20] That is, Wakanda must choose a new path that does not rely on just one man.

Aside from the content of his narrative, Coates's method of storytelling addresses the notion that no one man could adequately represent Wakanda. His multithreading approach alternates between scenes on T'Challa, the Midnight Angels, Shuri, Tetu and Zenzi, and Changamire. The narratives featuring secondary characters displace T'Challa's lone standing in *Black Panther*. Instead, others become well established too. In this regard, Coates reveals a multiplicity of Wakanda and Wakandans that have rarely been portrayed to this extent.

Coates's approach risks alienating some readers. *Black Panther* presumably tells the story of Black Panther/T'Challa, and the more time spent on other characters, the less time T'Challa receives. For superhero comic readers drawn to the adventures and daring deeds of a central character, Coates's approach to T'Challa could be disappointing. Some reviewers criticized the limited involvement of Black Panther. Robert Reed observed that at times during the series, T'Challa "has seemed a supporting player in his own book."[21] Prioritizing various characters, most saliently the Midnight Angels, meant that T'Challa inevitably had to cede page time and space.

In at least one case, even Coates expressed reservations about his approach. In a 2021 interview with Evan Narcisse, he reflected on his run on the comic, and he identified what he viewed as a problem with the first issue. "There are probably too many people [in that issue], I guess," said Coates. "There's probably too much going on."[22] When *Black Panther* #1 appeared, Coates was at the beginning of his career as a comic book writer and inclined to include as much as possible, not fully realizing what it meant to pace himself across issues. Additionally, though, such a tapestry of people appears and so much goes on in that first issue because Coates introduces the idea that a constellation of characters and opinions should represent Wakanda. He artistically renders the no one man idea. Fewer characters and narrative threads would have made for a tighter story and given greater narrative weight to T'Challa, but such an approach would not have accomplished the ambitious task of reconfiguring the system of government in Wakanda and the views of the key figures in the narrative.

As will be discussed more in subsequent chapters, Coates's approach positioned Stelfreeze, Chris Sprouse, Wilfredo Torres, and Leonard Kirk to present a spectrum characters and environments in Wakanda. It's not uncommon for comic books to showcase protagonists and their supporting cast. Nevertheless, few comics ever incorporated, let alone preserved, a cross section of African and African American characters. The scenes with dialogue from Zenzi, Tetu, Aneka, Ayo, Changamire, Shuri, and Ramonda ensured that they appeared throughout the twelve issues of "A Nation Under Our Feet." In short, they function as more than nameless extras. T'Challa retains his position as the star of the series, but his ensemble cast figures prominently and becomes integral to representations of Wakandans.

Black Panther #12 opens with major players throughout the series seated in a circle discussing the future of Wakanda. In a review of the issue, Robert Reed emphasized the staging of the scene as an example of Stelfreeze's talents as an artist. "This scene juggles a half dozen characters with at least four distinct arguments," noted Reed. "The way Stelfreeze is able to maneuver the characters so that there is both a progression in their role in the conversation as well as showing their own attitudes and moods with their body language is simply stellar."[23] Those scenes carry power and present the audience with this rare moment where a group of Black people participate in difficult discussions about the way forward for their nation.

Toward the end of "A Nation Under Our Feet," T'Challa informs Ramonda that in the coming months a council "representing every region of Wakanda" will be convened. The council would meet to produce a new constitution and government elected by Wakandans. The new government, he says, will hold the creed, "no one man." Ramonda responds that Wakanda still needs a king, and it must be T'Challa. He agrees but with a caveat, noting that Wakanda will have "one man who represents the nation, but not one who rules the people."[24] He further notes that Wakanda's governing institutions should match the brilliance of its people.

Stan Lee and Jack Kirby introduced T'Challa as a superhero who performed classic feats of valor, a pattern the character continued throughout his appearances. Coates infused the narrative with elements of a political thriller. After all, the recurring theme of "no one man" meditates on governmental representation. The conclusion of the twelve-part series, where characters debate and finally agree to draft a new constitution, confirms the centrality of politics in Coates's run. By decolonizing and questioning the traditional kingship, Coates encourages new visions for Wakanda and Black Panther.

In a review of *Black Panther* #4, Oz Longworth assessed that "Coates' internal narrative is every bit as poetic as you would expect from a scholar of his caliber." Longworth further determined that the overall narrative "has gone from being a superhero book to the Marvel comic version of a political thriller brimming with suspense and intrigue on par with your favorite Tom Clancy novel."[25] In a review of the trade paperback for issues 5–8 for *Entertainment Weekly*, Christian Holub noted that "political drama subsides" as the story progresses. "More time is spent on meditative digressions into folklore, rather than political intrigue or constant action," conveyed Holub, adding that "this collection is very 'talk-y,' especially when compared to Coates's first."[26] Striking the right balance between political thriller, superhero, action-filled comic book, and Wakandan folklore undoubtedly poses narrative challenges for Coates. The demand for more action from comic book fans, pointedly those interested in superhero stories, may have clashed with Coates's sensibilities as a long-form journalist, a writing style that tends to favor slower-paced, contemplative developments.

The presentation of T'Challa's thoughts coincides with the internal musings of Black men fictional characters and the authors of autobiographies by Black men. In this regard, Coates follows narrative paths explored by Frederick Douglass, Richard Wright, Ralph Ellison, James Baldwin, Ishmael Reed, Charles Johnson, Paul Beatty, and Colson Whitehead.[27] Like these writers, Coates shared introspective and sometimes expansive takes on central Black men characters and narrators. The display of T'Challa's interiority also links him to the central figures in poetry volumes by Cornelius Eady, Tyehimba Jess, and Adrian Matejka, where readers gain access to the ruminations of Black men.[28] Referencing this intertextuality situates Coates's portrayal of T'Challa along a continuum of Black literary expression that extends outside of comics.

Within the twelve issues of "A Nation Under Our Feet," T'Challa faces challenges, looks inward and outward for answers to tough questions, receives guidance and assistance from an array of people, and learns beneficial lessons to arrive at a new sense of himself. Extended journeys of Black men characters struggling to understand themselves and their circumstances occupy a central place in African American literature. The protagonists from James Weldon Johnson's *The Autobiography of an Ex-Colored Man* (1912), Ralph Ellison's *Invisible Man* (1952) and Toni Morrison's *Song of Solomon* (1977) face hardships and embark on journeys of self-discovery that correspond to the routes traveled by T'Challa. In other words, Coates's depictions of a superhero recall influential Black men characters in canonical novels. The corresponding character depictions and explorations between the works of a Black comic writer and the works of Black fiction writers suggest interconnected narrative practices of introspection, resilience, and transformation. Recognition of these shared practices can bridge African American literary and comic storytelling.

Coates's interrogations of T'Challa's place in Wakanda echo his reflections on his own place in the world, as detailed in his autobiographical works—*The Beautiful Struggle* (2008) and *Between the World and Me* (2015). In his journalism, he has likewise examined and written about Malcolm X, Bill Cosby, Barack Obama, MF Doom, and more Black men.[29] Connections among Black comic book writers, memoirists, and journalists prove crucial for acknowledging the breadth of Black creative production. Coates exemplifies this convergence, embodying all three facets in one figure. Prior to writing comic books, Coates spent years as a blogger, memoirist, op-ed writer, reporter, and long-form journalist examining his life and experiences as a Black man while also reflecting on the lives of other Black men. His rethinking of T'Challa's relationship to Wakanda, exemplified by the view that no one man should hold all the power, represents an extension of Coates's considerations of leadership, responsibility, and identity.

Chapter 5
Women of Wakanda

On July 22, 2016, just three months after the release of *Black Panther* #1, Marvel announced the upcoming spin-off *Black Panther: World of Wakanda*, which would launch in November 2016. As reporting of the then forthcoming comic book noted, one part of the series would be devoted to the Midnight Angels, co-plotted with Roxane Gay and Coates, and the other part would spotlight Zenzi, written by Yona Harvey. In an article announcing the new development, *The New York Times* observed that *World of Wakanda* would showcase women "on the page and behind it."[1] In his article for *Entertainment Weekly*, Christian Holub mistakenly referred to the new comic as "*Women of Wakanda*," an error based on the identity of the main characters and creators. "Many of the most famous Marvel superheroes are no longer white men," wrote Holub. "Captain America's shield has been taken up by a black man, a black girl will soon wear the Iron Man armor, the Hulk is Asian American, and Thor is a woman. Between Coates, Gay, and Harvey, Marvel is also upping its efforts to recruit more diverse writers to script these characters."[2]

Coates recruited both writers for *World of Wakanda*. When he and editors at Marvel considered potential writers for the new series, Coates recalled a zombie story that he heard Gay read at a conference and thought she would be an ideal candidate for writing the comic book. Coates and Harvey had been friends since their days as undergraduates at Howard University. Coates felt that Harvey's knowledge and experiences as a poet would make her well-suited for writing comics.[3] The introduction of two Black women writers to Marvel stood out as a newsworthy development, which spoke to Coates's power and influence in convincing the company to take a risk on two inexperienced comic book writers.

Coates had paved the way for *World of Wakanda* by making women characters central to the main storyline for *Black Panther*. In one discussion about his work on the comic book, Coates said that in the lead-up to his time writing the comic book, men close to T'Challa had been killed. The Wakanda that Coates inherited, therefore, included women, and so he wrote from there rather than reboot.[4] But Coates adopts an overly modest stance. Other writers may not have been as willing to reduce T'Challa's presence in the narrative to make room for such a litany of women characters.

Coates actively engaged in representational redemption. He, like others, realized the underrepresentation of Black women characters and creators in comics. He now held the power to address past and contemporaneous problems. As an advocate with decision-making power, he could recommend two Black women to become comic book writers. As a writer, he could present more women in principal positions in the storyline.

In the first few issues of *Black Panther* alone, we encounter a selection of Black women characters—Ayo, Aneka, Ramonda, Zenzi, Shuri, Mbali, and the griot who appears in the Djalia or the plane of ancient Wakandan memory. Coates had indeed passed the Sexy Lamp Shade test, that is, the informal gauge created by Kelly Sue DeConnick to determine whether women characters matter to the plot. If the characters could be removed from the plot and hardly anything would change, then the narrative fails.[5] Unlike the multitude of comic books that relegate women to the sidelines, Coates had succeeded in making women characters relevant to the storyline. Their actions shape consequential moments throughout the story.

During the 2010s, increasing numbers of comic readers pushed back against underrepresentation and sexualization of women characters, as documented by Carolyn Cocca in her book *Superwomen: Gender, Power, and Representation*. A mix of developments—including demographic and political changes, new and expanded fan bases driven by blockbuster films and the increased availability of comics on television, streaming platforms, in bookstores, and online—led to greater diversity of writers, artists, editors, and characters. "The number and frequency of panels depicting female characters in sexually objectifying ways has decreased since the 1990s," declared Cocca. "However, such representations are still pervasive."[6] Because fans, creators, critics, and scholars raised awareness about the history and recent instances of demeaning characterizations, depictions of women in comics began to improve.

Coates gained valuable insights from continuous dialogue surrounding the representation of women in comics. "The feminist critique is in the air now," he remarked in a blog entry. "If my rendition of *Black Panther* wasn't created by that critique, it breathed the same air." He attributed influence to ideas from comic creators such as Gail Simone and Kelly Sue DeConnick. For much of his time as a comic book fan, he had not questioned the depictions of women in comics nearly as much as he should have. Exposure to cultural criticism by and about women allowed him to deepen his understanding, and "the feminist critique of comics" encouraged him to interrogate and challenge sexist depictions.[7] He put what he learned into practice in his writing on *Black Panther*.

Ayo and Aneka make frequent appearances throughout "A Nation Under Our Feet" as they lead a resistance movement comprised in part of women and girls formerly enslaved and sexually assaulted by bandits in northern Wakanda. By labeling them the Midnight Angels early in the series, Coates indicates an interest in distancing the characters from their origins as Dora Milaje, the designation given to them when created by Christopher Priest. According to Priest, his editors Joe Quesada and Jimmy Palmiotti had encouraged the idea to give *Black Panther* female bodyguards.[8] During their first appearance in November 1998, the Dora Milaje also known as "the adored ones" and "kind of wives-in-training," wear revealing red mini dresses as they, at T'Challa's command, demonstrate their fighting skills by taking out a group of men.[9] The Dora Milaje that Priest presented belonged to a long line of sexualized women characters in comics designed to stimulate the interests of boy and men readerships. Coates, again exercising representational redemption by giving the characters more agency and dignity, chose to utilize the characters in far more empowering ways.

When we first see the Dora Milaje in Coates's *Black Panther*, they defend one another and women, not fighting at the command of T'Challa. "No one is coming to save us," explains Ayo to Ramonda, "and so we must save ourselves." She presents a video showing Aneka confronting and then killing a man who imprisoned and sexually assaulted girls. Ayo makes the case that Aneka's actions justified themselves given the circumstances.[10] Thus, in the opening pages, a member of the Dora Milaje performs as a kind of defense attorney and advocate for the protection of abused girls. Here and elsewhere, Coates and his collaborating artists redefine the representation of women in *Black Panther*, taking them well beyond their origins as sexualized fighting machines. Reginald Hudlin, who previously produced a run on *Black Panther*, provided models for elevating Wakandan women in storylines. In fact, Hudlin created the character Shuri, T'Challa's sister.

Superhero comic books have been historically defined by thrilling scenes showcasing heroic men performing daring feats. Consequently, a woman character, not T'Challa, leads the most spectacular action sequence in *Black Panther* #1. Ayo leads a courageous offensive on a prison to free Aneka. Ayo creates a tremendous explosion, blasts through a wall, outduels prison guards, and flies off with Aneka.[11] The most iconic and recurring rescue scenes in comics, film, and television involve men carrying women to safety. Despite that, in this opening issue, a Black woman clings to another Black woman who holds her securely in her arms as they soar in the air. This scene anticipates dynamic action sequences involving Black women throughout the series.

Shortly after the prison break and rescue, Ayo and Aneka sit alone together and regroup. Ayo says that a part of her died, "the part that was Dora Milaje. The part of me that once lived for our king." Ayo and Aneka then share a kiss, revealing an intimate relationship. In a review of the issue, L. E. H. Light, noted that the "relationship is carefully, tenderly portrayed and even in their black silhouettes they are made visible—strikingly, stirringly so" and "sets the tone for the entire series, establishing that a variety of women's perspectives, straight and queer, will be significant in how this story unfolds."[12] Presenting Ayo and Aneka as a couple constitutes a new depiction in the history of the Dora Milaje. In addition to no longer serving the interests of T'Challa, Ayo and Aneka show more of their own personal interests and choices, which further distances them from the limits of their initial character designs. Priest created the Dora Milaje as bodyguards and aspiring wife selections for T'Challa. Meanwhile, Coates revealed that Ayo and Aneka had no interest in serving as the king's protectors or suitors.

"I am tired of living and dying on the blood-right of one man," says Ayo. She gives voice to a critique of power being bestowed based on lineage. She expresses exhaustion and her rejection of sacrificing all for the royals. Aneka then mentions the Midnight Angel prototype suits, and in the next panel, the two of them stand together wearing their new blue armor uniforms with full-face masks.[13] These new uniforms appear visually impressive and equipped with cutting-edge technology, not overtly sexualized as previous attire had been.

First appearing in *Doomwar* #5 (2010) in a story by Jonathan Maberry, T'Challa introduces the Midnight Angels as "a special networks team of Dora Milaje elite." In Maberry's story, they assist the Fantastic Four, Deadpool, and T'Challa on a dangerous mission against Doctor Doom.[14] When Coates took on *Black Panther*, he aimed to present the Dora Milaje more progressively than in previous depictions. He was, understandably, critical of how they had been portrayed at times. He knew that the group's activities had evolved under writers such as Christopher Priest, Reginald Hudlin, and Maberry. While Coates could have introduced a new name for them, he preferred the nomenclature established by Maberry. Regarding his approach to the Dora Milaje, Coates stated that he sought to "think about them as whole characters and try to think about things from their point of view, not as appendages to T'Challa."[15] He clearly aimed to redeem and enrich the representation of those Black women characters.

In "A Nation Under Our Feet," the Midnight Angels become an insurgent force that delivers protection to those underserved by the official Wakandan government. With each victory, their numbers of supporters grow. In a report to T'Challa and his council, one of his advisers recounts Ayo's successful effort to free Aneka and notes that the two of them "have been marauding through the country ever since." As he discusses their actions, a sequence of images shows Ayo and Aneka leading a group of fellow Midnight Angels as they carry a body under a sheet toward a group of men. They eventually remove the sheet to reveal a dead body, previously identified as Mandla, who had taken over the Man-Ape mantle in the absence of M'Baku. When they show Mandla's dead body, he is shirtless, and the words "NO ONE MAN" have been written in blood on his chest, a brutal and searing message from the Midnight Angels that they will not accept rule from male tyrants.[16]

The narrative that Coates composed presents Black women as more than simply warriors. They also function as strategists who weigh political alliances and debate opposing positions and approaches in conversation with one another. They also show a willingness to take counsel from elders like Changamire and Mbali, a woman they rescued from a bandit compound in northern Wakanda. When the Midnight Angels hold a private meeting with Tetu to discuss potential partnerships, Mbali joins them and contributes.[17] Later during another meeting, Mbali serves as lead spokesperson for the Midnight Angels as she informs Tetu about "testimonies of mothers and daughters roughly treated, or forced into concubinage" by his army. "We understand that you are not wholly responsible for every act of your men," says Mbali, "but a revolution in Wakanda that overlooks half the country is no revolution at all."[18]

After concluding their exchange with Tetu, then Mbali, Ayo, and Aneka debate next steps with each other. Ayo and Aneka disagree on whether they should build an alliance with Tetu given the actions of his army. Aneka favors a coalition with Tetu only because "you go to war with the army you have, not the one you wish you had." Ayo counters that Aneka's comment sounds "like some warmongering barbarian out of the west." Mbali interrupts their conversation to alert them to another problem that they must consider.

With assistance from Zenzi, the Midnight Angels had defeated a force of T'Challa's men, the Hatut Zeraze, also known as the Dogs of War. Ayo and Aneka's group then imprisoned the men, and Mbali mentions that a few of the men tried to escape to which Ayo says, "then kill them."

Mbali responds, "Now who is the barbarian," redirecting Ayo's critique of Aneka, and then asking rhetorically, "And so we are to be butchers?"

Aneka joins in to point out, "We are to be warriors," and Mbali then addresses her saying, "And yet a moment ago, you were women."

Frustrated, Aneka says to Mbali, "Mother, I swear it, I am doing all that I can," and Mbali tells her, "And I am sorry, daughter, but you are going to have to do more."

She goes on to explain to the Midnight Angels that "you set out to destroy the reign of kings," but "what shall you build yourself?"

She closes by asking Ayo and Aneka, "Have you so soon forgotten the parable of Zami? 'A free house is not built with a slave-driver's tools.'"[19]

The parable of Zami references Black feminist poet, essayist, and autobiographer Audre Lorde, author of *Zami: A New Spelling of My Name* (1982). She also wrote the widely cited essay and adage "The Master's Tools will never dismantle the Master's House."[20]

The allusion to a Black feminist icon during a discussion involving African women engaged in a liberation struggle further incorporates Black aesthetics into the comic book. Dwayne McDuffie, Reginald Hudlin, John Jennings, Eve Ewing, and N. K. Jemisin, to name some African American comics creators, made references to Black writers and cultural figures in their storylines. What stands out about Coates's allusion in this instance is the suggestion that Lorde's ideas resonate within Wakandan lore. Mbali wants to make sure that Ayo and Aneka have not forgotten the parable of Zami. In this context, people expect Black women warriors and thinkers to know and absorb Zami's lessons. So more than providing a passing name drop, Coates positions Lorde as part of the intellectual history for Wakandan women guiding a movement.

These relatively brief exchanges between the Midnight Angels and Tetu and then Ayo, Aneka, and Mbali amount to quite remarkable steps in the struggles to represent Black people and their experiences with complexity. For one, what a rare depiction in comics and popular culture: an all-Black women's council of warriors and insurgent leaders negotiating with a potential ally, ultimately berating him, and then engaging in a discussion and debate with each other about their group's overall aims and values. Too few instances exist of Black women leaders holding forth and working through multifaceted political problems. Fortunately, we have plentiful representations of Black women fighting courageously and resisting unfair treatment, but in this scene, Mbali calls on Ayo and Aneka to do more. She urges them to embrace their identities as the architects of a new reconfigured nation.

Equally relevant, the storyline addresses the problem of soldiers abusing and sexually assaulting women and girls. The scene raises awareness about gendered atrocities committed during war, a serious issue that the general public sometimes brushed over or underdiscussed. Considerations of sexual assault involving Black women and girls rarely appear, largely due to their limited presence in comics. The Midnight Angels push Tetu—and audiences—to think about the appalling and oppressive actions of men who claimed to be fighting for liberation. By embedding this topic, Coates brings a salient Black feminist critique to comics.

Coates's larger effort involved reconfiguring and expanding the agency of the Dora Milaje, which included rejecting their original nomenclature in favor of the Midnight Angels. The incorporation of Lorde, whose *Zami: A New Spelling of My Name* celebrates the reclamation of identity, felt fitting for a group seeking to rebrand and repurpose itself. The Midnight Angels that Coates presents exude the kinds of pride and empowerment found in Black women's poetry, such as Maya Angelou's "Still I Rise" and "Phenomenal Woman," Mari Evans's "I Am a Black Woman," Nikki Giovanni's "Ego-Tripping," Lucille Clifton's "won't you celebrate with me," and June Jordan's "Poem About My Rights." In her poem, Jordan declares, "my name is my own my own my own" and "I can tell you that from now on my resistance / my simple and daily and nightly self-determination / may very well cost you your life."[21] Coates evoked these and other African American creative writers who envisioned empowering Black women in their works.

Coates's narrative does more than only highlight the experiences of the Midnight Angels controlling their own destinies by force on the fields of battle. He instead positions them conversing with each other and *planning*, which contributes to the weight of the scene with Tetu and the Midnight Angels. At the opening of the conversation, a wide shot of the room shows Tetu and Zenzi on a video screen and a group of seven Midnight Angels seated around a large table with Mbali standing. She leads the exchange with Tetu. Recall that Mbali, a character created by Coates and Stelfreeze, first appeared in a group of imprisoned and sexually abused women. She thus goes from unnamed prisoner to survivor to a primary spokesperson and adviser for the Midnight Angels.

Although only one panel presents the full group of seven Black women, which includes Ayo, Aneka, and Mbali, gathered around a table, the scene suggests that they have been meeting and discussing strategy. A long visual history in comics shows heroes or political leaders seated around tables discussing weighty matters. In DC Comics, images present the Justice League meeting together. Titles for Marvel show gatherings of the Avengers, including T'Challa, Captain America, Iron Man, and Captain Marvel, seated at a table discussing and debating plans. Multiple images from *X-Men* over the decades show Xavier meeting at tables with Storm, Beast, Rogue, Wolverine, and Cyclops. In that tradition, Coates and Stelfreeze give the Midnight Angels their table meeting moment.

In mass-market comic books, depictions of groups of Black women meeting and interacting with each other appear infrequently. Fans and commentators note how popular culture depictions fail the Bechdel-Wallace test, lacking conversations between women that do not pertain to men. Yet, in the continuum of African American literature, interactions involving Black women occur far more frequently. Zora Neale Hurston's *Their Eyes Were Watching God* (1937), Toni Morrison's *Sula* (1973), Alice Walker's *The Color Purple* (1982), Gloria Naylor's *The Women of Brewster Place* (1982), and *Mama Day* (1988) all portray Black women engaging in discussions about a breadth of subjects. Coates's depictions of Wakandan women, when viewed through the lens of African American literature, show how certain writers, particularly Black women, have long been invested in portraying multifaceted interactions between Black women characters. Coates advances popular culture renderings by depicting large groups of Black women assembling, strategizing, and taking collective action to lead a revolution.

Outside the rarity of a table meeting of Black women, the scene indicates that planning or careful strategic thinking and organizing occur within the circle of the Midnight Angels. The table meeting strategy session contributes to multiple scenes of Black women gathering together. In issue 2, Ayo and Aneka lead a daring night-time prison break and free a large group of women who celebrate their new liberated status by burning the message "No One Man" in the grass. In issue 3, they meet with Mbali, join hands, and resolve to eventually build an army of Midnight Angels. In issue 4, their force of women warriors delivers the dead body of Mandla to his soldiers, defeats them in battle, and convenes tribunals. In issue 6, they clash with the Hatut Zeraze and nearly lose until Zenzi intervenes and turns the battle in the favor of the Midnight Angels. These scenes and the discussions of weighty issues establish the centrality of these women of Wakanda.

Coates seems less interested in telling an origin story and more invested in illuminating a liberation narrative. Indeed, at one point as they prepare for their battle with the Hatut Zeraze, Aneka gives a motivational speech to her "sisters," reminding them that "we were once slaves to" Black Panther, and "we were bred by men solely to give our bodies to other men." Then she says, "We have seen how the woman became the enslaved. Let us now show them how the enslaved becomes a legend." Aneka's words appear above images of Ayo hurling her war club at an aircraft flown by the Hatut Zeraze, causing it to explode.[22]

Aneka's statement about women once enslaved becoming legends paraphrases a statement from the *Narrative of the Life of Frederick Douglass*, where Douglass writes that, "You have seen how a man was made a slave; you shall see how a slave was made a man."[23] Coates reveals his interest in crafting a liberation narrative by infusing the Midnight Angels with the spirit and words of our most famous ex-slave.

In addition to the Midnight Angels, Coates positioned Shuri as a central figure in "A Nation Under Our Feet" by interspersing her extended conversation with a griot in the plane of ancient Wakandan memory during the first issues. The griot takes the form of a woman and informs Shuri that "I am your mother, girl. All of them."[24] In West African societies, griots performed as storytellers who told narratives, parables, and folk tales concerning past activities of their ethnic groups. In some regions of Africa, people referred to the griot as "djali," hence the usage of "The Djalia" in Coates's *Black Panther* as the name for the plane of Wakandan memory. According to Amiri Baraka, the notion of griots grew in significance for African Americans due to our interconnectivity with "Pan-African diaspora." Baraka expounded that the purpose of the Djali or griot "was to raise us, with the poetry, the music, the history, the message, to take us up and out."[25] Consequently, Coates employs the services of a griot in *Black Panther* to strengthen Shuri and uplift Wakandan cultural frames of reference and storytelling. At the start, the griot takes the lead by telling parables of centuries past in Wakanda. Shuri listens and learns.

"I am a griot," the storyteller explains by way of introducing herself to Shuri, "a caretaker of all our histories, now lost to the acolytes of machine, and the prophets of this metal age." The griot and Changamire serve somewhat similar purposes, making a case for humanities and ideas in a nation known primarily for its technological prowess. The griot, though, considers Wakandan tales rather than philosophical concepts and history books. She tells Shuri that "you have forgotten the old ways, my queen, you have lost your soul." But no worries, because now, they reside in the plane of ancient Wakandan memory: "Here, we will arm you, not with the spear," but with "the power of memory, daughter, the power of our song."[26]

What a novel proposition in the history of *Black Panther* representations: the strength of Wakandans rests in their memories and stories, not necessarily vibranium. The griot seeks to restore Shuri's lost soul by sharing the stories of triumph and tragedy of her people. Her approach differs from prevalent depictions of Wakanda that foreground technology or the radiance of T'Challa/ Black Panther. Hardly anyone would have been inclined to suggest that the power of the nation rests on stories transmitted by a woman. For this Wakandan griot, stories and memories can yield vital lessons to a queen and nation.

Eventually, after recounting a few tales and responding to questions, the griot encourages Shuri to recall stories she heard as a child and to contemplate their meanings. Thus, the student-listener gradually becomes the teacher-speaker. Shuri presents a tale about a boy who initially struggled to win a race until he thought more of himself and his capabilities. Retelling the story similarly inspires Shuri to move forward with speed and power. Stories of past trials and triumphs, she learns, can be motivating.

Within the Djalia, at least two scenes function as key instances of visual foreshadowing. During one of their first sessions, a bird flies in and lands on the hand of the griot, who pets the bird before it flies away.[27] In a later session, the griot tells Shuri about the "blackbird's song," a tale about an enslaved woman forced into marriage and kept in a basement. When the woman is finally permitted outside to see the light, she achieves freedom. As the griot reaches that point in the story, she drops backward off a high cliff that she and Shuri had climbed. Shocked, Shuri screams out and reaches for her, but the griot suddenly transforms into a cloud of blackbirds soaring in the sky.[28] In retrospect, the birds in the Djalia foreshadowed or even inspired Shuri's new powers when she returned to the real world outside as she possesses the ability to transform herself into a flock of blackbirds.

Another scene of foreshadowing or inspiration occurs early in the story sessions when the griot mentions power and memory. As she speaks, she appears in a previously unseen black and blue uniform with white trimmings, scarf, and spear.[29] Later, when Shuri departs the Djalia, she appears, standing confidently, and informs T'Challa that "I remember everything."[30] On the one hand, her statements reference her recollection of the stories she heard and shared with the griot. At the same time, Shuri apparently remembers what she saw, as she wears the uniform that the griot appeared in during one of their early sessions.

The Djalia scenes appear in half of the twelve issues that comprise "A Nation Under Our Feet."[31] The sessions with the griot and Shuri ensure that exchanges between Black women receive strong representation in *Black Panther*. Historically, such representations remain uncommon in comics. After all, the Bechdel-Wallace test sheds light on how depictions of women in popular culture rarely show two women conversing about subjects other than men. Conversely, Shuri and the griot do not discuss T'Challa. Rather, they illuminate the power of stories and storytelling, where women characters primarily take the lead.

During her time in the Djalia, Shuri's physical appearance gradually changes. She initially appears with short black hair twists that somewhat pass her ears. In a later scene, her hair stretches further down her neck and has gray streaks. By her final lessons, her hair has grown longer and turned all gray and white, nearly matching the griot's. Thus, the Shuri who reappears outside the Djalia emerges looking visibly more mature and wiser than when she appeared in a comatose state. Her appearance complements her statement that "I remember everything."

The striking cover image for *Black Panther* #9 shows T'Challa and Shuri standing facing each other with their hands clasped. A flock of blackbirds emerges from Shuri's back. Later in the issue, as Aneka runs through a wooded area, she's startled when a flock of birds approaches and transforms into Shuri. In the next issue, revealing her powers, Shuri commands Aneka and Ayo to break their alliance with Tetu's armies who plan to attack the Golden City, the capital of Wakanda. Otherwise, she and the Wakandan forces will "march against you," and "your allies will not help. They will be too busy pillaging."[32] Shuri makes the case that T'Challa is honorable, a statement that even Ayo and Aneka cannot say of Tetu and his supporters.

Toward the end of the series, as T'Challa prepares to lead his forces into battle against Tetu, Shuri informs him and the council that "hope for Wakanda has never rested in one man, but in Wakandans themselves." The words move T'Challa: "When did you become the wise one, sister?"[33] Later, after they have defeated Tetu in battle, Shuri, not T'Challa, has the final words. "A new sea is upon us, beloved," she says. "And we are unmoored. How shall we live in this new land, so far from our old ways, our old myths, our old stories?" Since a close-up of Shuri's face appears in two panels beneath one showing the conquered Tetu in chains and surrounded by Wakandans, readers can reasonably presume she's the one speaking to him. Yet, on the next page, a full-page image reveals that Shuri is seated at a meeting table with the Midnight Angels. This image, which includes the words "a beginning" at the bottom of the page, indicates that a new direction for the nation involves a meeting and conversation involving women of Wakanda.

After the publication of *Between the World and Me*, Coates and more generally his work increasingly became the subject of gender-based criticism. Some Black women writers felt that the spotlight on Coates led or would lead to diminished interest in Black women writers and their interests.[34] These reviewers and commentators lamented that the public favored Black men over Black women, thus giving voice to a pertinent representation grievance. It is unfortunate, however, that more reviewers did not examine Coates's *Black Panther* run, which presented a strong presence of characters such as the Midnight Angels, Zenzi, and Shuri. Coates portrayed empowered and multidimensional Black women, offering a notable example of a Black man writer foregrounding women within a mainstream comic narrative.

Quite possibly, critiques about Coates's limited treatment of women in his previous work led him to place more deliberate narrative emphasis on women by the time he composed *Black Panther*.[35] Nonetheless, as noted, Coates said that he prioritized women because men in T'Challa's life had been killed in previous storylines.[36] Still, that explanation underappreciates the creativity and complexity of Coates's depictions of the Midnight Angels, Shuri, and additional women in the series. Keep in mind that the success of *Black Panther* and Coates's recommendations led to a writing venture for Roxane Gay and Yona Harvey. Significantly, Coates expanded representations of Black women in comics by increasing the narrative exploration of Wakandan women in the series, facilitating the development of a spin-off on the characters, and by creating professional avenues for Black women to enter comics. He revealed that a comic creator could positively affect the presence of Black women in comics on multiple fronts.

Chapter 6
Mapping an African Country

It's 2 a.m., March 20, 2016, in France, and Coates stays wide awake, mapmaking. He wants to make Wakanda feel real, first in his own mind, and later, in the minds of readers. Real places have maps, and so do some fictional worlds. So why shouldn't Wakanda? That's why Coates works deep into the night, working with software programs to bring Wakanda's geography to life.[1] He had tried one mapping tool that he found too complicated. "So I'm messing with this software Fractal Mapper," he told Evan Narcisse, "trying to come up with something which I'm assuming they'll then send to a designer who will do something else with it."[2]

Marvel eventually brought in a designer, Manny Mederos, who had designed the title pages of *Black Panther*. First though, Coates wanted to try it himself, taking a shot at "putting together a geographical vision of Wakanda." He experimented with Campaign Cartographer and Fractal Mapper before deciding to produce his maps of Wakanda using Photoshop.[3] Coates published one version of his map on April 22, 2016, a couple of weeks after the release of *Black Panther* #1. "This isn't much of a map," wrote Coates, "But it has the basics down in terms of where Wakanda exists in the world and what's around it." Coates explains that "in my imagination," Wakanda lies in East Africa, just west of Lake Victoria, and shares borders with fictive Marvel countries—"Mohanda to the North, Canaaan to the West, Azania to the Southwest, and Niganda to the Southeast."

Coates assessed the map he produced alone as subpar, but he indicated the appearance of a forthcoming higher-quality map. Nonetheless, the processes of constructing a map gave him a chance to participate in a useful learning experience. "And that was the whole reason to take this gig to begin with," he wrote, "to learn."[4] Coates approached the task of writing *Black Panther* by first experimenting with cartography, sharing his modest results on his blog, and signaling that he would soon collaborate with Marvel artists for a more polished version. In short order, Coates put forth a view of a Black writer as a mapmaker, blogger, and collaborator, all of which contrasted the conventional view of writers as solitary figures only writing narratives.

Beginning with issue 4, a map of Wakanda began appearing at the end of the comic book. Credit for the creation goes to Coates and Mederos. "On this map," a note reads, "are various cities beginning with the appellation 'Birnin'—Wakandan for 'city.' Each city on this map is named after a famous Black Panther, and each is actually more like a fortress than a city, protecting the entryways into Wakanda." The notation goes on: "Wakanda was navigable mostly by a system of rivers, and the political geography of the country is still dominated by this fact."[5] The appearances of the map in issues of *Black Panther* instilled a concrete view of Wakanda for monthly readers and strengthened a sense of the country's geography. The images showcased Coates's geospatial imagination.

The Wakanda map was not the first time that he participated in the creation of a map to complement his writing. His memoir *The Beautiful Struggle* (2008) contains a map of his Baltimore neighborhood. The map includes a legend and brief descriptions linked to episodes in his life covered more thoroughly within the narrative of the memoir. The top of the map shows a sword, and toward the center, the head of a dragon appears. Those small details suggest the maps of the game Dungeons and Dragons, a game that Coates recalled with fond memories during interviews. Similar to Coates's memoir, Colson Whitehead's *Sag Harbor* (2009) contains a map, showing memorable locales from the novel. Coates's interest in Dungeons and Dragons led to his interest including maps in *The Beautiful Struggle* and *Black Panther*. When Narcisse mentioned Coates's mapmaking resembled the map that came with Dungeons and Dragons, Coates responded, "That is exactly what I'm trying to do."[6]

Apart from reenacting elements of a children's game, Coates's mapmaking contributes to representation struggle, namely revising previous depictions of Wakanda. During the 1970s, Wakandan maps overused references to animals. "You can't do that," argued Coates, "You can't have Panther Island, Piranha Cove, Gorilla Peak. You can't do it buddy. You can't do it."[7] Coates's decision to name locations after famous former kings of Wakanda replaces and revises frameworks that may not have been sensitive enough to the long-standing problems of colonial approaches to naming African locales and countries. European settlers named countries such as "Ivory Coast," "Gold Coast," "Slave Coast," and "Northern Rhodesia," based on their own interests in those regions, not the preferences of the inhabitants of those areas. Coates participates in a decolonizing act by seeking to present names based on terms seemingly familiar to Wakanda. His renaming of Wakandan landmarks in the interest of addressing past troubling designations constitutes representational redemption.

Coates's map appealed to a spectrum of creators, as evidenced by its reproduction in books over the years. The map appears in the back of issues 1,

3, and 5 of *World of Wakanda* (2016–2017), and in issue 4, an image of the map appears as a holographic projection during the course of the narrative. The first issue of *Rise of the Black Panther* (2018), written by Evan Narcisse and drawn by Pau Renaud, recreates the map as part of the interior art. In one scene, N'yami, T'Challa's birthmother, works in a laboratory with the map projected on a computer screen.[8] In what is probably its largest book-version reproduction, the map appears in *Black Panther: The Illustrated History of a King* (2018), a publication with 11 x 14 dimensions. Shuri studies the map, which appears on a large screen in Eve Ewing's *Ironheart* #9 (August 2019).

In 2021, DK Books and Marvel Entertainment published *Marvel Universe: Map by Map*, which includes artist Adam Simpson's update to the Coates and Mederos version. The artist renders the map primarily in green, with the city structures in gold. Simpson's adaptation of the Coates and Mederos map appears near the beginning of issues 1, 3, 4, and 5 of *Wakanda* (2022–2023), a series written by an assemblage of contributors. Much like the Coates and Mederos map that appeared in the back of early issues, Simpson's version also appears in the back of *Black Panther* (2022–2023), written by Eve Ewing. A variation by Teo Georgiev appears in *Black Panther: Wakanda Atlas* (2022), and the *Black Panther Omnibus* (2022) includes a reproduction of the original Coates and Mederos map. These various reproductions, appearances, and adaptations of the map suggest that it held pronounced attention power and continuously attracted the creative interest of Marvel artists and writers. That enduring appeal speaks to the influence of Coates's geospatial imagination, which helped reframe Wakanda as a layered, mappable world.

The cartography and placement of Wakanda have evolved over the decades. The first map of Wakanda appeared in *Jungle Action* #6, published in September 1973. The map presented the Atlantic Ocean off the coast of Wakanda, which suggested the country's positioning in West Africa.[9] A slightly revised map of the country appeared in January 1974 in *Jungle Action* #8. This time, the Atlantic Ocean no longer appears, possibly serving as a corrective to the previous map. In 2008, *Marvel Atlas* #2 showed a map that placed Wakanda to the southwest of Ethiopia, to the north of Kenya, and to the northeast of Uganda. The earliest detailed map of Wakanda presented in *Jungle Action* gave prominence to forests and utilized drawings of huts to mark the residences of citizens. Coates takes a different approach.

He presents six Wakandan cities. In effect, he propels the idea that a highly developed African nation would contain distinct metropolitans. The map by Coates and Mederos displays cutting-edge high-rise buildings above the city names. The icon for Mena Ngai (the Great Mound) denotes a modernized factory. The depiction of these modernized buildings contrasts or counters illustrations of African locales and instead projects a country with highly modernized cities.

In 2014, historian Simon Stevens curated a collection of three dozen novel covers on Africa, all of which contained a familiar image: a sunset, an arid plain, and an acacia tree.[10] "Why is it that books about Africa always look the same?" asked Marta Bausells.[11] Elliot Ross criticized the fact that "the covers of most novels 'about Africa' seem to have been designed by someone whose principal idea of the continent comes from *The Lion King*."[12] According to graphic designer Peter Mendelsund, due to "deeply ingrained problems" tied to colonialism, "we're comfortable with this visual image of Africa because it's safe. It presents 'otherness' in a way that's easy to understand."[13] Decades removed from overtly racist characterizations of the so-called dark continent and its habitants, an abundance of contemporary depictions project Africa and Africans in overly simplistic and formulaic ways. Due to such depictions, Coates's efforts to imagine and portray the diversity of Wakanda made a critical intervention in struggles to adequately represent Africa.

In the first four issues alone of "A Nation Under Our Feet," Brian Stelfreeze and color artist Laura Martin deliver compelling, multidimensional illustrations of Wakanda that enrich the comic book as well as views of Africa. The backgrounds of Stelfreeze's covers for *Black Panther* #1 and #2 show sleek skyscrapers that resemble the skylines of innovative cities such as Singapore, Dubai, and Hong Kong. In the background, in the capital of Wakanda, just outside the window in an early scene from issue 1, a majestic scene of towering buildings appears.[14] Later, in Birnin Azzaria, pinnacle structures come into view outside the window of a classroom.[15] In yet another scene, T'Challa and Ramonda talk while relaxing on a platform located amid high-rise glass buildings. The projection of soaring cityscapes stands in opposition to abundant *jungle action* images that fill the pages of previous depictions of Wakanda.

Stelfreeze's drawings of the city influenced the production of a memorable scene produced by another creator. A Hip Hop Variant cover by Alitha Martinez for *World of Wakanda* #1 (2016) presents an aerial view of the African nation that recreates the look of Dr. Dre's album *Compton* (2015), which overlooks Los Angeles. On Dre's album, the iconic Hollywood Sign is replaced with the word "Compton," and in Martinez's version, "Wakanda" takes its place. The high-rise buildings in Martinez's drawing recreate those drawn by Stelfreeze. The drawings depict the architectural wonder of Wakanda.

Wakandan cityscapes presented by Stelfreeze and Martin anticipated depictions of Wakanda that captured the imaginations of millions worldwide with the release of the *Black Panther* film in 2018. "Brian Stelfreeze is an amazing artist," said Nate Moore, a producer for the film, "and some of his version of Wakanda and even Wakanda technology was stuff that we borrowed pretty liberally from."[16] Hannah Beachler, the production designer for *Black Panther*, acknowledged in interviews that Stelfreeze, one of the artists whose representations she used, guided aspects of her vision bringing Wakanda to the big screen.[17] When reviewers, commentators, and fans gushed about the splendor and Afrofuturist aesthetics of Wakanda presented in the film, they could have easily been referring to the Wakanda as rendered by Coates, Stelfreeze, and Martin. Or put another way, depictions of a sleek, innovative African city in *Black Panther* the comic book served as concept art for *Black Panther* the movie.

Of course, skyscrapers can be seen as embodying Western aesthetics, elements of which have been spread globally due to colonialism and cultural hegemony. Thus, towering buildings with glass facades in fictive African cities do not necessarily warrant celebration. In response to concept art of Wakanda revealed in 2017, a year before the film's release, Sam Keeper thoughtfully critiqued the placement of Western architectural style buildings in African cities. The lofty steel and glass structures suggest that this Western style "is so good inherently that Wakanda couldn't help but adopt it—that even though they weren't conquered they had to borrow" designs from the West. Keeper went on to note that "what's unsettling about this to me is the implication that the West's way of doing things is so universal that they can be extended to any other civilization on earth."[18] The widespread belief that exceedingly tall buildings signify a country's wealth, power, and prosperity makes it a struggle to represent Wakanda without large, imposing architectural structures. The magnificent city skylines that emerge in *Black Panther* the comic book and film inspire while also reminding us of the difficulty of imagining an African nation independent of Western aesthetic influence.

Still, the efforts by Coates and Stelfreeze to conceive of structures, cityscapes, rural areas, interiors of buildings, forests, and meeting spaces constitute a modernizing endeavor in the publishing history of *Black Panther*. As Narcisse observed in *Black Panther: Wakanda Atlas* (2022), in its first appearance in 1966, "Wakanda looked and felt a lot smaller." At that point, "Wakanda was primarily shown as an exoticized, unindustrialized realm," and "readers were given the impression that the majority of the populace held more closely to traditionally agrarian ways of life."[19] Poet and short story writer John Keene praised the comic book, noting that Coates had "imagined a more fully African Wakanda than the original," a suggestion that this representation surpassed the earliest depictions of the nation in the 1960s and 1970s.[20] Oz Longworth noted that following the series meant watching "Wakanda evolve from a novelty dot on a fictional map into a fully formed, realistic country that has varying states of geography and ideology."[21]

To their credit, Coates and Stelfreeze substantially expanded and enhanced the world-building of the African country. Their creative contributions influenced subsequent visual artists, writers, movie directors, and production designers who portrayed Wakanda, and they supplied readers with a more fully realized Black nation.

Another essential yet seemingly minor element of Coates's map indicated his interest in decolonizing Wakanda and Africa more broadly. Maps showing east-central Africa have designated the large body of water surrounded by Kenya, Tanzania, and Uganda as Lake Victoria. In typical colonializing fashion, English explorer John Hanning Speke bestowed that designation in 1858 in honor of Queen Victoria with no input from inhabitants. Late nineteenth-century and early twentieth-century cartographers mapped "Victoria Nyanza." The word "Nyanza" is a Bantu language designation, which means lake. For his map, however, Coates presented "Nyanza" as the official name, placing "Lake Victoria" in parentheses to register it as an alternative, less formal name. This seemingly minor change constituted a disruption to the prevalent colonial practice of remaking Africa in Eurocentric likeness and terminology.

Throughout "A Nation Under Our Feet," Coates provides labels for the setting of scenes, including "The Great Mound," "the Golden City, Capital of Wakanda," "The Nigandan Border Region," and "Birnin Azzaria, the Learned City." References to multiple Wakandan locations display multifaceted views of the country. Therefore, it's no small wonder that Coates worked on the maps at 2 a.m. The acts of thinking and writing about disparate locales necessitated long hours of plotting. That a litany of the settings corresponds to designations on Coates's map, which appears in issues of the comic book, trade paperbacks, and the hardcover editions, gives further weight to this fictive nation.

Black writers engage in the recurring practice of mapping distinct locales. In *Native Son* (1940), Richard Wright presents locations throughout the cityscape of Chicago. Toni Morrison maps the Midwest in her novels *The Bluest Eye* (1970), *Sula* (1973), *Song of Solomon* (1977), and *Beloved* (1987). Edward P. Jones charts a host of areas in Washington, DC, in his two short story collections, *Lost in the City* (1992) and *All Aunt Hagar's Children* (2006).[22] Colson Whitehead depicts New York City in his novel *Zone One* (2011) and documents Harlem in his crime fiction novels, *Harlem Shuffle* (2021) and *Crook Manifesto* (2023). Jesmyn Ward maps the Gulf Coast of Mississippi in her novels *Salvage the Bones* (2011) and *Sing, Unburied Sing* (2017) by presenting the fictive town Bois Sauvage. Walter Mosley charts Los Angeles in his Easy Rawlins mystery series. When these writers come up alongside Coates, the continuum of Black writers mapping distinct geographic locations in their works becomes clear.

The practice of Black writers mapping locales can be empowering based on the long history of representation. For centuries, white writers and mapmakers dominated descriptions of cities, regions, and even African countries, shaping spatial depictions that reflected colonial and Eurocentric frameworks.[23] By mapping out a mosaic of environments and locales in their works, African American literary artists have collectively created alternatives to the dominance of white-authored narratives, conveying geographic representations that foregrounded Black aesthetics and perspectives.[24] Coates's efforts to chart cartographies of Wakanda coincide with works by Jones, Morrison, Ward, Whitehead, and Wright that envision landscapes, both real and fictional, as sites of Black identity and possibility. These mapping processes challenge historical erasures and distortions by showing Black people's spatial and cultural positioning in various landscapes.

The Djalia, or Plane of Wakandan Memory, additionally manifested Coates's geospatial imagination, blending spiritual heritage with topographical design. This alternate dimension encompassed a mix of environments, including forests, open plains, landscapes, farming areas, villages, a mountain, and a cave. More than simply present a griot or Djali sharing tales, Coates and Stelfreeze created an expansive, transformative storytelling and learning space. The Djalia showed otherwise hidden areas of Wakanda. At one point, the griot tells Shuri of an ancient Wakandan territory known as Adowa while presenting farmlands and a village scene.[25] In another session, the griot discusses "the village of Nri—a place now lost to your written histories."[26] Thus, the Plane of Wakandan Memory recovers places and people and transcends the current timeline of the narrative.

The Djalia reflects Coates's ability to imagine new realms that enrich the history and geography of a fictive African country. He demonstrates his world-building capabilities by envisioning a previously nonexistent place in the *Black Panther* mythos. Stelfreeze, artist Chris Sprouse, and Martin skillfully materialize Coates's vision. The Djalia constitutes a useful addition to representation struggles. Historically, people portrayed Africa with racist images, and then more recently, people depicted the continent in overly simplistic ways as symbolized by the lone acacia tree in the sunset on book covers. The Djalia, by contrast, presents dynamic, multidimensional scenes of Africa and Africans.

During his run on *Fantastic Four*, Jonathan Hickman introduced Necropolis, also known as the city of the dead.[27] It is the place where past "Black Panthers go to die," and their spirits can be summoned to counsel the living, T'Challa above all.[28] Coates builds on Hickman's idea by incorporating the Necropolis during his run, and the Djalia emerges as a notable alternative. Unlike the Necropolis, which showcases primarily men, the griot of the Plane of Wakandan Memory takes the form of a woman and eventually creates space for Shuri to guide the storytelling. Moreover, the Djalia projects intricate scenes and shows Shuri and the griot traversing settings. In short, Coates, Stelfreeze, and Sprouse use the Djalia to further expand the territory of Wakanda.

The idea of the Plane of Wakandan Memory conceivably influenced an alternate reality space, which appears in the film *Black Panther*. In fact, when a trailer for the movie appeared in October 2017, some commentators speculated that one scene would include the Djalia. "A brief sequence showed us King T'Challa, dressed in his ceremonial white garb, walking among the African landscape at night, an ethereal aurora borealis lighting his way as black panthers, perched on a tree's branches, look upon him," wrote Ian Cardona. "It would appear that this could be our very first look at the mystical plane known as the Djalia."[29] In an article for *GQ*, Joshua Rivera disclosed that the trailer for *Black Panther* contains "loads of smaller surprises for people with sharp eyes and a bit of comics knowledge—like what looks like the Djalia, the spirit realm from the Black Panther comics, where T'Challa seems to be communing with the Panther god."[30]

The film names the area the Ancestral Plane, which makes use of the "plane" in Plane of Wakandan Memory. T'Challa travels there to meet with his deceased father, T'Chaka, and later, additional former Black Panthers join them. The scene includes a purple-tinted sunset and familiar acacia trees. The Ancestral Plane apparently blends elements of Hickman's and Coates's concepts. Like Hickman, Ryan Coogler's film presents T'Challa receiving counsel from former kings of Wakanda. In Hickman's books, they meet in Necropolis. The open plain that appears in the movie has more in common with scenes from the Djalia presented during Coates's run.

In the film, Killmonger enters the Ancestral Plane and visits his childhood home and meets with his father. In the sequel, *Black Panther: Wakanda Forever* (2022), Shuri visits the Ancestral Plane and encounters Killmonger in the Wakanda throne room. Thus, following the function of Coates's Plane, Coogler's Plane presents visitors in vastly different settings. In 2019, Nnedi Okorafor utilizes the Djalia in issues of *Shuri*.[31] In 2023, Eve Ewing presented the Djalia in an issue of *Black Panther*, and in 2024, Cheryl Lynn Eaton chose the Djalia for the opening of *Black Panther: Blood Hunt* #1.[32] The recurring appearances of the Plane of Wakandan Memory reveal that multiple artists found Coates's conception useful. The Djalia provides evidence of his inventiveness and extends Wakandan world-building. The ability to bring the country to life undoubtedly depended on his collaborating artists.

Martin deserves special recognition for her contributions to fully realizing T'Challa's homeland. Shortly following the release of *Black Panther* #1, Joseph Illidge pointed out that "the media coverage and praise seems to mostly leave out a significant player in the creation of this impactful comic book: The Color Artist." He stated that "for most of the history of American superhero comic books, Black people were colored in unflattering shades, and usually all of them the same shade in any given comic book." Hence, Martin's careful and virtuoso renderings of her subjects stand out. Illidge remarked that the first issue of the comic book "has at least seven scenes, and a different palette for each one. No palette is used twice."[33]

Martin deploys her coloring versatility throughout "A Nation Under Our Feet." She applies bright and dark hues, integrates shading and lights, and uses bold colors to highlight action scenes. Lush greens radiate the forest scenes in Wakanda, and light blues accentuate open-air scenes such as when Ramonda and T'Challa sit together amid skyscrapers.[34] At varied points, Martin applies a transparent coloring approach as characters project their portable screens. She introduces subtle contrasting colors within a single panel to differentiate images on the screens from figures within a room.

Martin's expert use of color in depicting Wakanda is far from trivial. The multilayered palette of hues invites interpretations and challenges simplistic views of an African nation. Martin brings Wakanda to life through a broad spectrum of colors and shades, ensuring consistency across recurring settings. In an interview with Marvel on her approach to coloring the comic book, Martin said that "I will play and manipulate the background colors in order to elicit different responses."[35] This approach draws attention to the uses of color in representing a Black country. Through her meticulous and vibrant color work, Martin presents Wakanda, and by extension, Africa, in a splendor rarely seen in comic books and other visual media.

Coates, Stelfreeze, Sprouse, and Martin enrich Wakanda's diverse locales by populating them with a wide array of Black characters. The series depicts Wakandans with varied physical appearances, diverse clothing and adornments, and different hairstyles. They shift through facial expressions and engage in different actions—walking, running, flying, fighting, embracing, conversing, and debating. This treatment of Black characters in numerous settings animates Coates's geographical vision. From the vibranium miners at the Great Mount and officials in the Golden City to students at Hekima Shulē and Midnight Angels in the Jabari Lands, Coates, Stelfreeze, and Martin present Wakanda as a nation teeming with a tapestry of identities.

Coates's map reveals the strategic positioning of soldiers from a neighboring country. The image shows Wakanda protected by mountains and the vast Lake Nyanza, except at its open southern border with Niganda, a poorer neighboring country.[36] Throughout the narrative, Tetu and his army gather in this unprotected region. Wakanda's vulnerability makes the activity and stationing of Nigandan forces in this region all the more apparent. The map also reveals that Nigandans believe the Alkama fields once belonged to them, providing a plausible motive for their aggression. In other words, Coates's maps suggest why Nigandans populate Wakanda and the border region.

One quietly revealing aspect of spatial arrangement in "A Nation Under Our Feet" lies in how Coates positions characters throughout the narrative. A cross-section of scenes depicts three or more characters gathered around a table or in a circle, engaging in discussions of weighty matters. At points, T'Challa meets with his council members to talk about recent disturbances in the country.[37] Other scenes show Tetu convening with the Midnight Angels.[38] Later, T'Challa gathers with a group of leaders who have suppressed revolutions.[39] Toward the end of the series, Shuri sits at a large circular table with six Midnight Angels while five more surround them.[40] In the final issue of the story arc, a large group, including T'Challa, Changamire, Shuri, Ayo, and Aneka, gathers in a circle in Changamire's garden to reflect on past events and chart a path forward for Wakanda.[41]

Coates uses these gatherings to map political discourse throughout the series. More than one-on-one exchanges, scenes involving three or more characters in *Black Panther* almost always involve crucial decision-making and pressing issues, manifesting assertions of power. The multiple scenarios where groups of Black characters come together to deliberate reflect Coates's interest in charting the convergence of divergent interests within Wakanda. These gatherings also project compelling aesthetic visions of large groups of Black people engaging with one another. Such assemblies function as salient instances of representational redemption. These gatherings counteract tokenism by challenging the pervasive pattern of depicting only one Black person at a time.

Chapter 7
A Breakthrough for Black People in Comics

Six months after announcing the release of the *Black Panther World of Wakanda*, Marvel revealed another upcoming spinoff on January 20, 2017, this one cowritten by Coates and Yona Harvey.[1] They teamed up to write *Black Panther and the Crew*, starring T'Challa, Storm, Luke Cage, Misty Knight, and Manifold. These spinoffs emerged in response to the tremendous sales achieved by *Black Panther*, above all Coates's debut issue. Marvel's investment in these projects, which foregrounded Black characters written by Black creators, marked a shift in its publishing priorities. In some respects, the company placed greater value on diversity than ever before.

In 2013, Joseph Hughes had raised concerns about the lack of Black writers in the comic book industry. By 2016 though, the landscape had begun to shift in visible ways. Coates, David F. Walker, John Semper Jr., Geoffrey Thorne, Roxane Gay, and Yona Harvey wrote for Marvel and DC Comics. At the smaller press Black Mask Studios, Kwanza Osajyefo released the first in his series *BLACK* about a world where only Black people possess superpowers. *BLACK* paved the way for later spinoffs—*BLACK [AF]: Widows and Orphans*, *BLACK [AF]: Devil's Dye*, and *America's Sweetheart*. Bryan Hill, now one of the more prolific African American comic book creators, wrote *Postal* for Top Cow Productions.

Developments on screen in 2016 inspired hope for audiences interested in diversity, particularly in the representation of Black people. For one, Chadwick Boseman made his debut as T'Challa in the film *Captain America: Civil War* in May 2016. The appearance in the Marvel Cinematic Universe began greatly expanding the popularity of Black Panther on a global scale in unprecedented ways. "The masterful performance by Chadwick Boseman as the ruler of Wakanda," Coates said, "it really feels like this is Black Panther's time."[2] Media coverage of the film and comic book further solidified links between Boseman and Coates, who first met as undergraduates at Howard University. Both men would be tied to Black Panther.

Luke Cage, released on Netflix on September 30, 2016, stood out as the other newsworthy development concerning diverse representation on screen. Luke Cage briefly appears in three successive issues of Coates's *Black Panther*.[3] However, the Netflix series boosted interest in the Harlem hero, which may have assisted in building interest in Coates and Harvey's work on *Black Panther and the Crew*. News reports on the *Luke Cage* series referenced the *Black Panther* comic book and the movie, which was in development at the time. "It seems like it's an interesting moment, because you're doing Luke Cage, Ta-Nehisi Coates is doing Black Panther, Ryan Coogler is working on the Black Panther film," said Jelani Cobb in an interview with *Luke Cage* showrunner Cheo Hodari Coker. "Do you think this is a breakthrough for black people in the comics arena?"[4] Other journalists and commentators also illuminated representation and Black creative interconnectivity.

In an article, "Luke Cage and the Year Marvel Finally Reckoned with Its Black Audience" for *Vanity Fair*, Joanna Robinson cataloged portrayals produced by or showcasing Black people. She listed Riri Williams, the casting of Zendaya as Mary Jane Watson in the then upcoming *Spider-Man: Homecoming*, Boseman as T'Challa, and Mike Colter as Luke Cage. Robinson pondered the implications of the increasing numbers of Black people in front-facing posts: "At a time when the national conversation around race has reached a boiling point, has Marvel recognized, in a way many entertainment companies have not, that black voices matter as much as black dollars?" Despite Marvel facing critiques about "a lack of black representation," Robinson relayed that "the conversation shifted dramatically in September 2015," when Marvel announced Coates as the upcoming writer for *Black Panther*. Hiring a writer with Coates's "prominence in the subject of racial identity signaled an even more dramatic commitment to the black perspective." Robinson determined that Coates, Coker, Coogler, who was then preparing the movie *Black Panther*, and Gay and Harvey, who would release *World of Wakanda*, together "represent a brave new world."[5]

Marvel's print and on-screen productions, along with the accompanying news dispatches, captured the intertextual resonance of representation.[6] Audiences discerned these productions as interconnected, commonly identifying the relationships between the works. Commentators spotlighted Coates in the conversations about Black artistic productions and notable Black creators emerging during this moment. Discussions of the *Luke Cage* series or Black Panther's appearance in *Captain America: Civil War* sometimes made mention of him. Coates's rising profile as a creative writer reflected a critical expansion of his professional identity. Previously known primarily as a journalist and commentator on race and racism, his move into comic books solidified his reputation as an influential artist.

At Comic-Con in 2016, Ryan Coogler discussed his developing work on the *Black Panther* movie and described Coates as "my favorite writer right now in the world." The director asserted that "Since being turned on to [Coates's] work, I'm reading everything that he does. His nonfiction work, especially. But what he's doing with *Panther* is just incredible. You can really see his background as a poet in some of the dialogue." Coogler said that he was impressed with the questions raised by Coates's and Stelfreeze's work, and declared that "it's just inspiring for [co-screenwriter] Joe Robert Cole and myself."[7] Coogler's comments circulated in assorted venues. Imagine how rewarding it must have felt for Coates to learn he had become the favorite writer of the director of one of the most anticipated Black films in cinematic history. Consider too that the cowriters for that upcoming film found Coates's work inspiring. Such affirmation would be quite encouraging. Coogler's comments undoubtedly added value to Coates's overall cultural capital.

Tara Betts, Matthew Teutsch, and Sarah Nicolas published articles documenting Black characters engaging with books and ideas throughout *Luke Cage*.[8] Nicolas enthused that the series "established Power Man as one of our own: a reader."[9] The depictions of reading, books, and book discussion in *Luke Cage* recall Coates's presentations of Wakandans reading and discussing books in *Black Panther*. In a review of *Luke Cage* for *The Hollywood Reporter*, Daniel Fienberg also cataloged the books and authors cited in the series. He observed that "once you throw in the references to Walter Mosley and Donald Goines and Ta-Nehisi Coates, it becomes clear that this show doubles as a superlative summer reading list."[10]

Coates became a go-to cultural reference for discussions on police brutality, interrogations of white supremacy, and serious Black thought. A February 22, 2016, episode of the television show *Black-ish* on police brutality referenced Coates's work. On October 5, 2016, *The New York Times* published "Sarah Jessica Parker and Ta-Nehisi Coates, on New Literary Paths" discussing their respective endeavors in publishing. Presenting Coates alongside a famed actress attested to his growing cultural relevance. "Coates has attained an exalted perch," wrote Sarah Nicole Prickett and Jody Rosen in the article, "the rare public intellectual whose reach extends from the ivory tower to the street."[11] A figure resembling Coates even appears in a comic book.

Howard the Duck #10 brings in a character named Ta-Nehi-C, modeled after Coates. Critics refer to the character as "the new golden boy" chosen to write *Black Panther*, a title they mockingly dismissed as a "C-lister." Another character, modeled after Wil Moss, Coates's editor for *Black Panther*, counters by stating, "Ta-Nehi-C really elevated T'Challa's story! It's one of the most popular relaunches we've ever done."[12] Beyond the breadth of reviews of Coates's work, this reference within a comic book further testified to his cultural prominence. His inclusion emphasizes his stature as both an accomplished writer and an acclaimed cultural figure.

In a June 2016 Supreme Court dissent, Justice Sonia Sotomayor cited Coates's book alongside W. E. B. Du Bois's *The Souls of Black Folk* (1903) and James Baldwin's *The Fire Next Time* (2015).[13] A November 2016 episode of *Saturday Night Live* contained a brief sketch about "The Bubble," a community of liberals, defined by preferences for hybrid cars, used bookstores, and small farms. As the speaker says, "used bookstores," the scene shows a white woman thoughtfully reading Coates's *Between the World and Me*.[14] In July 2018, during the opening scene of *The Equalizer 2*, the protagonist Robert McCall, played by Denzel Washington, rides a train as he reads *Between the World and Me*. These references to Coates and his works expanded his influence in the public imagination. The citations augmented Coates's cultural capital and attention power, ensuring that mentions of his name and books could attract notice.

Coates vigorously and admirably resisted claims that positioned him as a singularly exceptional Black person. He wanted to counter the pervasive practice of tokenism and one-at-a-time celebrations of African Americans. In an extended blog entry for *The Atlantic*, published on June 2, 2016, responding to characterizations of him as a stand-alone phenom, Coates identified the accomplishments of more than a dozen of his fellow Black journalists and affirmed that his writing grows out of a large community of Black writers.[15] Similarly, as a comic book writer, he belonged to networks of Black creators. For one, he followed Christopher Priest and Reginald Hudlin as writers for *Black Panther*. Like novelists Mat Johnson and Victor LaValle, Coates had built a reputation for himself as a writer in other genres and then entered comics. As a Black comic book writer, Coates joined a field that included David F. Walker, Geoffrey Thorne, Bryan Hill, and Kwanza Osajyefo, all produced titles during the same period.

As a writer with expansive reach, Coates occupied a strong position to promote others, and he did so. In another blog entry in June 2016, Coates recalled an informal meeting during the late 1990s when a literary artist and mentor, Joel Dias-Porter, introduced him to Henry Dumas's poem "Rootsong." As a poet and short story writer, Dumas associated with participants in the Black Arts Movement, the cultural enterprise of the 1960s and 1970s. A transit police officer tragically ended his life on May 23, 1968, when he was just thirty-three years old. His friend and literary executor, Eugene B. Redmond, worked to promote and oversee editions of Dumas's work, which Toni Morrison published for Random House during the 1970s. In light of the circumstances of Dumas's death, Redmond, Morrison, and others felt especially motivated to participate in efforts to circulate and extend the publishing life of the poet.[16] Coates contributed to that effort by publishing excerpts from a Dumas poem in *Black Panther #3*.

Coates expressed his fondness for "Rootsong" and stated that "what stunned me about the poem is how it used black myth to construct a narrative of the diaspora before and after colonialism and enslavement." He then presented a brief excerpt from the poem and added that "'Rootsong' always struck me as romance—not so different from the kind of romance you'd see in Marvel's *Thor*." Coates saw a link between verse and sequential art storytelling. "Poetry is a natural cousin to comic books. Comic book writing, like poetry, requires a ruthless efficiency with words," wrote Coates. "The art is the hero and if I may say so myself, the art in *Black Panther #3*—particularly in the pages using "Rootsong"—is heroic."[17] In an interview for *The New Republic*, Coates said that he included Dumas because "I wanted to incorporate the poets from the Black Arts Movement into the canon of comics."[18]

In an entry, Coates blogged that he first encountered Dumas's poem "during one of my many study sessions with the poet Joel Dias-Porter." He further disclosed that Porter actively mentored "a whole crop of young writers—Terrence Hayes, Yona Harvey, Jelani Cobb—who happened to be in the DC area." Each of those three went on to build distinguished careers as writers. During one of their informal sessions in 1995 or 1996, Porter shared a collection of poetry by Dumas with Coates and introduced him to "Rootsong."[19] Who could have known that casual exchange would eventually lead to the words of a lesser-known Black poet appearing in the pages of a Marvel comic book? The publication of Dumas's poem in *Black Panther #3* testifies to the value and power of informal Black poetry study sessions. The appearance of "Rootsong" also confirms Coates's deep ties to African American literary artists and compositions.

Coates's dedication to promoting and incorporating Black artists into his work shaped his identity as a writer and his commitment to embedding Black aesthetics in his writing. He invokes the words and ideas of African American artists and activists, including Frederick Douglass, Malcolm X, Audre Lorde, Notorious B. I. G., and Jay-Z. By fusing these and other Black artists in his work, Coates demonstrates his admiration for their thoughts and compositions while placing himself in conversation with them. In *Between the World and Me*, Coates discusses his blossoming love for the arts, with an affinity for poetry, noting that "older poets introduced me to artists who" inspired them. He emphasizes the importance of recognizing these influences so "you know that I have never achieved anything alone."[20] For Coates, producing work as a Black writer involves acknowledging and repurposing the works of other Black writers.

Coates's references to multiple Black historical figures and cultural icons constitute what we might call a "concentrated cultural catalog." The practice of African American writers citing copious Black people, ideas, and artistic compositions within a single work or series of interrelated works spans multiple genres. In his poem "Dope," Amiri Baraka mocks preachers as he critiques a plethora of cultural productions and circumstances involving Black people, and in "Digging Max," he name-checks and pays tribute to dozens of jazz musicians.[21] Paul Beatty incorporates hundreds of cultural figures and ideas in his novel *The Sellout* (2015), and Nafissa Thompson-Spires references African American television show characters, novelists, and rappers in her short story collection *Heads of the Colored People* (2019). In *The Boondocks*, both as a comic strip and television series, Aaron McGruder critiques and satirizes Black political figures and entertainers.[22] Through these processes of citation and cataloging, Coates, Baraka, Beatty, Thompson-Spires, and McGruder embed Black aesthetics within their compositions. Their ability to weave names and concepts into their works exemplifies artistry and deep cultural knowledge.

Coates's career exhibits a compelling vision for being a multi-genre Black writer. In 2016, he actively produced works as a blogger, journalist, cultural critic, and comic book writer. As a blogger for *The Atlantic*, Coates held a platform that allowed him to share his thinking and writing processes on *Black Panther* in a high-profile venue. Between December 2015 and July 2016, Coates published five blog entries and an additional article about aspects of his comic book work. From his initial blog entry, he made it clear that he produced the work in collaboration with others and under the guidance of those with more experience and expertise. He informed readers that he would write scripts early "in order to give Brian [Stelfreeze], and my editors, a chance to tell what I am doing wrong." His previous writing projects had been "a lonely exercise," he noted. That changed when he became a comic book creator. "Black Panther has been different," he blogged. "There's a lot more collaboration and conversation. Barely three days go by in which I don't talk to Brian or my editor, Wilson Moss."[23]

Coates's strengths as a commentator led to a discussion of Black Panther in a venue separate from his blog. Marvel launched a series of YouTube videos with appearances by Coates discussing aspects of "A Nation Under Our Feet." In a description of the project in *The Hollywood Reporter*, Borys Kit revealed that "with *Black Panther* one of the biggest comics hit in years, Marvel is hoping to keep the momentum going by taking a page out of the Hollywood marketing playbook." The company partnered "with production house Bow & Arrow to produce hip-hop-driven trailer recaps that aim to build buzz ahead of each new issue."[24] In addition to promoting the comic book, the videos conveyed Coates's knowledge concerning *Black Panther* and his deep interest in his subject. He spoke earnestly about the challenges that T'Challa faces and the circumstances confronting Wakandans.

His commentary across venues contributed to the growing body of cultural criticism on Black artistic productions, which increasingly included Coates. The previously mentioned high praise from Coogler, the citations in the coverage of *Luke Cage*, and the inclusion of his work in end-of-the-year roundups of "best of" lists all added to Coates's visibility. In "The 7 Best New Comics of 2016," Alex Abad-Santos wrote, "No comic book enjoyed as much fanfare and anticipation in 2016 as *Black Panther*." Coates's run "breaks new ground in building out the vulnerability of its title character and the world he protects."[25] In an article for *Entertainment Weekly*, Christian Holub identified Coates and Stelfreeze's *Black Panther*, and so did Gavia Baker-Whitelaw in an article for *The Daily Dot*, noting that Coates's work "strikes an ideal balance between a thoughtful, complex political narrative and a traditional, action-heavy superhero adventure."[26] The appearance on those and associated lists situated Coates, in his first year as a comic book writer, alongside veteran writers like Marjorie Liu, James Tynion IV, Scott Snyder, Tom King, and Greg Rucka.

On the one hand, the publicity for Coates and *Black Panther* amounted to a win for Black representation in comics. Between 2013 and much of 2015, people bemoaned the absence of Black writers. Hardly anyone foresaw a comic book written by a Black writer becoming a bestseller and widely discussed in 2016. On the other hand, the abundant analyses that Coates received did not extend to other Black writers. They struggled to gain notice. They did not receive plentiful interviews and profiles in mainstream venues. Unlike Coates, they primarily gained popularity within the comic book industry.

Nonetheless, looking back, 2016 marked a pivotal year in the publication of Black comic books and characters. Along with Coates and Stelfreeze's work, the on-screen appearance of T'Challa, and the *Luke Cage* series on Netflix, formative developments took place. Marvel published first issues for *Nighthawk*, *Mosaic*, *World of Wakanda*, *Power Man and Iron Fist*, and *Occupy Avengers*—all written by Black writers. Several Black artists participated in the production of Hip Hop Variants. DC Comics published *Cyborg*. Black Mask Studios published *BLACK* by Kwanza Osajyefo and Jamal Igle, and the series generated a noteworthy amount of buzz for a title that neither Marvel nor DC published. These publications marked a shift toward greater representation and recognition of Black talent in the comic book industry.

In 2015, Bryan Hill began cowriting *Postal* with Matt Hawkins, and in 2016, Hill took on sole writing duties for the title. Later the same year, he wrote a miniseries, *Eden's Fall*, which, like *Postal*, Top Cow Productions published. He then wrote another miniseries *Romulus*, published by Image Comics. Hill had been publishing since 2009, but his 2016 runs on *Postal*, *Eden's Fall*, and *Romulus* constituted a breakthrough. This period foreshadowed Hill's reputation as a prolific writer in the industry.

Two years before the release of the film *Black Panther*, with interest in Black comic books anticipated to surge, a large roster of Black writers came into focus. Hill, Walker, Osajyefo, Gay, Harvey, and Coates published in 2016, and expanded the terrain for diverse representation in the comic book industry. While Coates received most of the media emphasis, those other writers made contributions and laid the groundwork for future endeavors. At the time, they did not appear in discussions as a designated cohort or school of writers. Yet in retrospect, their collective involvement as Black creators in the history of comic books and representation made this moment significant.

Marvel's success bringing Coates, a nonexperienced comic book writer, into the field would carry over to other Black writers in direct and indirect ways. Those writers belong to what we might refer to as the Coates Comics Tree, people linked to him through their work on *Black Panther*-related narratives.[27] Alongside the previously discussed writing opportunity that he made for Gay and Harvey, Coates facilitated Evan Narcisse's debut as a comics writer. Narcisse built his career as an experienced pop culture journalist who wrote about comic books. Still, like most people, he had not acquired an inside contact to write a comic book miniseries writing assignment with Marvel. A casual friendship between Coates and Narcisse allowed the two of them to participate in a sweeping interview in 2016, two weeks prior to the release of *Black Panther* #1.[28] During the course of the conversation, Narcisse showcased his deep knowledge about comic books, which impressed Wil Moss, Coates's editor at Marvel. Conversations about Narcisse between Moss and Coates led Marvel to offer a writing job, and *Rise of the Black Panther*, which Narcisse wrote, appeared in 2018.[29] For the last issue of *World of Wakanda*, published in 2017, Coates brought on fellow journalist Rembert Browne to write the issue. The assignment gave Browne a platform to take part in the expanding universe of *Black Panther* titles and creators.

In 2016, Brian Michael Bendis created the character Riri Williams, and when Bendis eventually left Marvel, the company hired Eve Ewing, who wrote *Ironheart*, following Riri. Ewing had no prior experience as a comic book writer, but neither did Coates when Marvel first hired him to write *Black Panther*. The company had reason to believe that a nonveteran writer could succeed in the field. When Marvel hired her, Ewing sought guidance from Coates.[30] Since their debuts with Marvel in 2018, Ewing and Narcisse went on to author additional titles for the company.

In December 2017, Marvel released an online comic book, *Black Panther—Long Live the King*, written by novelist Nnedi Okorafor. She would go on to write additional titles with Marvel, including *Shuri* and *LaGuardia* with Dark Horse Comics. In 2021, DC Comics published a comic book *Far Sector*, written by acclaimed science fiction and fantasy novelist N. K. Jemisin. Although no formal statement acknowledged Coates, it seems clear that his entry into the industry served as a model for the decisions made to hire Browne, Ewing, Gay, Harvey, Jemisin, Narcisse, and Okorafor. From that viewpoint, these writers and Coates appeared linked. To varying degrees, his experiences with Marvel influenced their ability to enter the field of comics.

An increased number of Black writers in comics is, of course, reason to celebrate. Yet representation often brings layered implications. While the debut of new Black comic book writers marked a positive development, it also raised concerns. The industry's interest in hiring accomplished Black creators with no prior comics experience may have resulted in more seasoned African American writers being bypassed or overlooked. Black comic writers who made decisions and sacrifices to move up the professional ladder within the field in the conventional way may have felt slighted. In the imperatives to diversify the comic book industry, companies somewhat surprisingly overlooked Black creators who had at least some experience writing comics. In July 2016, Karama Horne published an article listing more than forty Black women writers who produced comics.[31]

Horne's list functioned as an important, if underacknowledged, resource and practice of advocacy. Rarely has anyone ever published such a long list of Black women creators who have written comics or webcomics and not yet been employed by major publishers. A lack of knowledge about those women motivated Horne to create the list. People would ask her if there were "any black women out there actually writing comics, (I get this question at least once a week)."[32] Her list, which included Felicia Henderson, Barbara Brandon-Croft, and Mikki Kendall, emphatically challenged those who say diverse women creators did not exist or had no experience. Additionally, her useful checklist promoted artists who had previously gone overlooked.

Later in 2016, Nilah Magruder became the first Black woman to write for Marvel. Others, including Okorafor and Cheryl Lynn Eaton, would write for Marvel as well. The acclaimed that Coates garnered may have led Marvel and corresponding publishers to look outside of the comics industry when looking to employ Black writers. The discovery of someone like Coates could bring new diverse readers and lead to favorable reporting. As noted, the downside to such an approach involved bypassing Black writers who had been toiling within the field.

Alitha Martinez, better known as a visual artist, earned a spot on Horne's list. Martinez took on the drawing duties for *World of Wakanda* with Gay. Martinez had been working in comics since the 1990s, doing work on *Cable*, *Bat Girl*, and *Iron Man*. In 1998, she had done penciling and inking work on *Black Panther* during Christopher Priest's run. Her work on *Black Panther* for Marvel, particularly with Priest, proved to be a significant professional milestone. However, twenty years after producing that work, in an interview with Horne, Martinez expressed regret about having depicted the Dora Milaje when they "were wearing little impractical tops and little skirts while fighting with spears." In retrospect, she felt remorse for the drawings. "Please tell your audience I'm sorry for that," said Martinez to Horne, as she reflected on those early drawings of the Dora Milaje. "I was young in the business and I inked whatever they told me to," said Martinez.[33]

The act of drawing the women of *World of Wakanda* gave Martinez a means for representational redemption, allowing her to revisit portrayals of Black women characters and address past shortcomings. She regretted depicting these women in demeaning and impractical ways years ago, but she could now draw them in more practical clothing, not limited to miniskirts, and within the context of their own story. In *World of Wakanda*, she presented empowering images of Black women, free from an uncritical male gaze. Moreover, Martinez had the privilege of bringing to life the script of a Black woman writer, a circumstance far less available in 1998 when she drew and inked for *Black Panther*. Twenty years after her initial portrayals of the Dora Milaje, Martinez depicted them under much better circumstances. Coates played an instrumental in creating these conditions, elevating the Midnight Angels and facilitating the spinoff. This surge in visibility, in turn, ensured that Martinez received more acknowledgment in the industry than she had in the past.

Gay and Martinez writing and drawing, respectively, *World of Wakanda* constituted an instance of a Black writer-and-artist team, a combination that had not been frequent, at least not with top-tier publishing companies. In a review of Coates's *Black Panther* #1 and #2, acclaimed painter Kerry James Marshall shared that in 2009, Reginald Hudlin and Ken Lashley formed the first Black writer-and-artist team on *Black Panther*.[34] Later, Coates and Stelfreeze worked together, and while their collaboration drew the most public interest, other Black teams produced work. Complementing the work of Gay and Martinez, *World of Wakanda* included a story starring Zenzi written by Yona Harvey and Coates and drawn by Afu Richardson. Kwanza Osajyefo and Jamal Igle produced *BLACK*.

David F. Walker participated in quite a few projects that employed Black visual artists. In 2016, Walker and artist Sanford Greene produced *Power Man and Iron Fist*, also known as Luke Cage and Danny Rand. That same year, Geoffrey Thorne and Khary Randolph wrote and drew, respectively, *Mosaic*, and Walker wrote *Shaft: Imitation of Life*, drawn by Dietrich Smith. In 2017, Walker wrote *Luke Cage*, drawn by Nelson Blake, and in the same year, Walker and Sheena C. Howard cowrote *Superb*, drawn by Ray-Anthony Height. In 2017, Victor LaValle published *Destroyer*, which Dietrich Smith drew. In 2018, Walker and Chuck Brown cowrote *Bitter Root*, which Greene drew. Nalo Hopkinson and Domo Stanton teamed up on *House of Whispers* (2018), and Tee Franklin and Alitha E. Martinez produced *Jook Joint* (2018). In 2019, Walker and Brian Michael Bendis cowrote *Naomi*, which Jamal Campbell drew, and in the same year, Walker published *The Life of Frederick Douglass: A Graphic Narrative of a Slave's Journey from Bondage to Freedom*, illustrated by Damon Smyth.

The participation of Black writer-and-artist teams on individual comic book titles during this period did not receive much analysis. Nonetheless, their emergence constituted a pertinent development in representation. Black creators collectively wrote and drew sequential art and demonstrated what increased diversity across creative and editorial functions could entail. The creators took on more control of comic book production than when only a Black writer or Black visual artist contributed to titles. The formation of the teams reflected an intentional effort by publisher officials, editors, and creators to bring Black writers and visual artists together.

When readers view Coates in relation to other Black comic creators, the narrative moves away from isolating him as a seemingly exceptional individual Black writer to recognizing a broader creative network. This network, which includes Black writer-and-artist teams, attested to the collaborative and interconnected nature of their contributions. A full recognition of this network depends on appreciating the multiplicity of its artistic productions. Their works expanded representation and challenged industry norms by increasing the number of Black-authored titles. Although artists within this network continued to receive inadequate notice, their collective contributions remain significant, marking a breakthrough moment for Black creators in the comic book industry.

Chapter 8
Diversity Doesn't Sell

A year after Coates debuted to considerable fanfare with *Black Panther* #1, an intense conversation began to take shape about the limits of diversity sales in the marketplace. In late March 2017, the site *ICv2* interviewed David Gabriel, senior vice president of sales and marketing for Marvel. He remarked on shifts in the industry, with an emphasis on sales and people spending less in October and November the previous year in part because of the economy. "There was a lot of unease in the market," said Gabriel, and "there was probably a little too much product going out at that time."

The interviewer, Milton Griepp, followed up and asked Gabriel if the apparent slumping sales had anything to do with other factors. "I think also it seemed like tastes changed because stuff you had been doing in the past wasn't working the same way," said Griepp, "Did you perceive that or are we misreading that?" Gabriel tentatively agreed. Griepp asked a follow-up wondering why those tastes changed. Gabriel said he thought that was a better question for retailers who had a clearer sense of audience interests. Then, he went a little further. "What we heard was that people didn't want any more diversity," he said. "They didn't want female characters out there. That's what we heard, whether we believe it or not. I don't know that that's really true, but that's what we saw in sales."

He continued making observations about how audiences appeared to respond or not respond with respect to diversity based on the bottom line. "We saw the sales of any character that was diverse, any character that was new, our female characters, anything that was not a core Marvel character, people were turning their nose up against," he said. "That was difficult for us because we had a lot of fresh, new, exciting ideas that we were trying to get out and nothing new really worked."[1] He probably regretted not doing more to contextualize his comments about diversity. Vague declarations about sales, diversity, and audience interest or disinterest can be a minefield.

Gabriel's comments drew immediate criticism on social media and on comic book forums. To temper the angry responses, he reached out to *ICv2* to clarify his statements. "Contrary to what some said about characters 'not working,'" his statement read, "the sticking factor and popularity for a majority of these new titles and characters like *Squirrel Girl*, *Ms. Marvel*, *The Mighty Thor*, *Spider-Gwen*, *Miles Morales*, and *Moon Girl* continue to prove that our fans and retailers ARE excited about these new heroes." He went on to add, "And let me be clear, our new heroes are not going anywhere! We are proud and excited to keep introducing unique characters that reflect new voices and new experiences into the Marvel Universe and pair them with our iconic heroes."[2]

The attempt at damage control may have been too late. The next day, April 1, *CBR* ran an article with the headline, "Marvel Exec Clarifies Comments That 'People Didn't Want Any More Diversity.'" The article shared that "Gabriel's statements drew a lot of criticism online, leading him to clarify his remarks in a subsequent statement to *ICv2*."[3] The widespread online backlash reflected the collective power of fans to collectively shape conversations about diversity. In this case, their critique of a Marvel executive's remarks led to swift clarification to mitigate the fallout. Such reactions may have encouraged comics professionals to be more thoughtful when discussing diversity.

Also on April 1, *The Mary Sue* published an article by Marykate Jasper titled "Marvel VP Said Sales Slumped Because 'People Didn't Want Any More Diversity.'" The article included a subheading quotation, presumably from the VP, stating, "They didn't want female characters out there." Jasper opened by noting, "This one's not an April Fools' joke, dear readers." She then noted that while Gabriel cited a litany of factors for declining sales, he had "also pointed to readers' changing tastes." The article recounted key aspects of Gabriel's remarks and also heightened criticism of Marvel's stance or lack thereof on diverse representation.

Gabriel's comments came across as "representative of a constant, recurring problem for media which features marginalized protagonists," explained Jasper. "When confronted with sales drops for diverse characters, executives blame the diversity. Time to cancel those series! When sales for 'traditional' (read: white, male) characters drop? Instead, it's time to change up the creative teams, look at the storylines, and bump those ad dollars!"[4] Jasper expressed a long-standing complaint: Marvel and associated publishers too quickly canceled titles built around diverse characters or creators. Meanwhile, executives at those companies showed more support to white men characters and creators.

In the ensuing days, other publications, including *The Guardian*, *Entertainment Weekly*, *Polygon*, NPR, and *The New York Times*, published articles covering the "diversity doesn't sell" debate. Writing for *Vox*, Alex Abad-Santos commented that "the rapid response to Gabriel's words isn't just about one quote from one interview." Marvel had been involved in a years-long initiative that pushed for "representation and diversity" with respect to characters and creators. "Gabriel's response, and the reaction to it, represents a flare-up of long-simmering issues on both the business and artistic sides of the industry, issues that boil down to one complicated question," wrote Abad-Santos. "What is the value of comics diversity, and how do we measure that value?"[5]

The comic book industry has historically depended on a distinct model for generating sales, most heavily at the level of comic book shops.[6] As Abad-Santos reported, "[I]t basically comes down to comic book shops having limited space, not being able to return stock, and making the savviest orders." Thus, shop owners gravitate toward the safest route for returns which includes "A-list comic books featuring well-known heroes." As a result, the system appears "difficult to break into or change" and tends to "skew toward the status quo, instead of toward breaking new ground."[7]

The orientation toward the status quo partly explains the difficulty Black writers have breaking into the industry and securing enough sales to justify extended runs on titles. An assumption that audiences prefer stories following white and male heroes would explain why publishers have not done more to recruit diverse creators. "Blaming readers for not buying diverse comics despite the clamor for more is a false narrative," wrote Alex Brown. "Many of the fans attracted to 'diverse' titles are newbies and engage in comics very differently from longtime fans." Brown brought up that quite a few of these newer comic book readers tended to wait and purchase trade paperbacks and digital issues rather than print, so their interests and purchasing patterns went uncaptured when only considering how comic book shop owners responded. "Every comics publisher is struggling to walk that customer-centric tightrope," noted Brown, "but only Marvel is dumb enough to shoot themselves in the foot, then blame the rope for their fall."

As evidence that diversity can result in substantial financial returns, Brown cited the $150 million domestic earnings gained by the film *Get Out* and the fact that "*Black Panther* #1 was Marvel's highest selling solo comic of 2016."[8] Indeed, in some respects, *Black Panther* indicated a departure from the status quo. A Black character protagonist and Black writer-and-artist team had achieved extraordinary success with sales and enthusiastic appraisals. Coates presented a storyline that placed Black characters and ideas at the narrative core in ways not always common in comics. Likewise, Coates paved the way for additional Black creators to break into the industry.

At the same time, and as a reminder about the persistence of representation struggle, Coates's collaboration with Marvel illuminated the substantial cultural capital and attention power required for a Black writer to gain notice and excel in the comic book industry. His successes revealed that diversity could thrive under optimal conditions such as when a comic book writer already ranks among the best-selling authors. Apparently, only a certain kind of diversity sells. Talented and experienced writers without similar accolades and name recognition still face high barriers to advancement in the field. So, while Coates's achievements disprove the notion that diversity doesn't sell, they also speak to the challenges Black comic book writers face in gaining industry traction.

Coates's run on *Black Panther* included fifty total issues, a rare feat for Black comic book writers. But the two spinoffs from the comic book did not fare as well. Marvel canceled Roxane Gay's *Black Panther: World of Wakanda* and Coates and Yona Harvey's *Black Panther and the Crew* after only six issues. In an article reporting the cancelation of *World of Wakanda*, Jessica Lachenal linked the demise of the series to Gabriel's comments. "Though [Marvel] hasn't offered any sort of explanation," wrote Lachenal, "it's pretty easy to draw a line from this cancellation to Marvel's fairly recent knock against 'diverse titles.'"[9] According to Alex Abad-Santos, the straightforward reason that Marvel canceled *Black Panther and the Crew* and *World of Wakanda* stemmed from the books' low sales. A compounding factor resulted from the comic book industry's outdated approach to distribution, which made it difficult for some titles to gain the necessary audience and sales to justify continued publication.[10]

Amid the cancelations and debates about the marketability of comic books, Coates continued writing and publishing his second *Black Panther* story arc titled "Avengers of the New World." Coates took his story arc title from Lauren Dubois's book *Avengers of the New World: The Story of the Haitian Revolution* (2004). As he had done with "A Nation Under Our Feet," he chose to adopt a Black history book as the frame of reference for his story. The use of "avengers" corresponded to a familiar term in Marvel discourse. Known collectively as the Avengers, the team of superheroes includes Thor, Hulk, Iron Man, and Captain America. Coates suggests that those gathering to fight on behalf of Wakanda represent their own Avengers collective.

Coates's multifaceted story arc traces threats to Wakanda from forces known as the Originators—a group of species that include Simbi (snake-men), ape-like creatures, sea creatures, and the Anansi (half spider, half man beings). The Originators had preceded humans in the region that became known as Wakanda, and through mysterious portals, they returned to reclaim their lands. Adding to the challenges, T'Challa and his allies must thwart the villainous efforts of Ulysses Klaw, Zeke Stane, Doctor Faustus, Zenzi, and the Fenris twins who collectively seek to control Wakanda. Early on, the threats led Wakandans to question whether they had been forsaken by their Orisha, or the gods of Wakanda. T'Challa uses his intelligence to outmaneuver his adversaries, and he draws on the assistance of Shuri, Storm, the Midnight Angels, Manifold, and Eliot Franklin (also known as Thunderball). "Avengers of the New World" is infused with weighty political and philosophical undertones, making it a rich exploration of *Black Panther*. Just as important, the story arc displays Coates's imaginative capabilities and skills as an emergent comic book storyteller.

For one, he looked back, far back, and greatly extended the temporality of Wakandan cultural memory. In the opening pages of the series set in New York City, T'Challa, in a conversation with Storm, discusses the Wakandan Orisha — Bast (the Panther Goddess who bestows the Black Panther title), Kokou (the God of War), Mujaji (Goddess of sustenance), Ptah (the shaper of alloys like vibranium), and Thoth (God of Wisdom). In the meantime, in Wakanda, Eden, also known as Manifold, looks through books in the Wakandan Royal Library for information about the appearance of the Simbi. Shuri arrives and informs him that "there is the history of this country — the one you find in books like these — and then there is something older. The story of the land and its peoples long before they took the name 'Wakanda.'" Those aspects of pre-Wakandan history reside, Shuri says, in the "deep past."[11] The effort by Coates to recall distant or hidden Black histories corresponded to artistic practices employed by Toni Morrison, Octavia Butler, Colson Whitehead, and comparable African American creative writers.[12]

Coates also involved Wakandan ancestors in the story, making a distinction between them and the gods. The ancestors, past Black Panther leaders, occupy a spirit realm and function as a royal council that passes knowledge along to the current ruling Black Panther, which at this point means T'Challa. The council of ancestors sits at a large table, a recurring motif in Coates's stories, and converses with T'Challa and each other. Some of the past Black Panthers, like T'Chaka and Mamadou Fall, had appeared in previous storylines by other creators. Then, Coates introduced ancestors such as Negus and Benhazin. The presentation of familiar and new characters revealed his interest in blending continuity and new creations. The presentation of the Black Panther ancestors allows Coates to further showcase Wakandan histories.

Much later in the narrative, T'Challa joins Shuri on a voyage to the Djalia to seek out the source of the Originators. In the course of the story relayed to him, T'Challa learns that the Originators preceded the earliest Wakandans who "first came as pilgrims." Early on, the pilgrim Wakandans and Originators coexisted, but eventually a war took place. The pilgrims initially lost, but with the emergence of their Orisha, they conquered their foes. "And upon the land of the Originators, upon the lands seized by the pilgrims and their young gods…, we built the most advanced society ever known to man." T'Challa reacts with shock upon learning this ancient history, of the way his earliest ancestors seized the homeland of others and remade it as their own. He feels hurt when he realizes that "there will be no reparation for the Originators."[13]

Coates represented and at the same time unsettled views of a Wakandan past. The history that he narrated matched African American accounts that highlight how European colonists and settlers often built their empires on lands that originally belonged to others. Comic creators often present Wakanda as a proud nation legendary for its innovation and independence. Coates raises the possibility though that the country's early history has been far from spotless. Like other nations, Wakanda's success came at the expense of the violent downfall of others. The act of imagining a complicated past for Wakanda enriched its complexity and plausibility.

T'Challa's experience learning about the history of his country, and, essentially, about Black history, places him in league with several protagonists in African American fiction. Most notably, Milkman, the lead character from Toni Morrison's *Song of Solomon*, goes on a journey of self-discovery and knowledge growth as he learns about his near and distant relatives. Literary scholar Courtney Thorsson applied the phrase "research narrative" to describe a genre of African American novels where a protagonist undergoes "a frustrating and pleasurable pursuit of knowledge through long, intense periods of textual study, sometimes requiring the reader to mirror a protagonist's scholarly endurance." Research narratives use elements of detective novels where protagonists seek clues to solve mysteries.[14] These genres—detective fiction and research narratives— shed light on "Avengers of the New World." The story arc involves instances of T'Challa seeking out new knowledge, questioning potential witnesses or people with useful information, and looking for clues to address unsolved cases. In essence, he takes on the responsibilities of a researcher and detective.

Early in the arc, the council informs T'Challa that a sorcerer, Zawavari, who resides beneath Nyanza (a massive lake) might have answers to difficult questions. T'Challa travels to the destination, meets with Zawavari, poses questions, receives some answers, and develops a partnership.[15] At another point in the story, T'Challa goes to the exact place in Riverside Park in New York City where an ally, Asira, had been kidnapped. T'Challa takes a knee, holds dirt in his hand where someone fired blasters and a struggle took place, and reimagines what happened.[16] In other words, like a detective, he visits a crime scene, looks for clues, and mentally recreates the circumstances of the crime. As previously mentioned, T'Challa travels with Shuri to the Djalia to learn more about the deep past in the region that became Wakanda. Late in the story arc, after defeating and unmasking a villain, Ras the Exhorter, T'Challa and his allies express shock learning that the foe turned out to be a former friend. The revelation of a surprise villain, a friend turned secret culprit stands as a hallmark of detective fiction.

Black Panther still functions as a comic book with superheroes, science fiction, fight scenes, and dramatic action. Coates enhanced or extended the comic, however, by adapting detective fiction and research narrative elements into the story. Coates crafted a T'Challa who leads as a hero and king and engages as an investigator and scholar pursuing knowledge. This framing brought the character's strength and intelligence to the forefront. Coates showed T'Challa as a leader who valued wisdom and inquiry as much as power and action.

"Avengers of the New World" keeps with the conventions of team building in comic books by presenting situations where T'Challa works with allies who ultimately join him in battles against groups threatening Wakanda. Manifold and Shuri stand with him in his efforts, as do Akili and the Hatut Zeraze. T'Challa requests and receives assistance from Storm, Zawavari, N'Kano, Asha, and Thunderball. Elsewhere in the narrative, T'Challa meets with the royal council of Black Panther ancestors, and he makes a brief appearance before the new Wakandan Constitutional Council. The Black alliances that T'Challa forms may be common for a leader based in Africa, but superhero depictions have yet to widely embrace such storylines.

White characters typically dominate team-building narratives in comics, while the level of Black representation continues to fall short. For long stretches, T'Challa remained the lone Black character on the Avengers. Cyborg continually filled the role of the sole African American with the Teen Titans and the Justice League. Storm appeared as the Black character with the X-Men. This kind of tokenism reflects the long-standing marginalization of Black characters in comics.

In *Black Panther*, Coates projects alternatives. He assembles all-Black teams in "A Nation Under Our Feet" and "Avengers of the New World." While T'Challa has his circle, Tetu and Zenzi, along with their supporters, constitute a team. Ayo and Aneka, joined by the army of Midnight Angels that they amass, comprise a team as well. "I assure you," Shuri informs a villain at one point, "I never fight alone."[17] That idea of never fighting alone operates as a guiding philosophy for Coates, who shows Wakandans relying on one another and other Black allies.

Coates showed a clear interest in Black teams beyond *Black Panther*. He facilitated the spinoff *World of Wakanda*, which spotlighted Ayo, Aneka, and the Dora Milaje. Along similar lines, he rebooted *Black Panther and the Crew*, which brought together T'Challa, Storm, Luke Cage, Misty Knight, and Manifold. Coates extended diverse representation in comics by forming and foregrounding all-Black teams across titles. The appearances of teams in *World of Wakanda*, *Black Panther and the Crew*, and *Black Panther* boosted the visibility of varied casts of Black characters and gave them occasions to collaboratively participate in dramatic action sequences.

The inclusion of Storm ranked among the more pivotal additions to "Avengers of the New World." She made brief appearances in Coates's first story arc, but she became a much more prevalent supporting character in the second arc, where she and T'Challa began to rekindle their relationship. The Storm–T'Challa relationship in fact bookends the arc, which opens with the couple conversing, and closes with them talking, sharing a kiss, and professing their love for one another. Storm, being more than just T'Challa's love interest, speaks with Black Panther about political matters, and she assists in battle. With Storm here, T'Challa must balance what it means to be in relationship along with performing his royal duties. "I came back for you because I love you," he tells Storm at one point. "But I am, what I am—King of Wakanda. And I cannot wish that away, any more than I could wish you out of my heart."[18] In a battle toward the end of the series, when T'Challa and his allies are nearly overwhelmed by the Originators, Storm swoops in and provides cover. "Yet again," she tells T'Challa, "the damsel must rescue her champion."[19]

Storm contributes to the roster of formidable women characters that Coates presents during his run. Unlike Ramonda, the Midnight Angels, and Zenzi, Storm already existed as a famous comic book character prior to her appearance in *Black Panther*. Coates chose to involve a character with arguably more backstories than even the protagonist, T'Challa. Specifically, he revisited a familiar storyline: T'Challa and Storm once shared a marriage before annulling their union. In "Avengers of the New World," the two heroes renew their relationship, showcasing a somewhat rare depiction in comics: a loving partnership between Black heroes.

At various points in the series, illustrators Wilfredo Torres, Chris Sprouse, and Leonard Kirk, along with color artist Laura Martin, create thrilling images of Storm soaring through the air. *Black Panther* #16 opens and closes with her flying amid a ferocious storm of tornadoes, strong winds, and lightning. She does not wear her signature X-Men suit; instead, she initially appears in a simple black shirt and white pants. Later in the series, she dons a red long-sleeve crop top and a long skirt. She wears casual clothing while performing super heroic deeds, which allows her to blur the lines between her everyday identity and her status as an iconic, mythic figure. When Storm arrives in an area of the Alkama fields and promises to assist the people in danger of being harmed by the Anansi, a villager informs Storm that "your presence is proof enough" that their fortunes will change. He goes on to say people of the region refer to her as "The Hadari Yao. In the old Alkamite tongue: Walker of the Clouds, the goddess who preserves the balance of all natural things."[20]

The emergence of Storm as a key figure led Marvel to begin taking steps to launch a series with the character in a solo title. In October 2017, Dawn Fallik, writing for the *Philadelphia Inquirer*, reported that Coates "has confirmed that he is writing a comic book about X-Men character Storm with Marvel Comics illustrator Jen Bartel."[21] Other publications followed up and expressed excitement about the series. Rich Johnston, of *Bleeding Cool News*, pointed out that Storm "has had solo series before but they have been short-lived things.

This may have the chance to go a little longer."[22] But it never came to pass. To the disappointment of fans looking forward to the Storm series, the busy schedules of Coates and Bartel prevented them from finding time to collaborate and produce the book.[23] Nonetheless, the favorable responses to the possibility of a Storm stand-alone series based on her presence in "Avengers of the New World" spoke to Coates's ability to stimulate interest in the Walker of the Clouds.

While the inclusion of Storm gave Coates a vehicle to reintroduce a familiar character, bringing in the less widely known character Thunderball served as an instance of representational redemption. Thunderball, whose civilian name is Dr. Eliot Franklin, is an African American character affiliated with a villain group known as the Wrecking Crew, who first appeared in comics in 1974. As Dr. Franklin explains to fellow team member Piledriver (also known as Brian Philip Calusky) when the two first appear in Coates's *Black Panther*, "You know, Brian, before the Wrecking Crew, I was a scientist. Dignified and respectable. They used to call me 'The Black Bruce Banner.' Why am I still down here?" working with the Fenris twins. Piledriver responds to the question noting that he stays *down here*, performing menial tasks "for the same reason they didn't call Banner 'the white Eliot Franklin.'" In other words, Franklin's race prevented him from being more well established.

After defeating the Fenris twins and their crew, T'Challa has all of them taken away except Thunderball, who the king greets by noting, "Dr. Franklin. It is an honor. I do not think I have ever told you this, but I studied your research as a student. It was impressive."[24] T'Challa is referring to Franklin's research on gamma radiation. Franklin, expressing self-pity, assumes "the Black Bruce Banner" label is how T'Challa knew him. No, the king counters, he knows the scientist by his full name, "Dr. Eliot Augustus Franklin." T'Challa continues, "The names these people give us—as though they know us better than our fathers, or our own deeds. They have no imagination, Dr. Franklin. To them we are only shadows of their glory, never our beautiful, original selves." The comments to Franklin implicitly critique the tendency of people to frame Black accomplishments in white or Eurocentric terms. Some deployed and viewed "the Black Bruce Banner" as a compliment, but T'Challa exposes the moniker as a racially prejudiced slight. The Wakandan king says that "you do not have to answer to whatever they call you, Dr. Franklin. It is not too late to recover your own name."

Later, T'Challa and Shuri free Franklin from imprisonment on the condition that he assist them in tracking subsonic energy signatures created by Klaw. Soon after, the scene shows Dr. Franklin in a Wakandan room, dressed in a white lab coat over his Wrecking Crew uniform, ready to investigate the energy signatures. The contrast between past and present responsibilities becomes starkly evident. The scientist Dr. Franklin thus overshadows his identity as

Thunderball. The transformation from a Black man in America who achieves his goals through brute force to a Black man using his intellect and scientific knowledge to solve complex problems constitutes a powerful representational redemption.

Coates further positioned the Midnight Angels as integral to the series. *Black Panther* #169 stands out as a vividly captivating sequence where Aneka frees herself from capture and rescues Ayo. This largely silent issue joins the ranks of other notable wordless comics, such as *G.I. Joe* #21 (1984), *Daredevil* #28 (2001), *Punisher* #7 (2001), and *Hawkeye* #11 (2013). The issue opens with the villain Zeke Stane activating a device that emits intense sonic energy, rendering people unable to hear. As the sound transmits, henchmen escort Aneka, shackled in chains and wearing a prisoner mask, while blank speech bubbles indicate that their words go unheard. Fully black panels denote intermittent power outages, during which Aneka seizes the moment to strike. She uses her helmet as a weapon, swiftly overcoming her captors as the panels oscillate between darkness and visibility. Aneka then stealthily enters a room to confront Zenzi and Dr. Faustus and free Ayo from captivity. As they make their escape, an army of Midnight Angels arrives to assist, attacking the facility that held Ayo and Aneka.

Issue 169 testifies to Coates's ability to orchestrate a riveting narrative with minimal words. He organizes a salient silent counterstatement to those who described his first story arc as "talky and boring."[25] In a public discussion about his experiences writing *Black Panther*, Coates mentioned "getting out of the way" of the artist and color artist. Holding issue 1 in his hand, he said, "sometimes, I get these pages back, and I like cut stuff." He pointed to one page and said, "this is too many words."[26] His effort to say less in his writing and create space for the artist and color artist to say more may have influenced the extended wordless action scenes in issue 169. The issue rewarded readers who had tracked the series, delivering on earlier subtle references to the devastating sonic device. The issue also harks back to issue 1 when Ayo rescues Aneka from prison. This time, Aneka acts as the hero and saves Ayo.

One sequence of panels stands out for its action and intensity. A guard aims his gun at Aneka's face, preparing to shoot. Just before he fires, a panel shows the prisoner's helmet at Aneka's feet, followed by a panel of the guard aiming, and then another of Aneka kicking the helmet, which in the next panel strikes the guard's head. On the next page, bullets from another gunman barely miss Aneka as she dodges and hurls the helmet and chain toward him, tangling his arms and roughly dragging him to the ground. Next, a guard wielding two knives then attacks and manages to cut Aneka on her face, one of the rare instances of blood being shown in the series. He then kicks Aneka, sending her near a gun. In one panel, she holds the gun near the man's face as he looks on in shock. The next panel shows Aneka with a determined expression, followed by a panel of the gun firing, apparently at point-blank range. The twenty-three-panel sequence, from the guard pulling his gun on Aneka to her shooting another guard, delivers a violent, action-packed, and masterfully rendered moment of agency rarely seen with Black women characters in comics.

"This is by far the most action-heavy issue of *Black Panther* since Ta-Nehisi Coates began his run," wrote Robert Reed in a review. While praising the artwork of Leonard Kirk and Laura Martin, Reed added that "credit must also go to Ta-Nehisi Coates for the staging this issue." Reed explained that the issue showed "the growth" of Coates's writing on the comic which had been previously "criticized for being verbose and lacking in action." However, Reed also acknowledged the issue's problem with "the lack of focus on T'Challa." He wrote, "*Black Panther* #169 is a well-crafted book that arguably puts too much of the series' focus on T'Challa's supporting cast. How much one likes this issue will largely depend on how well Coates won you over on Ayo and Aneka in the first place."[27]

Reed's point indirectly touches on the "diversity doesn't sell" debate. What difference, for instance, would it make to audiences if a Black woman, rather than T'Challa, took the lead in an action-packed issue of *Black Panther*? To what extent would depictions of Black women comic book characters drive sales? Questions and debates about the profitability of diverse characters had been taking place in comics and popular culture, and soon the discussions would intensify and expand. The issue dedicated to Ayo and Aneka came out on January 24, 2018, just a month before the *Black Panther* franchise reached incredible new heights with the release of the film.

Chapter 9
Diversity Sells

Black Panther generated incredible buzz. Long before its February 2018 release, people couldn't contain their excitement. At a conference in July 2017, Roxane Gay proclaimed that she planned to repeatedly view the film, regardless of its quality: "I'm going to see that movie 20 times."[1] She had plenty of company in her enthusiasm. In an article for *The New York Times*, Salamishah Tillet disclosed that weeks before its release, the film had "already become a kind of shared language." When two Black men strangers passed each other in the mall, they gave each other a head nod before one said, "'*Black Panther*'s in a month yo.' That was his version of 'what's up.'"[2] The internet overflowed with expressions of joy and anticipation. In one of the viral memes and short videos that emerged ahead of the movie's debut, a group of elated Black children dance on tables after learning that their school would be taking a trip to see the film.

The movie became a blockbuster juggernaut. Shattering expectations, *Black Panther* "was a revolution at the box office, becoming the highest-grossing movie ever (at $1.3 billion) featuring actors of color."[3] The movie broke records, including the largest February opening and the biggest solo superhero film debut in history. Apart from its financial success, the cultural impact of *Black Panther* resonated far and wide. Reviewers and commentators celebrated the film for its breathtaking portrayal of African culture and its talented and diverse cast. The film's success energized discussions about the importance of representation in Hollywood and created opportunities for other Black cultural productions.

The contrast between the 2017 debate over whether diversity sells and the achievements of the 2018 film exemplified the shifting dynamics of representation struggles. Black screenwriters wrote the film, a Black cast headlined it, a Black filmmaker directed it, and the story unfolded in an African nation. One year, in the world of comic books, people debated diversity as a possible liability for profits. The next year, in the world of film, the conversation shifted to the ever-growing accolades and box office success of *Black Panther*. Apparently, the perceived value of diversity shifted depending on time and context. "There are few films in the last decade that have had as much of a cultural impact as Ryan Coogler's *Black Panther*," wrote Terence McSweeney. The film earned the largest opening weekend box office for a movie by a Black director in film history and also became "the first superhero film ever to be nominated for an Academy Award for Best Picture."[4]

Even though *Black Panther* received widespread praise, the film contained some questionable depictions. Hardly any of the top-billed Black actors cast to play Wakandans came from Africa. Toward the end of the film, white CIA Everett Ross assists T'Challa and his forces in achieving victory. "However given the intelligence agency's checkered history, especially in Africa," wrote Lynn Stuart Parramore, "the CIA's star billing and heroic turn in a celebration of black empowerment feels a touch off-key."[5] The seeming representational redemption of a white CIA operative in Africa is ironic and worrisome in light of the long history of terrible misdeeds that the agency committed, as thoroughly documented in Susan Williams's *White Malice: The CIA and the Covert Recolonization of Africa*.[6]

In an article titled "*Black Panther* Is Not the Movie We Deserve," Christopher Lebron identified ways the film presents troubling depictions, including the uplift of "the African noble at the expense of the Black American man." Lebron points out that the *Thor* villain Loki "gets multiple, unearned chances to redeem himself no matter what damage he has done," while no such possibility is allowed for Killmonger, despite the value of his interest in critiquing anti-Black racism. The only Black American woman depicted in the film, Lebron observed, "has, by my count, less than fifteen words to say in the movie and is unceremoniously murdered." She is "disposed of by Black-on-Black violence," and she is "invisible and nearly silent."[7] Lebron's perceptive critiques of *Black Panther* revealed that a tremendously successful and beloved Black movie could nonetheless contain troublesome depictions. Indeed, representation involves gains and losses.

Despite any shortcomings, *Black Panther* positively affected prospects for Black comics creators. Interest in the film led Marvel to produce spinoffs with Black characters written by Black writers. In December 2017, Nnedi Okorafor began writing an online miniseries, *Black Panther: Long Live the King*. In January 2018, Evan Narcisse made his comic book writing debut with *Rise of the Black Panther*, a miniseries that introduced readers to the background on T'Challa and Wakanda. Okorafor later wrote *Shuri*, a miniseries that began in October 2018, and in December 2018, Bryan Hill began writing the miniseries *Killmonger*. These projects, building on the overall interest in the growing *Black Panther* fictional universe and franchise, expanded professional pathways for Black comics creators.

Titles anchored by Black characters and Black writers in 2018 extended well beyond *Black Panther* spinoffs. Image Comics published *Farmhand*, written and drawn by Rob Guillory; *Jook Joint*, written by Tee Franklin with art by Alitha Martinez; and *Bitter Root*, created by David F. Walker and Chuck Brown with artist Sanford Greene. Fiction writer Nalo Hopkinson began writing *House of Whispers*, a DC Comics title within the *Sandman* universe, while DC's Vertigo imprint published Bryan Hill's thriller *American Carnage*. Meanwhile, Nnedi Okorafor launched *LaGuardia*, published by Dark Horse Comics. Black Mask Studios expanded the *BLACK* universe with Kwanza Osajyefo's *BLACK [AF]: Widows and Orphans*, and Valiant Comics released *Livewire*, written by Vita Ayala. Rodney Barnes wrote *Quincredible*, published by Lion Forge, and Eve Ewing made her comic book debut with Marvel's *Ironheart*. Taken together, these and corresponding titles released in 2018 exemplified the vibrancy of Black artistic production in comics, coinciding with the release of the highest-grossing Black movie of all time.

Coates undoubtedly benefited from the ubiquitous coverage generated by the *Black Panther* film. Journalists covering the movie routinely referenced Coates's work on the comic book. "Though my colleague Ta-Nehisi Coates played no direct role in the film," wrote Christopher Orr in an article for *The Atlantic*, "his recent work on the Black Panther comics was a substantial inspiration."[8] In their podcast *Still Processing*, Wesley Morris and Jenna Wortham analyzed the film and brought in Coates as a guest commentator.[9] In his otherwise unfavorable view of *Black Panther*, Christopher Lebron praised the depiction of women in the film by giving a nod to Coates: "The Black women of Wakandan descent are uniformly independent, strong, courageous, brilliant, inventive, resourceful, and ethically determined." Lebron continued, "I take it that a good deal of this is owed to Ta-Nehisi Coates's success at elevating the series' women to central characters with influence and power that turns more on their minds and integrity than their bodies."[10]

Journalists and organizers incorporated Coates into reporting and events surrounding *Black Panther*. A *Variety* article by Ramin Setoodeh on Chadwick Boseman and director Ryan Coogler mentioned that Coogler and filmmaker Ava DuVernay worked near each other at Disney as they worked on post-production for separate projects. DuVernay wrapped up *A Wrinkle in Time* as Coogler completed *Black Panther*. One day at the studio, wrote Setoodeh, "Coogler introduced DuVernay to one of her heroes, the author Ta-Nehisi Coates."[11] *Black Panther* #170, released in February 2018, includes an interview between Coates and director Ryan Coogler. On February 27, 2018, the Apollo Theater in Harlem and *The Atlantic*, coordinated an event "Black Panther in Conversation: Featuring Chadwick Boseman and Ta-Nehisi Coates."[12] The conversation also included actress Lupita Nyong'o who appeared as Nakia in the film. Coates's inclusion in the discussions and promotion of the *Black Panther* movie further extended his visibility and enriched his overall cultural capital.

On February 28, 2018, amid *Black Panther* mania, Coates made a momentous announcement about the future of his career in comics. On *The Atlantic* site, he revealed his new assignment with Marvel in his article, "Why I'm Writing *Captain America*." He stated, "For two years I've lived in the world of Wakanda, writing the title *Black Panther*. I'll continue working in that world. This summer, I'm entering a new one—the world of Captain America."[13] News organizations, including *The New York Times*, *The Guardian*, *Polygon, Slate*, and *The Hollywood Reporter*, immediately responded with articles about Coates's announcement. Remember once again that in February 2013 and 2014, Joseph Hughes and Joseph Illidge, respectively, scrutinized the absence of Black writers for top-tier comic book companies.[14] Now, in early 2018, a Black creator had been slated to write one of the most famous American superheroes. And the news about his new assignment emerged, not coincidentally, in Black History Month.

Coates emphasized that "writing, for me, is about questions—not answers. And Captain America, the embodiment of a kind of Lincolnesque optimism, poses a direct question for me: Why would anyone believe in The Dream?" He added that "What is exciting here is not some didactic act of putting my words in Captain America's head, but attempting to put Captain America's words in my head. What is exciting is the possibility of exploration, of avoiding the repetition of a voice I've tired of."[15] In 2003, Robert Morales wrote the limited series *Truth: Red, White and Black*, which introduced Isaiah Bradley, an African American subjected to experiments during World War II in an attempt by the US Army to create super soldiers. Morales presents Bradley as an African American Captain America. Coates's assignment to write Steve Rogers, that is, the white Captain America represented a representational breakthrough in comics.

Coates was not the first Black comic book creator to write canonical white heroes. Reginald Hudlin wrote issues of *Spider-Man*, and Christopher Priest wrote *Spider-Man* and *Conan the Barbarian* for Marvel and *Batman* and *Green Lantern* for DC Comics. Priest also penned the series *Captain America and the Falcon* in 2004 and 2005. In 2016, David Walker wrote *Power Man and Iron Fist*, which paired Luke Cage and the white character Danny Rand. While it wasn't entirely unheard of for Black comic book creators to write stories on white characters, the announcement that one of the most well-known Black writers in the country would pen a comic book about one of the most storied white comic book heroes marked a pivotal development.

The announcement that Coates would write *Captain America* drew immediate media attention. "It's hard to overstate how fertile the thematic ground is here," wrote Abraham Josephine Riesman for *Vulture*. "The notion of putting one of the most prominent and thoughtful critics of the American experiment in charge of a character who is, in many ways, supposed to be that experiment's living embodiment? That should be interesting."[16] Graeme McMillan, writing for *The Hollywood Reporter*, noted that "In what is likely to be the most high-profile announcement of its Fresh Start initiative, Marvel Entertainment has revealed that Ta-Nehisi Coates will write a new Captain America comic, launching this July."[17] The tone of the dispatches on Coates confirmed that excitement about him as a writer persisted at a high level, which would, along with other outcomes, translate to sales upon the release of the comic book.

Marvel made a provocative choice by selecting Coates to write *Captain America*, when taking account of his more pointed assessments and critiques of the United States. According to Jonah Engel Bromwich in an article for *The New York Times*, "This could make the character an interesting match for Mr. Coates, who throughout his career has written about his complicated relationship with and views about patriotism, and has often been accused of being pessimistic about the United States' future."[18] In an article for *Polygon*, Susana Polo remarked that "Coates' most high profile career moments have been his examinations of race in American history, and his writing on how the United States can move forward as a country struggling with deeply embedded systemic racism."[19] Once again, write-ups about Coates's work in comics diverged from those about others in the field. Reviewers and commentators referenced his noncomic work in ways that did not apply to his fellow creators.

In his announcement about his new writing assignment, Coates gave credit to "Axel Alonso, who first broached the idea of me writing Cap."[20] Alonso had stepped down as editor in chief at Marvel in November 2017, but his efforts to promote diversity at the company endured. On the one hand, Alonso faced criticism during his tenure as Marvel's leader. "As one of the public faces for Marvel, Mr. Alonso sometimes found himself at the forefront of controversies," wrote George Gene Gustines.[21] Some observers criticized Alonso in discussions surrounding the "diversity doesn't sell" debates and faced scrutiny for Marvel's perceived lack of diverse writers under his leadership.

On the other hand, in 2014, Alonso helmed Marvel when the company introduced an African American Captain America and a woman as Thor. As previously noted, that same year, the company introduced Kamala Khan as the new Ms. Marvel. A 2015 article in *Time* magazine pointed to Alonso's "imperative to create comic books starring women that could sell."[22] He also spearheaded the development of the much talked-about Hip Hop Variants, which drew inspiration from a Black musical art form and included visual artists of color. When news broke in 2016 about the cancellation of *Nighthawk*, David F. Walker, the writer for the series, expressed gratitude for the backing of the editor in chief: "Marvel has been very supportive of *Nighthawk*, especially Axel, who has been in our corner.

But the market is not supporting the book."[23] Notably, Alonso served as editor when Marvel hired Coates. He ultimately oversaw and influenced consequential developments in Marvel's diversity efforts. The setbacks and progress during his tenure exemplified the notion of representation as a continuous negotiation.

In addition to Alonso, toward the end of his *Captain America* announcement, Coates thanked his network within the comic book industry. First, he identified "a community of comic creators (Matt Fraction, Kieron Gillen, Jamie McKelvie, Ed Brubaker, Kelly Sue DeConnick, Chip Zdarsky, and Warren Ellis, among others) who've embraced me and helped me learn the form." He then expressed gratitude to editors Sana Amanat, Wil Moss, Tom Brevoort, and C. B. Cebulski, who had replaced Alonso as the editor in chief at Marvel.[24] The people Coates listed constitute an enviable group of supporters for any creator, but definitely for a Black writer relatively new to comics. A famous Black writer entering comics could bypass the years it took most to build a large social network of well-connected insiders. Less than two years into his tenure within the field, Coates could thank a group of veteran and accomplished creators and editors who had directly assisted him.

In contemporary literature, particularly with poetry, elite institutions and well-connected friends provide access to social networks vital to achieving success, which often means winning prestigious prizes. Juliana Spahr, Stephanie Young, and Claire Grossman have conducted a series of studies examining prize-winning trends in poetry.[25] For one study, Spahr and Young compiled and analyzed a data set of 429 winners of eight hundred poetry prizes. Their findings revealed that "over half have a degree of some sort from a cluster of eight schools: Harvard, University of Iowa, Stanford, Columbia, Yale, New York University, University of California, Berkeley, and Princeton." Furthermore, "around 60 percent of the poets who get tapped to judge [poetry prizes] attended that same small cluster of schools." Spahr and Young concluded that "reciprocity defines this subculture," where small "overlapping groups of poets" select members from their own networks, who later reciprocate when they become judges.[26]

Prizes do not shape success and career trajectories in the field of comics to the same extent as in poetry. Nevertheless, much like in poetry, membership in influential social networks brings rewards. Ta-Nehisi Coates's insider status as a writer for *The Atlantic* connected him to Sana Amanat, which led to opportunities at Marvel and access to editors and creators who lent essential guidance and support. At Marvel, decision-makers paired Coates with accomplished and exceptionally talented visual artists. For *Black Panther*, he collaborated with Brian Stelfreeze, Chris Sprouse, Wilfredo Torres, and color artist Laura Martin. For *Captain America*, Coates would work with, "the incredible Leinil Yu on interior panels and Alex Ross on covers. Both Leinil and Alex are legends."[27] For poets, success commonly rests on winning prestigious literary prizes and honors. For a comic book writer like Coates though, success meant receiving assistance from experienced editors and working with veteran and skillful visual artists.

The support Coates received, compared to dozens of other Black creators in comics, spoke to the visibility disparity that exists in the field. One Black writer secured tremendous backing as others received far less recognition and fewer opportunities. Coates's career trajectory, including his noteworthy assignment to write *Captain America*, amounted to an outstanding series of breakthroughs. At the same time, his narrow and improbable path confirmed the rarity of such opportunities for Black writers in the industry. This disparity pointed to the systemic barriers that prevented inclusion and equity for Black comics creators.

To close his announcement about *Captain America*, Coates paid tribute to three African Americans who influenced him. "Finally, but most importantly," he wrote, "I have to thank the black comic creators I admired as a youth, often without even knowing they were black—Christopher Priest, Denys Cowan, Dwayne McDuffie, specifically—without whom none of this would be possible."[28] McDuffie built his career as a comic book creator and television writer whose pioneering Black superheroes won him widespread praise. He cofounded Milestone Media, which introduced characters like Static Shock, Icon, Rocket, and Hardware. When McDuffie died in 2011, his fans and admirers mourned, including Coates who published a blog entry, "Dwayne McDuffie, the Icon," describing how McDuffie's work on the animated series *Justice League* influenced his approach to memoir and his views on art.[29]

Trailblazers like Priest, Cowan, and McDuffie opened the door for Coates to pursue opportunities in comics. He wrote, "There has long been a complaint among Black comic creators that they are restricted to Black characters." With this statement, Coates disclosed a representation grievance: white writers have historically enjoyed the privilege of depicting leading characters of diverse races and genders, but Black writers have again and again been denied similar freedoms. Coates, however, recognized that his own career benefited from certain privileges that allowed him to bypass some of the barriers faced by Black creators. "I don't know what it means to live in a world where people restrict what you write," he observed, "and the reason I don't know is largely because of the sacrifices of all those who were forced to know before me. I have not forgotten this."[30]

By announcing his role on *Captain America* himself, Coates exercised a valuable form of self-representation agency. In most cases, comic book companies circulate press releases, or newspapers run interviews or profiles announcing a new development. Rarely do comic book writers have the opportunity to make the announcements themselves in widely available venues like *The Atlantic*. Here was Coates, though, breaking the news on his upcoming endeavors. When news outlets and magazines reported on the development, they cited Coates's announcement. In effect, he participated in controlling the narrative about his work.

By publishing a personal essay about his experiences, Coates followed the long-standing tradition of Black autobiographical writing. Like Frederick Douglass, Richard Wright, Maya Angelou, James Baldwin, and additional African American writers, Coates conveyed deeply felt accounts in his own voice. The field of comics, in comparison to fiction and poetry, has relatively few Black voices. Thus, Coates's essays in *The Atlantic* about writing *Black Panther* and *Captain America* both stood as uncommon and compelling acts of African American self-representation agency. These writings showcased a creator actively defining and communicating his creative process and concerns to a wide audience.

On May 5, 2018, for Free Comic Book Day, Marvel released a special issue of *The Avengers* written by Jason Aaron. The issue included a bonus *Captain America* story by Coates. On July 4, 2018, Marvel released *Captain America* #1, and the issue drew large numbers of readers. Coates's debut on the title sold more than 167,000 copies, making it the third best-selling title, after *Amazing Spider-Man* #1 and *Batman* #50, for the month of July.[31] *Captain America* #1 ranked 15th out of 1,000 for units ordered by comic book shops in 2018.[32] The only other title by a Black writer in the top 100, *Black Panther* #1, came from Coates.[33]

As the sales units suggested, this new writing assignment further bolstered his identity and reputation as an accomplished comic book writer. His new role, writing an iconic white hero diversified his writing portfolio. It's ironic that Coates diversified his portfolio by writing a comic book showcasing a white character. Diversity in comics typically refers to the incorporation of nonwhite characters. For Coates, Black people had been central, focal figures in his large body of published works. Within this context, Steve Rogers gave him a chance to further diversify his subject matter and characters.

Captain America #1 received news accounts in comic book venues and mainstream media. In a review of *Captain America* for *The Washington Post*, David Betancourt suspected that "Coates seems to have found his Marvel writing groove."[34] Brett Schenker assessed that the skills Coates demonstrated in *Captain America* surpassed those he exhibited in *Black Panther*.[35] In the same vein, Justin Partridge praised Coates's work as "far more focused and pointed than his Black Panther debut," describing *Captain America* #1 as "helmed by a steadily-improving writer who has no problems delving into the political ramifications of superheroes and their world." Patridge went on to remark that Coates successfully rejuvenated the series after its "divisive" previous run, delivering a much-needed positive restart. "*Captain America* #1 is a triumph for one of Marvel's A-listers who was in dire need of image rehab," wrote Patridge.[36]

In a review of *Captain America* #1 for *IGN*, Jesse Schedeen thought this newest volume "isn't quite the immediate home run as other recent relaunches like Venom and Thor." According to Schedeen, the issue "packs in some clever ideas," but ultimately, "this issue fails to establish a clear sense of direction or momentum in its opening chapter." In the process of reviewing the title, Schedeen, like other reviewers, made mention of Coates's concurrent work in comics. "His past two years on Black Panther," wrote Schedeen, "have shown him to be an intelligent, capable writer with a unique perspective and an ability to blend real-world politics with outlandish superhero concepts."[37] Along these lines, in his review of *Captain America* #1 for *Black Nerd Problems*, Keith Reid-Cleveland determined that writing the title "gives Coates another opportunity to use his extensive experience covering politics and social thought in comic book form alongside his work with the Black Panther."[38] In her review, Gavia Baker-Whitelaw pointed out that "*Captain America* #1 is harder to get into than the electrifying first issue of Coates' *Black Panther*," which she reviewed in 2016. In her *Captain America* #1 review, she also mentioned that "[i]n his non-comics career, Coates writes about race and politics in America, examining the country's deep internal divides."[39] Commentators made Coates's reputation as a political writer a fixture in the treatments of his work in comics.

Even Coates anticipated that people would expect him to infuse his politics into *Captain America*. In his announcement about taking on the title, he wrote, "What is exciting here is not some didactic act of putting my words in Captain America's head, but attempting to put Captain America's words in my head."[40] Upon the release of the comic book, Coates echoed those sentiments in remarks that he made to Kwame Opam in a story for *The New York Times*. "The opportunity of writing 'Captain America' wasn't to make Steve Rogers talk like the son of somebody who had been in the Black Panther Party," said Coates. "The opportunity was the son of somebody who had been in the Black Panther Party to talk like Steve Rogers. To get into that perspective."[41] The framing of Coates, the political writer and thinker, may have downplayed appreciation for the artistry of his storytelling.

An emphasis on the politics over the artistry of Black creative writers unfortunately persists. Across fields of artistic production, commentators have routinely appraised the political and sociological implications of compositions by Black writers and overlooked aspects of their artistry. In an interview in 1984, Toni Morrison said, "I don't think it is possible to discuss a literature without taking into consideration what is sociologically or historically accurate, but most of the criticism in this country stops here."[42] Again and again, assessments of Black artistic productions stop at political and sociological framings. What endures amounts to aesthetic underrepresentation, whereby craftsmanship, stylistic innovations, and artistic decisions employed by Black writers go underexplored.

Throughout history, Black writers, including Frederick Douglass, Richard Wright, Toni Morrison, and Amiri Baraka have published works labeled as "politically charged" or "controversial." Similar labels have certainly been applied to Coates's "The Case for Reparations," *Between the World and Me*, and other writings. The tendency to frame the works of Black writers primarily through political and sociological lenses contributed to the underrepresentation of their artistry. Serious issues pertaining to race and racism addressed in these works understandably motivated reviewers and commentators to attend to their political significance. Yet this approach perpetuated the suppression of Black artistic appreciation and ultimately undervalued aesthetic contributions.

Coates's work on *Captain America* nonetheless gained widespread praise. The publicity for the first issue suggested that taking on the title would expand Coates's overall audience. Though some overlap existed, several publications that provided reviews for *Captain America* #1 had not covered *Black Panther* #1 (2016) and *Black Panther* #1 (2018), indicating that even more reviewers and audiences engaged Coates's work. This expanded reception suggested that in some instances, Coates's *Captain America* would be read through a fresh lens, distinct from topics explored in *Black Panther*. The shift in audience indicated the broader appeal of *Captain America*.

Black Panther had, relatively speaking, only recently risen to prominence, but *Captain America* had been a prevalent and enduring title for decades. In 2018, the legacy numbering placed *Black Panther* #1 at 173 and *Captain America* #1 at 705. This difference clarified the reach and historical weight of *Captain America*, positioning Coates to engage with a larger and more deeply rooted fan base. Coates's success and visibility writing *Black Panther* paved the way for the opportunity he received to pen *Captain America*, and now the coverage of *Captain America* brought renewed visibility to his work on *Black Panther*. This reciprocal dynamic ultimately increased Coates's cultural capital and stood as an additional counterpoint to recent claims that diversity doesn't sell.

At the same time that Coates began his run on *Captain America*, he embarked on a groundbreaking take on *Black Panther*. In April 2018, he concluded his "Avengers of the New World" story arc, and the following month marked the launch of his new series, "The Intergalactic Empire of Wakanda." On February 20, 2018, prior to Coates's announcement about *Captain America*, Marvel unveiled its "Fresh Start" initiative, promising "news series, new creative teams, new directions, and new beginnings."[43] Marvel's previews for upcoming titles teased "A bold new direction for the Black Panther!" with revelations that "Wakanda is much bigger than [T'Challa] ever dreamed."[44] Charles Nicholas Raymond described the upcoming *Black Panther* series as showcasing its "hero exploring a Wakanda that has expanded its territory into the vast reaches of space."[45] For the first twenty-five issues of *Black Panther*, Coates had thoroughly explored Wakanda, and for his closing twenty-five issues on the comic book, he would boldly pursue cosmic exploration.

Chapter 10
Star Wars for Black People

On the evening of Tuesday, February 27, 2018, two stars of the recently released *Black Panther* film came home to Harlem. Coates moderated a conversation with Chadwick Boseman and Lupita Nyong'o at the Apollo Theater. The audience cheered as Coates and the two movie stars made their way to their seats on stage. Coates began the discussion by referencing a notable assessment of the blockbuster movie and the jubilant response it received. "Somebody who is much, much wiser and much smarter than me," he said, "called it 'Star Wars for Black People.'"[1]

The next day, articles in *Rolling Stone* and *The Guardian* attributed the statement to Coates, despite his comment that he had borrowed the phrase from someone else.[2] The original utterance came from Steven Thrasher who, writing for *Esquire*, recalled, "It was during the scene in which T'Challa (Boseman) is set to take over the kingdom from his late father and roams through the vibrant, bustling streets of Wakanda that I started to consider the notion that *Black Panther* is *Star Wars* for Black people." Thrasher continued, describing the scene as "wondrous" and "teeming with colorful life" akin to the cantina in *Star Wars: A New Hope* or the Imperial Senate in *The Phantom Menace* with one significant difference: "all the characters are Black humans."[3] Coates's use of the phrase at the Apollo Theater left the notion of *Black Panther* as "*Star Wars* for Black People" open to interpretation. Writing for *Rolling Stone*, Andy Beta indicated that the analogy implied that *Black Panther* "has the potential to inspire much like Star Wars did for kids back in the 1970s and today."[4] In *The Guardian*, Jake Nevins echoed Coates's view that *Black Panther* was "an incredible achievement."[5]

Few discussed at the time that Coates had other reasons to be contemplating *Star Wars* and adventures to galaxies far, far away. On February 20, a week before the event at the Apollo with Boseman and Nyong'o, Marvel announced its "Fresh Start" initiative, which included Coates's involvement in an upcoming

Black Panther story. With few details available, Coates's title received relatively little discussion. Besides, at the time, the recently released *Black Panther* film ruled most of the national conversation about Black artistic representation in popular culture. News about comic book developments could wait. Then, a day after Coates's appearance at the Apollo, he revealed that he would be writing *Captain America*, a revelation that quickly became the headline news story about him and his work in comics.

In retrospect, the writer of an upcoming series titled "The Intergalactic Empire of Wakanda" needed to prepare readers for a narrative shift and thus fittingly began a public discussion by drawing parallels between *Black Panther* and *Star Wars*. The influence of George Lucas's space opera on Coates's comic book writing became evident with the publication of his new story arc set in the outer cosmos. *Black Panther* #1 fittingly debuted in late May, the same time of year when films from both the original and prequel *Star Wars* trilogies premiered. May 4th, now widely celebrated as Star Wars Day, marks the connection. For Coates, the *Star Wars* films served as conceptual inspiration and frameworks for the world-building that transported Wakandans far from Africa and Earth.

Coates's "The Intergalactic Empire of Wakanda" story arc boldly reimagines *Black Panther* by taking central Wakandan characters into the vastness of space. The narrative unfolds in a future timeline where Wakandans have built a spacefaring society infusing high-level technology with their cultural values. What began as a peaceful outpost of Wakandans in outer space eventually gave rise to conquest, expanding their reach to planets and solar systems. T'Challa, stripped of his memories, struggles to reclaim his identity and navigate this spacefaring Wakandan empire. By combining *Star Wars*-like intergalactic escapades with Black diasporic themes, Coates explored questions concerning power, freedom, and cultural memory, and he greatly expanded the scope of Wakanda's story.

Several factors made "The Intergalactic Empire of Wakanda" an artistically ambitious production that showcased Coates's formidable capabilities as a comic book storyteller. For one, the series explored a rare and unique concept in both comic books and science fiction: the portrayal of abundant numbers of Black people in space engaged in daring action sequences. Indeed, Black intergalactic representation remains a rarity. Additionally, Coates incorporated Black diasporic terminology throughout the narrative, embedding distinct cultural concepts and values into the storytelling. Drawing on an enduring practice in African American artistic culture, Coates also depicted representations of slavery and struggles for liberation. He skillfully tapped into an evocative African American literary trope by weaving an intricate narrative about a Black protagonist battling the plunder of his cultural memory. Coates brought forth remarkable geospatial imaginative capabilities, exploring the outer reaches of the universe and interdimensional travel. Finally, in the closing issues, he orchestrated what may have been the largest assemblage of Marvel's Black heroes united in battle to protect Wakanda, a moment that we might describe as "Avengers for Black people."

Any of these elements—Black intergalactic representation, Black diasporic terminology, representations of slavery and liberation struggles, grueling efforts to reclaim cultural memory, stirring displays of geospatial imagination, and the unprecedented assembly of Marvel's Black heroes—would be commendable and generative to explore individually in a comic book series or other artistic productions. Coates achieves an ambitious feat by integrating all these elements into a single multifaceted story arc. Reviewers praised individual issues and the trade paperbacks of "The Intergalactic Empire of Wakanda" for its tremendous world-building, captivating storytelling, and visually arresting artwork.[6] Despite these appraisals, discussions of Coates's groundbreaking depictions of Black people in deep space have largely been confined to the realm of comic book reviews, without extending into African American literary and cultural studies. That's unsurprising, as comics rarely receive recognition as serious literature. Scholars have primarily examined Coates's acclaimed works, "The Case for Reparations" and *Between the World and Me*. Nonetheless, examining "The Intergalactic Empire of Wakanda" gives us occasions to recognize a Black writer's most innovative creative work and to think about expanded possibilities for Black representation in comic books.

The idea of Wakandan space travel emerged years before Coates's run. "The rise of the Wakandan space empire is a throwback to the very first issue of Jonathan Hickman's *New Avengers*," disclosed Kieran Shiach, "when a group of Wakandan teenagers succeeded in a trial to unlock the secrets of an undiscovered solar system."[7] In that issue, published on January 2, 2013, T'Challa informs those teenagers that "Wakanda now possesses the preeminent space program on the planet… but we must do more, go farther… to somewhere no human has ever been."[8] The discussion of interstellar travel is interrupted as mysterious visitors from another planet arrive. Another version of the scene occurs again in *Secret Wars* #9, also written by Hickman, published on January 13, 2016. This time, the scene extends and shows a rocket launching into outer space, and T'Challa says, "This is where it begins. That rocket is for Earth Command to support local system travel. We will drag mankind to the stars on the back of Wakandan science."[9]

Coates built on aspects of what Hickman presented in *New Avengers* #1 and *Secret Wars* #9. He began developing the story arc for what became "The Intergalactic Empire of Wakanda" as early as 2017, when his "Avengers of the New World" series appeared. A single page from the upcoming series appeared in *Marvel Legacy* #1, written by Jason Aaron, published on September 27, 2017.[10] The four-panel page consists of interstellar images, including a scene of stars and planets identified as "Benhazin Star System," another panel presented as "The

Planet of Bast," and two additional panels showing space jets, humans, other beings, and Black Panther iconography, all of which fall under the designation "The Intergalactic Empire of Wakanda." On May 23, 2018, and in the first seven issues of the story arc, *Black Panther* opens with a slightly adjusted version of that four-panel page.

"Two thousand years ago," the narration of issue 1 reads, "a detachment of Wakandans established a small, desolate colony on the outer edges of the cosmos." Eventually, these Wakandans extended their territory as they "pushed their country's traditional notion of self-defense to racial ends—true self-defense meant the conquest of all potential foes." The narration explains how a colony had transformed into an empire, "spanning five galaxies," and some of those Wakandans sought further expansion. The description closes by noting that "this is the story of the only man who could stop them—a king who sought to be a hero, a hero who was reduced to a slave, a slave who advanced into a legend."[11] The phrasing here invokes Frederick Douglass's statement: "You have seen how a man was made a slave; you shall see how a slave was made a man."[12] Thus, T'Challa syncs with the venerable former fugitive slave.

The connections to Douglass and representations of slavery continue in the opening scenes, which show T'Challa, unaware of his name at the time, being forced to work with others under grueling conditions. They live as enslaved people, whom their captors refer to as "dumb mules." T'Challa battles his captors, escapes briefly, but ultimately faces recapture and a return to servitude. Later, a fellow slave attacks T'Challa, who pummels the aggressor, nearly killing him until another enslaved bystander advises T'Challa to restrain himself and not behave like "a beast." The bystander goes on noting, "They have stolen your name, your culture, your God. Do not let them steal your mind!" *Black Panther* #1 delivers a powerful blend of ideas: a futuristic world that at the same time draws on historical tropes associated with slavery and struggles for liberation.

With his exploration of enslavement throughout "The Intergalactic Empire of Wakanda," Coates channels an expansion creative domain whereby Black artists have depicted physical bondage and efforts of Black people to free themselves. *Black Panther* #1 begins with an enslaved person attempting to escape, a familiar trope in African American artistic discourse. The planet that held T'Challa and his fellow captives bears the name Goree, derived from the Senegalese Gorée Island known as a key post in the Transatlantic Slave Trade from the fifteenth through nineteenth centuries. Years after including Goree in *Black Panther*, Coates made his first visit to Gorée Island and wrote about the experience in his book *The Message* (2024). In the opening issue, a group conspiring against the Empire plans an assault on Goree to liberate and enlist the captives there. The group planning the attack goes by the name "maroons," a term used to describe Black people who escaped and resisted enslavement in the Americas as early as the sixteenth century. The Jamaican Maroons who resisted British colonial forces for decades receive enduring reverence. In *Black Panther* #1, the maroons first appear aboard their spaceship, the Mackandal, a name derived from François Mackandal, a Haitian Maroon leader. The police force and enslaver overseers go by the name Askaris, the name assigned to African soldiers who served the interests of European colonial powers.

So in the first issue, readers encounter references to Frederick Douglass, Gorée Island, maroons, African colonialism, and a Haitian slavery resistance leader, along with depictions of enslavement, intra-racial conflict, cooperation, and wisdom sharing between enslaved people and slavery resistance. Taken together, these references imbue the comic with Black aesthetics. Such depictions enrich the comic book form and correspond to the flood of representations of slavery in African American literature. Slave narratives by Frederick Douglass, Harriet Jacobs, Henry Box Brown, and William and Ellen Craft emphasize resistance and escape. Later, neo-slave narratives such as Margaret Walker's *Jubilee* (1966), Ishmael Reed's *Flight to Canada* (1976), Toni Morrison's *Beloved* (1987), and Colson Whitehead's *The Underground Railroad* (2016) explore the conditions of enslavement and struggles for liberation. Coates's main storyline in "The Intergalactic Empire of Wakanda" extends this continuum, linking his work to a large body of writings on representations of slavery and liberation. His adaptation of these themes in a comic book format expands their reach, marking a rare instance where an esteemed African American literary artist writes for comics.

In addition to producing a large volume of blog entries on the Civil War and slavery, Coates further explored these themes in his artistic work in noncomic mediums. On September 24, 2019, he published a novel *The Water Dancer*, a neo-slave narrative about an enslaved man, who as a boy discovers that he possesses superhuman powers, much like a comic book hero. The protagonist, Hiram Walker, wields an ability called "conduction," which allows him to transport himself and others across distances. This power proves vital for Black people seeking freedom from physical bondage. Conduction parallels the teleportation abilities of Marvel character Eden Fesi also known as Manifold, who serves admirably alongside T'Challa throughout Coates's *Black Panther* story arcs. Hiram and Eden establish discernible links between Coates's work in comics and his novel, bridging these realms of artistic production.

Reviewers responded favorably to the descriptions of slavery and resistance in *Black Panther* #1. Deron generally asserted that the presentation of a slave working to recover his past "helps to create a deeper mystery that is infinitely interesting to see play out."[13] Based on the opening scenes, T'Challa is "a badass and almost leads a one man slave revolt," emphasized Logan Dalton.[14] "This issue plants the seeds for a nuanced discussion of imperialism, slavery, and identity without breaking its fighting, running, shooting stride," stated Charles Martin. "It also has some top-notch history content delivered with impressive subtlety. While you absolutely do not need to study up to fully enjoy this issue, both you and the author will be very pleased if it inspires you to plug terms like 'Maroons' and 'Askaris' into Wikipedia."[15] Indeed, the first issue alone evokes an array of aesthetics that signal Black culture and history.

Black Panther #1 sold resoundingly well, with 122,000 units ordered by comic book shops, making it the fifth highest-selling title out of five hundred in May 2018.[16] By the end of the year, Black Panther #1 ranked thirtieth among one thousand titles published that year, and it secured an achievement as one of only thirty comic books to exceed 130,000 units ordered by shops.[17] *Black Panther* #1 (2018) ranked Coates's third best-selling title, following *Captain America #1*, his second highest-selling, and *Black Panther #1* (2016), his highest-selling. The year 2018 marked a landmark year for releases by Black comic book writers, including David F. Walker, Eve Ewing, Bryan Hill, Evan Narcisse, Rodney Barnes, Nnedi Okorafor, and Nalo Hopkinson. Nevertheless, visibility disparities held steady, with Ta-Nehisi Coates receiving significantly more reporting than his peers. This imbalance partly stemmed from his dual work on *Captain America* and *Black Panther*, two high-profile properties bolstered by their long-standing reputations and by Marvel's substantial promotional efforts. The successes and challenges shed light on the importance of representation struggles, which revealed the accomplishments and barriers for Black comic writers faced.

Throughout the first issues of "The Intergalactic Empire of Wakanda," T'Challa experiences hazy memories and dreams of a mysterious woman with white hair who beckons him to "come back home." This woman, of course, is Storm, and T'Challa struggles to recall both her identity and his own. He, along with countless others in the universe, have had their memories wiped. His disorientation and quest for clarity become shared with the readers, drawing them further into the story as they seek to unravel the unanswered questions about his identity and past. These themes of identity, memory, and self-discovery occupy central places in African American literature and receive compelling explorations in works such as James Weldon Johnson's *The Autobiography of an Ex-Colored Man* (1912), Ralph Ellison's *Invisible Man* (1952), and Toni Morrison's *Song of Solomon* (1977). T'Challa's journey, as told by Coates, corresponds to this African American literary continuum where Black protagonists endeavor to gain a deeper understanding of their cultural heritage and personal identity.

While the representations of slavery and explorations of cultural identity place *Black Panther* in league with African American literary works, Coates's narrative also undeniably follows a *Star Wars* continuum. Terminology and concepts from George Lucas's fictional universe such as the Galactic Empire, the notion of spacefaring rebels opposing an oppressive system, and interstellar travel permeate "The Intergalactic Empire of Wakanda." Like Luke Skywalker, T'Challa begins his journey unaware of his origins. Emperor Palpatine and Darth Vader ruthlessly control the Empire and serve as composites for Emperor N'Jadaka in Coates's narrative. In a review titled "Black Panther Meets Star Wars in 'The Intergalactic Empire Of Wakanda,'" Anthony Composto explained that "The space battles all look and feel like something out of the Original Trilogy" of *Star Wars*. He assessed the connections as positive. "This is a mashup that we didn't know we needed, but now that we have it, it's so fulfilling."[18]

One unmistakable homage to a famous *Star Wars* action sequence takes place in *Black Panther* #2. T'Challa leads a daring fighter jet battle against the Empire, where he courageously outmaneuvers foes and commands the skies with his prowess as a pilot. The scene recalls Luke Skywalker's feats in the Battle of the Death Star, where he decides to turn off his computer targeting system and trust in his own instincts. Similarly, during his battle, T'Challa instructs his computer system to "disengage protocols," relying on his manual flying skills to combat his enemies. T'Challa's allies watch in awe as he performs death-defying moves. "How is he doing this?!"[19] shouts Nakia, after witnessing T'Challa evade and then destroy a group of adversary imperial fighter pilots. According to Matthew Peterson in a review of *Black Panther* #2, "The first half of this issue really feels like the climactic battle of 'Star Wars' to me, as Black Panther takes on the role of Luke Skywalker and takes down one ship after another."[20] Robert Reed described the issue as "a sci-fi actioner," referencing the swift pacing of the story, driven by the jetfighter battle that dominated the narrative.[21] Like *Star Wars*, "The Intergalactic Empire of Wakanda" gave audiences a thrilling, high-stakes space battle paired with a hero's journey.

The deep-space setting, interstellar travel, and speculative technology, all framed within a story that places Black people at the forefront, exemplify Afrofuturist aesthetics. According to Adam Bradley, "Afrofuturism uses literature and the graphic arts, music and dance, film and television to imagine Black people into a future long denied them."[22] Mainstream comics and pop culture have rarely depicted large numbers of spacefaring Black people. By contrast, Coates and his artist-collaborators engage in Afrofuturist world-building on a grand scale, both through storytelling and visual composition. In the universes of *Star Wars* and *Star Trek*, Black characters usually occupy subordinate parts or function as token representations in mostly non-Black casts. Alternatively, Coates envisions a narrative with a Black protagonist, supported by a majority-Black cast, fully engaged in interstellar life. In this regard, "The Intergalactic Empire of Wakanda" marks a commendable step forward in the history of Black space representations.

Afrofuturist aesthetics in Coates's writing link him to a continuum of Black science fiction writers, including Samuel R. Delany, Octavia Butler, N. K. Jemisin, and Tananarive Due. Black science fiction and fantasy writing have a long history. In "A Crash Course in the History of Black Science Fiction," author Nisi Shawl presents an annotated list of forty works, spanning Martin R. Delany's *Blake, or the Huts of America* (1859), Charles Chesnutt's "The Goophered Grapevine" (1887), and Pauline Hopkins's *Of One Blood* (1903) to Octavia Butler's *Fledging* (2005), Shawl's *Filter House* (2008), Mat Johnson's *Pym* (2011), and Nnedi Okorafor's *Akata Witch* (2011).[23] Coates's *Black Panther* contributes to this rich history of speculative ideas, expanding the creative discourse of Black sci-fi imaginings in literature. His work with Marvel ensured that depictions of Black characters piloting space voyages reached a wide audience.

Coates's work, with its Black and Afrofuturist aesthetics, dramatic action, and multilayered storytelling, indeed embodies abundant artistry. His writing also exudes sharp political commentary. At one point, M'Baku critiques oppressive forces: "Like all Empires, the Empire of Wakanda is counterfeit. It is a Confederacy of villains who've elevated criminality to galactic law…. It enlightens no one. Because, as the great Changamire taught, 'Empires do not enlighten, they plunder.'" He further charges that the Empire amassed its power and wealth from "the memories of the millions they've enslaved."[24] M'Baku's critique of the Wakanda Empire echoes critiques of historical empires, such as the British Empire or the concept of American Empire. Scholar Daniel Stein spoke to this parallel:

> Western civilization, and especially the United States (note the allusion to the Southern Confederacy and how the powers of vibranium recall the antebellum cotton economy), are unmasked as a gigantic fraud: a false claim to cultural and technological superiority derived from knowledge of the colonized that is stolen, stored in the archive, and then used against the disempowered, disenfranchised, and disinherited.[25]

M'Baku's use of the term "plunder" proves noteworthy, as the term pervades much of Coates's writings outside of comics, when he examined the exploitation of Black communities throughout American history. In his studies and writings on the Civil War and slavery, Coates discussed how "the seizure of free blacks and escaped slaves" by the Confederate army "was widespread, systematic, and countenanced by officers up to the highest levels of command."[26] He continued using the term intermittently before applying "plunder" as a central concept in "The Case for Reparations." The article framed the term as foundational: "America begins in Black plunder and white democracy, two features that are not contradictory but complementary." He described enslaved Africans as "plundered of their bodies, plundered of their families, and plundered of their labor."[27]

From there, "plunder" became a mainstay of Coates's work. He deployed the term throughout *Between the World and Me* (2015), with excerpts appearing in *Literary Hub* under the title "Of Plunder and the Killing Fields" and in *Truthout* as "The Plunder of Black Life Was Drilled into This Country in Its Infancy."[28] In his 2017 essay "The First White President," Coates wrote of Donald Trump: "Land theft and human plunder cleared the grounds for Trump's forefathers and barred others from it."[29] Overall, "plunder" has appeared more than 140 times in more than thirty of Coates's publications since 2010, solidifying it as one of his defining intellectual frameworks.

Just as plunder operated as a conceptual frame for "The Case for Reparations," Coates made theft of labor, ideas, and culture central to "The Intergalactic Empire of Wakanda." As M'Baku suggested, the Empire rose to power and flourished through its ability to steal cultural memories and violently extract free labor from otherworldly populations. Plunder rests at the core of the narrative—along with the struggles the maroons endure to reclaim what has been stolen from them. After informing T'Challa that the Empire has stolen much "from us all," a fellow maroon declares, "but now is the hour of restoration."[30] Not coincidentally, restoration ties closely to reparation, the concept that first catapulted Coates to national prominence in 2014. However, whereas reparations aim to make amends for past wrongs, restoration emphasizes acts of retrieval, repair, or reclamation.

Further enhancing the theme of plunder, Coates's main villain, Emperor N'Jadaka, wears a Symbiote-Panther suit throughout "The Intergalactic Empire of Wakanda." With the symbiote, N'Jadaka extracts life and energy from others, either by using their bodies as hosts or by stealing their power. In one pivotal battle, N'Jadaka drains divine power from Bast, the Panther Goddess.[31] Later, the symbiote, after being separated from N'Jadaka, possesses the body of Changamire.[32] From there, it takes over the previously dead body of Killmonger, resurrecting him and engaging in a conflict with him over control.[33] Ultimately, through the use of his symbiote, Emperor N'Jadaka epitomizes plundering.

Conversely, T'Challa, initially portrayed as nameless and enslaved and struggling to retain a sense of his past, spends the full story arc learning, growing, and working with others to reclaim or restore his and their memories. In his first story arc, "A Nation Under Our Feet," Coates chose to question and, in the end, disassemble a monarchial system of government in Wakanda, which meant interrogating and critiquing his protagonist king. Storylines in the series also regularly displaced T'Challa in favor of exploring side characters such as Shuri and the Midnight Angels. For these reasons, the approach in "The Intergalactic Empire of Wakanda" of tracing a protagonist evolving from slave to hero made for a more riveting narrative for readers, certainly those with specific interests in Black Panther. In his review of issue 1, Trevor Richardson noted that his interest with T'Challa presented as the focal point, which marked a difference from the previous two story arcs—"A Nation Under Our Feet" and "Avengers of the New World—"where it felt like T'Challa didn't do as much as his incredible supporting cast."[34]

Throughout the early issues, as he embarks on missions with the maroons, T'Challa exhibits incredible skills but disobeys the orders of his superiors. In *Black Panther* #2, he disregards commands to return to base and instead engages imperial fighters. Again, in *Black Panther* #8, he defies orders again when faced with an opportunity to help enslaved people. "'The King' is writing his own orders again," remarks M'Baku, speaking to T'Challa's pattern of insubordination. Nakia responds, "We have to be patient with him. He's a great warrior," to which M'Baku quips, "and a poor solider."[35] Presenting T'Challa as a skilled and heroic protagonist who occasionally acts recklessly creates chances for him to learn from his mistakes and grow into a responsible leader. His development over the course of two dozen issues endears him to readers. As Matthew Peterson concluded, "Coates' run on *Black Panther* changed the rules and made for stories equal to the MCU version of T'Challa, a development that is as surprising as it is pleasant."[36] This counts as high praise, since the cinematic characterizations and Chadwick Boseman's celebrated performances propelled T'Challa's prominence.

The development of T'Challa places him in concert with commonly referenced historical figures and protagonists in African American literature, including autobiographical depictions of Frederick Douglass and Malcolm X, as well as fictional lead characters like the unnamed narrator from Ralph Ellison's *Invisible Man* (1952), Milkman from Toni Morrison's *Song of Solomon* (1977), Lila Mae Watson from Colson Whitehead's *The Intuitionist* (1999), and Percival Everett's protagonist from *James* (2024). By charting T'Challa's evolution, Coates joins Douglass, Malcolm X, Ellison, Morrison, Whitehead, and Everett, who have contributed to the continuum of Black character development. Comic book writers, particularly African Americans, rarely receive opportunities to produce fifty issues of a single title and thus fully develop a main protagonist over an extended narrative arc. While myriad Black characters exist in comics, individual writers seldom fully develop these figures. Among the relatively few Black comic book writers who have reached the fifty-issue milestone, Coates, Christopher Priest, and Dwayne McDuffie stand out, with Reginald Hudlin following closely, having produced forty-seven issues of *Black Panther*. The rarity of Black creators producing extended runs built around Black characters confirms persistent representation struggles. At the same time, Coates's in-depth depictions of T'Challa mark an achievement, which he acknowledged, noting that he wished he had even more time to further develop aspects of the character's story.[37]

Protagonists who undergo dramatic transformations appear in popular culture, most visibly in movies. In "The Intergalactic Empire of Wakanda," T'Challa parallels Luke Skywalker from the original *Star Wars* trilogy and elements of Anakin Skywalker from the prequel trilogy. Like Luke and Anakin, T'Challa rises from humble beginnings and gradually learns that his ascent is seen as destiny. At one point, a video report shows N'yami asserting to her comrades that she has uncovered T'Challa's true potential, which, at the time, he and others do not know. "While I am convinced of his identity, it will take some effort to convince the champion himself," she says. "The chronicles say that T'Challa of Wakanda Prime preferred the warrior's spear to a king's crown. It is said that he had to grow into what he ultimately became. And so it is with our king returned." After N'yami's death, T'Challa reviews the report, sheds tears, and then takes hold of his ceremonial spear, resolved to join his fellow maroons fighting for freedom.[38] Over the course of issues, audiences witness a once-nameless slave transform into a renowned Wakandan leader.

Although Coates's first and last issues of "The Intergalactic Empire of Wakanda" received positive reviews, issues within the twenty-five-issue run garnered underwhelming assessments. "Black Panther gears up for a new phase in its intergalactic odyssey, but is moving with feet of clay," wrote Chase Magnett in a review of #19. While it's "a competently created comic book," the issue "struggles to rise above an overwhelmingly large herd of similar material at the end of 2019."[39] The copious number of available comics, along with increasing audience demands for exciting content, makes it difficult for titles to maintain high interest month after month. Still, the ambitious narrative and themes of Coates's run, combined with the stature he had earned, ensured continued support from Marvel for the full series.

Marvel released *Black Panther* #22 on March 25, 2020, but due to an extended pause in comic book distribution caused by the global pandemic, *Black Panther* #23 did not appear until almost a year later, on February 24, 2021. With national and global disruptions and transformations, much transpired during the gap between these issues. This period constituted profound societal shifts and deeply personal losses that resonated spanning communities, including those connected to the *Black Panther* legacy. The killing of George Floyd by a white police officer in Minneapolis, Minnesota, on May 25, 2020, ignited nationwide protests and a reckoning on race.

Just months later, on August 28, Chadwick Boseman died after a long, private battle with cancer. Amid the mourning, Marvel honored his legacy by including a tribute—"Rest in Power. Chadwick Boseman"—in comic books released on September 30. The tribute, drawn by Brian Stelfreeze, accompanied a eulogy from Coates, who reflected on his first encounter with

Boseman when they attended Howard University. "I met him leading a protest with my friend Kamilah Forbes to preserve the dignity of Howard's fine arts college," wrote Coates. "What I am saying is that before I knew Chad the artist, I knew Chad the warrior." He went on to explain that he watched Boseman's blossoming career over the years from theater to television to film until he was "finally cast as T'Challa. He was perfect. He had T'Challa's royal spirit, the sense that he did not represent merely himself, but a nation." Coates closed by merging his tribute to Boseman with *Black Panther* mythos, by noting that "just as Chad once walked into the City of the Dead and harnessed the energy of those who'd gone before him, so he too may be harnessed, by all those warriors to come."[40]

The closing issues of "The Intergalactic Empire of Wakanda" continue Coates's exploration of resilience and solidarity, moving toward a climactic ending where T'Challa draws on assistance from a cohort of allies as they defend Wakanda from Emperor N'Jadaka and his forces. T'Challa proves himself in a battle trial with the spirits of past Black Panthers, thus winning their support, and Queen Ramonda bargains a commitment from the Originators to assist. Coates orchestrates a grand assemblage of Black Marvel heroes to stand with T'Challa and Wakanda: Luke Cage, Nick Fury, Miles Morales, Thunderball (Eliot Franklin), Prodigy (David Alleyne), Gentle (Nezhno Abidemi), Patriot (Rayshaun Lucas), Patriot (Eli Bradley), Frenzy (Joanna Cargill), Okoye, Ironheart (Riri Williams), Doctor Voodoo (Jericho Drumm), Misty Knight, Spectrum (Monica Rambeau), Falcon, White Tiger (Kasper Cole), War Machine (James Rhodes), Storm, Ayo, Aneka, Vibraxas (N'Kano), Cloak (Tyrone Johnson), Bling! (Roxanne Washington), Manifold (Eden Fesi), Bast, and Zenzi.[41]

Although relatively few characters have speaking parts, the inclusion of such a large roster of Black heroes marks an unprecedented gathering of Black representation in comics. By assembling over two dozen Black heroes, Coates manifests his dedication to the art of concentrated cultural cataloging. In doing so, he matches figures such as Amiri Baraka, Paul Beatty, and Tyehimba Jess, as African American writers who weave an abundance of Black cultural references into their works. This approach showcases and facilitates African American encyclopedic cultural knowledge and Black aesthetics.

Coates's remarkable Black hero assemblage also stands as a counterpoint to the large-scale gatherings of primarily white characters presented in comic books such as *Avengers vs. X-Men* (2012), *Secret Wars* (2015), and the *House of X* (2019) and in films *X-Men: Days of Future Past* (2014), *Justice League* (2021), and most notably *Avengers: Endgame* (2019). In these instances, ensembles of heroes gather for epic closing battles. Coates diversified the template of these alliances. *Black Panther* #24 and #25 advance a groundbreaking vision of Black hero solidarity. An interstellar tale of an enslaved figure laboring to reclaim his memories culminates in a diverse and far-reaching cast of characters. In short, "The Intergalactic Empire of Wakanda" is *Star Wars* and *Avengers: Endgame* for Black people.

Conclusion

On February 26, 2021, *Shadow and Act*, a website dedicated to news about Black cinema and television and part of the entertainment site *Blavity*, dropped an exclusive news story: "Ta-Nehisi Coates to Write Upcoming Superman Film from DC and Warner Bros." According to the article, "The film is very early into the development process with no start or release date targeted." The article included a statement from Coates, where he asserted, "I look forward to meaningfully adding to the legacy of America's most iconic mythic hero." Aside from identifying J.J. Abrams as a producer, additional details on the film such as the director and the actor who would play Superman had yet to be released.[1] But the revelation that Coates, a journalist turned notable blogger turned best-selling author turned comic book writer turned novelist, would now become a screenwriter for a potential big-budget movie marked a noteworthy announcement.

By the end of the day, media organizations gave momentum to the news. "Ta-Nehisi Coates tapped to write new Superman movie produced by J.J. Abrams" read a headline for *Entertainment Weekly*. "A New 'Superman' Is Coming from J.J. Abrams and Ta-Nehisi Coates" and "Superman Movie Reboot in Works with Ta-Nehisi Coates, J.J. Abrams" read headlines for *ScreenCrush* and *Polygon*, respectively.[2] Joanna Robinson, writing for *Vanity Fair*, remarked that by breaking the news with a site that covers "African diaspora arts," Coates may have been indicating that "his version of Kal-El will very directly engage with his Black identity."[3] In an article for *The Hollywood Reporter*, Borys Kit and Aaron Couch wrote, "According to sources, the project is being set up as a Black Superman story."[4] Days later, commentators actively discussed Coates's "possible Black Superman."[5] *Bleeding Cool* reported that copies of comic books with iterations of a Black Superman had dramatically increased in value on eBay as a result of the Coates announcement.[6]

Once again, Coates and his upcoming work generated significant buzz. It felt like 2015 all over again, when Marvel announced he would write *Black Panther*, or February 2018, when he unveiled his *Captain America* assignment. But maybe the *Superman* announcement amounted to something bigger, something new. His involvement typified how a Black writer could shape the superhero genre in formative ways. Superhero comic books attract large audiences, but superhero blockbuster movies operate on a separate plane of cultural influence and financial profitability.

Either way, Coates has charted an amazing path as a writer for superheroes. He moved from writing *Black Panther* to *Captain America* and then to the possibility of penning a screenplay for a Black Superman. Studio executives saw the overwhelming success of *Black Panther* as clear evidence of the profitability of Black superheroes. And if Coates could craft compelling publications and comics then surely, so the thinking went, he could compose a screenplay about Superman. Once again, he advanced Black representation in the industry-wide realm of comics properties.

In addition to further elevating Coates's reputation as a creator and cultural figure, the new items on his potential *Superman* movie deepened the visibility disparity between him and kindred Black writers. Uneven media emphasis and opportunities prioritize select African American writers over their peers. This imbalance poses distinct challenges for historically underrepresented groups, who already face limited models and gateways for success. What entry points exist, for instance, for Black writers who do not fit Coates's mold? Moreover, the celebration of an exceptional writer's career trajectory can obscure the barriers and limited openings that exist for most Black writers.

In April 2016, Evan Narcisse published an interview with Coates, conducted just before the release of *Black Panther* #1.[7] On May 26, 2021, Narcisse published another exchange with Coates, timed to coincide with the release of the final issue of his run on *Black Panther*. In the conversation, Coates reflected on concluding his fifty-issue arc, explored the thematic elements of his work, and discussed his enjoyment of writing the characters Changamire, Bast, T'Challa, and Zenzi. He also spoke about coming to terms with his growing prominence as a cultural figure. "I had to reconcile myself to some small amount of fame. It's not really something I love or something I do," said Coates. "The sheer intensity of scrutiny was new for me," he went on to note. "There is no ability to have something that is high profile and not invite scrutiny. That's just what it is."[8]

During the interview, Coates also diverged from the main topic of reflecting on *Black Panther* to advocate for fair compensation for comic book creators whose works influenced the highly profitable superhero movie market. "I wish that Marvel found better ways to compensate the creators who helped make Black Panther *Black Panther*," he said. "I wish that they found better ways to compensate the folks who made Captain America *Captain America*." He was not speaking about himself. Instead, he wanted Marvel to more adequately reward someone like Ed Brubaker, who had produced memorable runs on *Captain America*, which greatly influenced the Hollywood blockbusters. Coates took issue with the Marvel Cinematic Universe (MCU) earning "billions over top of billions" and showing little willingness to engage writers like Brubaker.[9]

Journalists reported about Coates's comments on behalf of Brubaker and the apparent criticism of Marvel and its parent company, Disney+. In a *Screen Rant* article titled "Black Panther Writer Criticizes Marvel's Treatment of Comic Creators," published a day after the Narcisse interview, Robert Wood summarized Coates's remarks about Brubaker. Wood closed noting, "Hopefully, the comments of Ta-Nehisi Coates and others can be part of challenging that increasingly unjust status quo."[10] In a *Gizmodo* article titled "Black Panther Writer Ta-Nehisi Coates Wants Better for Creators Bringing These Stories to Life," Charles Pulliam-Moore recounted the comments from the interview. Pulliam-Moore concluded that although it "is the nature of for-hire work" for companies to own the rights to the characters, "it's an aspect of the industry worth considering as publishers and studios alike continue to turn these stories into big screen and streaming spectacles for audiences to consume."[11] Later, JB Augustine wrote an article about the lack of compensation for comic creators and brought to light that Brubaker and artist Steve Epting "have a prominent supporter in Black Panther and J.J. Abrams Superman writer Ta-Nehisi Coates."[12] These articles suggested that Coates's critiques and opinions carried weight. His creative voice mattered, and so did his willingness to advocate for the recognition and fair treatment of the creators behind the stories that captivate global audiences.

His influence and ability to shape conversations in comics expanded rapidly. When Marvel announced Coates as the writer for *Black Panther* in 2015, commentators hailed it as a milestone for diversity. Over the years, his stature as a writer grew, along with his cultural capital and ability to command attention. By 2021, a commentator could easily identify him as a "prominent supporter" for speaking out against how a major corporate entity allegedly mistreated a white comic creator. In the public discourse, Coates moved beyond mere beneficiary of a diversity initiative and assumed the role of an influential advocate.

In the introduction to *Wakanda: World of Black Panther*, Narcisse commented that Coates ushered in a "big evolutionary phase for the Black Panther mythos" when he began writing the comic book for Marvel. "The start of his tenure," pointed out Narcisse, "sparked headlines."[13] Pairing a famous Black comic book character with a famous Black writer generated far-reaching public interest for both. The release of dozens of comic books each week, month after month, year after year, means that Coates's contributions to *Black Panther* might be easily forgotten or overlooked, which says nothing of the works produced by less well-known Black comic book writers. Yet, Coates's influence and contributions linger.

For one, his writing on *Black Panther* deepened interpretations of T'Challa, extending understandings of him beyond earlier versions. Coates began his run at an inflection point right before T'Challa and Wakanda appeared in the MCU. By one telling, Coates's work assisted in accelerating the production of the film. In his book *The Ride of a Lifetime: Lessons Learned from 15 Years as CEO of the Walt Disney Company*, Robert Iger recalled feeling deeply moved by Coates's work on *Black Panther*. Iger enthused that he "was amazed by the elegant storytelling and the way Ta-Nehisi had added such depth to the character." Even before he finished reading the series, Iger "placed *Black Panther* on the list of must-do Marvel projects."[14] Others, too, found themselves influenced by Coates's work on the comic. Both films, *Black Panther* (2018) and *Black Panther: Wakanda* (2022), revealed Coogler's debts to Coates's storylines and artistic visions, including depictions of strong women characters like the Midnight Angels and the Plane of Wakadan Memory.

The critique and dismantling of Wakanda's monarchial system of government persisted in stories produced after Coates. John Ridley's fifteen-issue run on *Black Panther* from 2021 to 2023 picked up where Coates left off, delving into Wakanda's transition to a democratic form of government. Eve Ewing's ten-issue run on the title from 2023 to 2024 also maintains the overarching structures introduced by Coates. The miniseries *Wakanda*, with contributions from Narcisse, Stephanie Williams, Adam Sewer, and Ridley, published from 2022 to 2023, extended storylines initially introduced by Coates. These subsequent runs confirmed the lasting impact of his vision.

More than just character development and governmental systems, Coates enriched renderings of Wakanda. Early on, he produced a map of the African country, which has since appeared in scattered iterations in works such as *Rise of the Black Panther* #1 (2018), *Marvel Universe Map by Map* (2021), *Marvel Black Panther: Wakanda Atlas* (2022), and *Wakanda* #4 (2023). His story arc, "The Intergalactic Empire of Wakanda" took Wakandans far from their homeland and Earth, creating scenarios to envision Black people in the farthest reaches of the universe. These groundbreaking representations of Wakanda testify to the power and creativity of Coates's storytelling. His contributions reshaped or enhanced a significant sector of the imaginative landscape of *Black Panther*.

The scope of Coates's efforts to expand Black representation among comic book writers became evident. The omnibus *World of Wakanda* brings together contributions from Narcisse, Roxane Gay, Yona Harvey, and Rembert Browne. Coates directly facilitated their entry into the world of comics. These writers contributed to the *Black Panther* universe, but they also stood as branches of the Coates Comics Tree. Their involvement illustrated how Coates used his platform to bring new Black voices into the industry.

The Coates Comics Tree further extends to include a large assemblage of visual artists. Brian Stelfreeze, Chris Sprouse, Wilfredo Torres, Laura Martin, Karl Story, Daniel Acuña, Paul Reinwand, and Jen Bartel contributed interiors. Approximately ninety-five artists produced covers and variants for *Black Panther*. That number grows even larger when we include the many creators who worked on Coates's *Captain America* series. The scale and scope of participation are impressive. The Coates Comics Tree extends across a broad network, reflecting the collaborative efforts that supported his storytelling and boosted the visibility of many visual artists associated with his lauded work.

Fans and commentators had advocated for more diverse creators in comics, and Coates leveraged his power as a best-selling writer for Marvel to influence the company to employ more Black writers. Too, his success undoubtedly shaped industry dynamics, encouraging Marvel and DC Comics to bring in more Black writers. Their decisions to hire Eve Ewing and N. K. Jemisin to write *Ironheart* and *Far Sector*, respectively, despite neither having prior comic book writing experience, marked a clear outcome of this influence. Separate from his own storytelling, Coates served as a catalyst for expanding access to comics for Black creators. His emergence in the field created momentum and visibility that assisted in shifting possibilities.

Since Coates completed his runs on *Black Panther* and *Captain America*, no new high-profile Black comic book writers have garnered widespread media emphasis, with accolades extending past the comic book industry. There has been no comparable buzz surrounding Black writers akin to the enthusiasm that followed announcements of Coates's new assignments. Marvel and DC Comics have not assigned Black writers to helm canonical white superhero titles, as Coates did with *Captain America*. Just as telling, journalists have not collectively produced sweeping descriptions of other Black writers as they did for Coates. In short, no other Black comic book writers have received such remarkable receptions for their works.

Nonetheless, plenty of veteran and rising Black writers produced comics over the last few years. Bryan Hill, David F. Walker, Ewing, Ridley, Narcisse, Cheryl Lynn Eaton, Victor LaValle, Jemisin, Brandon Thomas, Kwanza Osajyefo, Nilah Magruder, Rodney Barnes, Justina Ireland, and John Jennings have contributed to the field. Their collective work has expanded the standing of Black creators and characters in comics. In 2014 and early 2015, commentators rightly voiced concerns about the lack of Black comic book writers. While the industry still has room to grow, crucial progress has been made.

Without Coates in the field, Black comic book writers do not have to contend with the visibility disparity or the halo effect, where the prominence of one figure overshadows all others. The enthusiasm that greeted the initial announcement that Coates would write *Black Panther*, including pronouncements that he stood as the best living writer on race, inadvertently contributed to the narrative of a lone savior concerning diversity problems. The celebration of good news on one acclaimed hire may have also taken pressure from Marvel and analogous comic book companies to address structural challenges. With Coates no longer in the field, publishers arguably had an incentive to promote new diverse voices. Theoretically, this shift created space for additional Black creators to emerge and be recognized.

On the other hand, the absence of attention-getting unifying figures diminishes avenues for visibility on developments in a field. In some cases, a distinguished figure can advocate for or accelerate progress. Such figures function as focal points, showcasing aspects of the field and galvanizing efforts around shared interests. They also provide a platform for bringing forward voices that commonly go unheard. Coates encouraged Marvel to hire Black writers that the industry may have otherwise overlooked. Furthermore, his experiences and body of work attested to the fact that with sufficient backing, Black comic book writers could attain extraordinary success.

Over the course of the fifty issues he produced for *Black Panther*, Coates infused the comic book with numerous Black aesthetics, including historical and cultural figures as well as diasporic terms and concepts. He referenced Frederick Douglass, Audre Lorde, Biggie, Jay-Z, Ken Saro-Wiwa, and François Mackandal. He deployed maroons, Goree, Djali, Askari, and corresponding terms that channel realms of Black history and culture. In the process of writing *Black Panther*, Coates produced an encyclopedic concentrated cultural catalog, tapping into domains of Black knowledge. Accordingly, Coates's work resonated with continuums of African American literary art. Indeed, he echoed themes and artistic approaches that appear in compositions by Amiri Baraka, Paul Beatty, Toni Morrison, and Colson Whitehead.

Throughout this study, I pinpointed links between Coates's *Black Panther* and the contributions of authors in a modest attempt to encourage more examinations of Black comics through the lens of African American literary studies. Comics and Black literature rarely enter into conversation with each other, as evidenced by a review of dozens of syllabi for courses on comics and African American literature. Coates bridges these fields, based on his status as both a decorated Black author and a comics creator. What's more, the thematic and artistic components of his *Black Panther* run echo compositions in African American literature. These connections deepen our understanding of Coates's work and enrich our views of Black artistic writing across diverse fields.

Although an increasing number of universities now offer comic book courses and academic concentrations in comics studies, the institutional longevity of African American literature courses presents unique prospects to merge Black literary studies and comic book studies. Coates's explorations of identity, slavery, history, intra-racial struggles, Black aesthetics, and more in *Black Panther* resonate with African American literature curricula. He demonstrates what it means for a contemporary Black comic creator to repurpose ideas raised by Frederick Douglass in his autobiography, using them to enrich a comic book narrative about a captive Black protagonist seeking freedom. The pronounced Afrofuturist aesthetics throughout *Black Panther*, markedly in "The Intergalactic Empire of Wakanda," place Coates alongside Octavia Butler, N. K. Jemisin, and associated Black writers who prioritize Black representation in science fiction. In April 2025, Nigerian fantasy and science fiction writer Suyi Davies Okungbowa published *Black Panther: The Intergalactic Empire of Wakanda*, an adaptation that further situated Coates's work in the realm of speculative fiction. Considered within this literary field, Coates's comic book writing brought to light the interconnectivity between comics and African American literature, expanding the scope of both artistic continuums.

The inclusion of a series like *Black Panther* in an African American literature course can contribute to enrollment growth. Quite a few students show a strong interest in comic books over conventional literature and forms of art. In 2021, when the French government gave every eighteen-year-old in the country $350 to make cultural purchases, an overwhelming number of them bought comic books.[15] Coates's comic book writing can open a useful gateway into African American literature. The cultural and artistic contexts that inspired or shaped his writing can lead readers and researchers to trace connections across comics, novels, poems, short stories, and essays.

Coates and Colson Whitehead share a notable distinction. In 2016, Coates's *Black Panther* #1 emerged as the most widely covered comic book by a Black writer, and Whitehead's *The Underground Railroad* stood as the most widely covered novel by a Black writer.[16] Since that time, they continued to be two of the most cited contemporary Black writers. The merging of comic book studies and African American literary studies requires attention to parallel developments in the reception of publications. Considerations of the rise of two Black writers to prominence in their respective fields lay the groundwork for comparative work at the intersection of disciplines.

Coates's career expands how scholars of African American literature might view the trajectory of a major Black writer. Traditionally, research in the field has privileged authors such as Zora Neale Hurston, Richard Wright, Ralph Ellison, and Toni Morrison, known for writing novels. The study of a prominent African American comic creator opens a unique route to examine a writer who has garnered notice in an alternative medium. Apart from the benefits of analyzing his writing, Coates's comic book work encourages scholars to explore his collaborations with visual artists and assess the responses to his writing.

Examinations of his work can expand and diversify African American literary studies by stretching into comics, which have been underexplored in the field.

Of course, African American literature has much to impart to Coates. Frameworks for studying Black publishing histories make possible the documentation of the incredible production of his work—and that production has been incredible. After concluding *Black Panther*, Coates continued publishing for a few months, wrapping up his *Captain America* run in July 2021. Even after he stepped finished, Marvel released comic books bearing his name. Later in 2021, Marvel released trade paperbacks of his comics. In 2022, the Folio Society published a collector's edition of *Black Panther: A Nation Under Our Feet*, and Marvel published the *Captain America* Volume 2 hardcover, following Volume 1's release in 2020. On October 4, 2022, Marvel released the omnibus *Wakanda: World of Black Panther*, which collected Coates's work on *Black Panther and The Crew* and *Black Panther: World of Wakanda*, along with contributions from Evan Narcisse, Roxane Gay, Yona Harvey, and Bryan Edward Hill. Two weeks later, on October 18, Marvel published the omnibus *Black Panther*, with Coates's full 2016–2021 run on the title. On July 25, 2023, they followed with the omnibus *Captain America*, compiling all thirty issues he wrote for the series. On February 4, 2025, Marvel released a hardcover edition of *Black Panther: The Intergalactic Empire of Wakanda* and a *Marvel Premier Collection* edition of *Black Panther: A Nation Under Our Feet*. These individual publications form an impressive body of work, which is outstanding for a creator who wrote comics for only about five years.

Despite the publications showcasing *Black Panther* and the sweeping reception Coates received, his contributions and those of other Black comic creators still face a strong likelihood of neglect or erasure. The rapid and continuous production of comics makes it difficult for underrepresented creators, even leading ones, to maintain long-term visibility. Without the kind of repeated inclusion that novels, short stories, and poems enjoy in African American literature courses, Black comic books can easily fade from public consciousness. Ten or twenty years after Coates's debut in comics, his contributions may be reduced to a footnote, and those of lesser-known Black writers may be overlooked entirely. This affirms the centrality of African American literary studies and literature courses in maintaining and transmitting the legacy of Black writers. If Coates's comic book writing and that of other Black creators secured a place in African American literary studies, it would increase the probability of these works being preserved in cultural memory.

Coates appears in the fourth edition of *The Norton Anthology of African American Literature* (2025). From one vantage point, editors missed an opportunity by excluding his comic book work. What if, instead of his largely unknown essay "The Legacy of Malcolm X," they had selected an excerpt from his best-selling *Black Panther* #1? Reproducing images in a course anthology may have been cost-prohibitive, and there is, as yet, no precedent for including comic books in such collections. Despite these obstacles, the inclusion of Coates's debut issue in a volume dedicated to significant literary works could expand students' understanding of African American creative expression. As the best-selling single issue of a comic book by a Black writer in the 2010s, and possibly ever, *Black Panther* #1 warrants high regard in histories of comics and African American literature.

Readers and critics could easily overlook the tremendous and sometimes subtle fan advocacy that paved the way for Coates and his peer Black comics creators. Without documented histories of fans, journalists, and cultural critics urging comic book companies to diversify their rosters of creators, new generations of readers may falsely assume that these changes happened organically. Everyone remembers dramatic scenes from *Black Panther*—both the comic books and the film. But without intentional documentation, few will recall the contributions of Joseph Hughes and Heidi MacDonald from February 2013, or Joseph Illidge from February 2014, who raised awareness about the lack of Black comics writers, or the impassioned critiques of cultural appropriation in comics presented by J. A. Micheline.[17] On September 22, 2015, the widespread optimism surrounding the announcement of Coates's entry into comics reflected a larger hope that Marvel, DC, Image Comics, Boom! Studios, Dark Horse Comics, IDW Publishing, and Dynamite Entertainment would address their diversity problems. That hope fueled interest in *Black Panther* #1 and Coates's tenure in comics. The act of preserving the histories of these developments ensures recognition and remembrance for the people who assisted in orchestrating changes.

For now, comic book collectors, scholars, and enthusiasts will lead efforts to ensure that information about momentous developments in comics is passed on to audiences and from one generation to the next. Believe it or not, comic book fans interested in diversity and scholars of African American literature share some notable similarities. Both groups hold central characters and creators in high regard. They keep abreast of publishing trends in their respective fields and continually seek out news and hidden histories. They also engage in discussions about representation. In addition, they perform as critical cultural witnesses, chronicling landmark developments through collecting and reflecting on what they have noticed over time. And look, in the case of this project, the comic book fan and scholar of African American literature converge as one.

In retrospect, the idea of comic book fans serving as indispensable observers and interpreters became fully evident in the interviews Narcisse conducted with Coates in 2016 and 2021. Their discussions covered T'Challa's portrayal over the decades, Black and white superheroes, Marvel's approach to diversity, writing in comics, the visual aesthetics of the medium, their childhood experiences with comics, Black creators, gender representation, and more. Recollections of past readings and realizations shaped their 2016 exchange. "Who was the first comic book creator that you remember knowing who was Black?" Narcisse asked at one point.[18] By 2021, with *Black Panther* complete, Coates could now look back on writing the Wakandan king. "I had a lot of fun, obviously, writing T'Challa, especially in the opening for Intergalactic Empire," Coates reflected. Later, he remarked, "If it was up to me—and this just doesn't cohere with how comics work—I would have spent 20 issues before T'Challa figured out who he was, in terms of the Intergalactic part."[19] Throughout the two interrelated interviews, Narcisse and Coates bear witness to a constellation of thoughts and activities and in the process produce a fantastic cultural catalog on comics and Black representation.

Narcisse and Coates work as comics creators, experienced journalists, and cultural critics. In those interviews, though, they revealed that above all else, they identified comic book fans. Encounters with wide-ranging, published dialogues between Black men who consider themselves comic book fans, such as the Narcisse–Coates interviews, seldom appear. There would be no surprise if a famous Black writer, described as a preeminent commentator on race and racism, participated in an exchange about characters inhabiting the novels of Ralph Ellison and Toni Morrison. But the idea of such a writer seriously discussing superheroes, comics creators, and the histories of Marvel storylines continues to be uncommon. In many quarters, comic books simply do not register as intellectually serious or consequential. Yet the depth, vulnerability, and intellectual curiosity revealed in the Narcisse–Coates interviews stand out as both admirable and instructive. Their exchange affirmed that a field populated by superheroes and deep space adventures can communicate valuable ideas about devoted readers, narrative world-building, racial representation, and shared cultural memory, all of which can complement and enhance African American literary studies.

Coates's entry into comics proved enormously beneficial, though it fell far from a solution to the structural barriers confronting Black writers. In writing *Black Panther*, Coates engaged in transformative character development, crafted the epic tale of "a slave who advanced into a legend," and reimagined a fictive African country alongside its intergalactic empire.[20] His involvement with Marvel energized conversations about control of Black narratives in mainstream visual culture. Reading *Black Panther* opened countless possibilities, prompting deeper considerations of African American literary artists and the progress and stagnation affecting Black comic book writers. Ultimately, tracing the diversity advocacy of cultural critics, the rise of a Black comic book writer, and the interplay of successes and setbacks made clear that representation remains an ongoing struggle.

Acknowledgments

I told folks I had turned my attention to writing about comic books, but they somehow took that as an opportunity to demonstrate their own superpowers. First, my parents and siblings, Phillis and Kenton, revealed their uncanny abilities to generate endless supplies of generosity and guidance. What a marvel: boundless lessons bestowed by C. Liegh McInnis, Eugene B. Redmond, Maryemma Graham, Cleo Thomas, Jr., William J. Harris, Donald Garcia, Cynthia Neal Spence, and the late, great Jerry W. Ward, Jr.

Donavan Ramon, Jessica C. Harris, Jessica DeSpain, Meg Smith, Cindy Reed, Tisha Brooks, Tori Walters, Kim Poteet, Taylor Cross, Daria Spencer, Danielle Hall, and Courtney Thorsson formed my own personal Justice League. At some point, I realized I had never seen Stefan Bradley and Earleen Patterson in the same place at the same time as the Avengers. A succession of emergent scholars miraculously transformed themselves into heroic research assistants: Rae'Jean Alford, Nicole Dixon, Ashley Hamilton, Rie Holmon, M. Mallon, Al Smith, Sierra Taylor, Lakenzie Walls, and Jalen White.

I benefited from the access I had to a comic book human encyclopedia, who often assumed the mild-mannered public persona of Stephyn Phillips. The supernatural, active problem-solver Elizabeth Cali continually delivered novel solutions. Amy Martin and the folks at Bloomsbury displayed their incredible ability to spot needles in haystacks. Hence, they found me.

Once every other week for more than twenty years, my longtime barbers, Keith Shackleford and Will King, at Shack's in St. Louis worked their magic to somehow make me look so fresh and so clean, while passing along crucial knowledge in the process. Finally, faster than a speeding bullet and quite capable of leaping tall buildings in a single bound, Psyche Southwell came to my rescue and showed me a way out of no way more times than I can count.

Appendix: Coates Comics Trees

The following lists of contributors comprise the *Coates Comics Trees*—a term used in this book to describe the branching networks of writers, artists, editors, and other collaborators associated with Ta-Nehisi Coates's run on *Black Panther* and related titles. While the main text refers to the *Coates Comics Tree* as a unifying metaphor, here I offer multiple trees that highlight the various individuals who shape these comics.

For additional context and visual examples, visit: blackpanther.siue.edu.

Appendix A: *Black Panther* Interior Contributors (Issues #1–18 and #166–72; 2016–2018)

Appendix B: *Black Panther* Interior Contributors (Issues #1–25; 2018–2021)

Appendix C: Writer Contributors to *Wakanda: World of Black Panther* Omnibus (2022)

Appendix D: Checklist of Cover and Variant Artists for *Black Panther* #1 (April 2016)

Appendix E: Checklist of Cover and Variant Artists for *Black Panther* #1 (May 2018)

Appendix A: *Black Panther* Interior Contributors (Issues #1–18 and #166–172*; 2016–2018)

[*Marvel resumed legacy numbering with Issue #166 as part of its initiative to honor the accumulated history of the *Black Panther* series.]

Illustrators (Artists, Penciler, Layout Artist)

- Brian Stelfreeze—Artist (#1–4, 9, 12)

- Chris Sprouse—Penciler/Layouts (#5–8, 10–12, 16–18, 168)
- Wilfredo Torres—Penciler (#13–15, 18)
- Leonard Kirk—Penciler (#166–67, 169–72)
- Jacen Burrows—Penciler (#14)
- Adam Gorham—Penciler (#15)

Inkers and Finishers

- Brian Stelfreeze—Inker (#12)
- Karl Story—Inker/Finishes (#5–8, 10–12, 16–18)
- Walden Wong—Inker/Finishes (#8, 11, 16, 168, 172)
- Goran Sudžuka—Finishes (#11)
- Roberto Poggi—Finishes (#11)
- Scott Hanna—Inker (#12)
- Leonard Kirk—Inker (#168, 169–72)
- Jacen Burrows—Inker (#14)
- Adam Gorham—Inker (#15)
- Terry Pallot—Inker (#14–15)
- Dexter Vines—Inker (#16–17)
- Marc Deering—Inker (#172)

Color Artists

- Laura Martin—Color artist (#1–18, 166–67, 169–72)
- Matt Milla—Color artist (#11–12, 167–168, 172)
- Larry Molinar—Color artist (#11)
- Rachelle Rosenberg—Color artist (#11)
- Paul Mounts—Color artist (#11)
- Andrew Crossley—Color artist (#13, 16–17)
- Chris Sotomayor—Color artist (#168)

Lettering and Design

- Joe Sabino—Letterer (#1–12)
- Rian Hughes—Logo Design (#1–12)

Editors

- Chris Robinson—Assistant Editor (#1–18, 166–72)
- Charles Beacham—Assistant Editor (#13–18, 166–72)
- Sarah Brunstad—Associate Editor (#13–18, 166–72)
- Wil Moss—Editor (#1–18, 166–72)

Appendix B: *Black Panther* Interior Contributors (Issues #1–25; 2018–2021)

Artists

- Daniel Acuña—Artist (#1–5, 13–17, 20, 22–25)
- Jen Bartel—Artist (#6, 12)
- Kev Walker—Artist (#7–11)
- Chris Sprouse—Artist (#18)
- Ryan Bodenheim—Artist (#19–23)
- Brian Stelfreeze—Artist (#25)

Inkers

- Marc Deering—Inker (#11)
- Karol Story—Inker (#18)

Layout Artists

- Paul Reinwand—Layout artist (#6)
- Kris Anka—Layout artist (#12)

Color Artists

- Triona Farrell—Color artist (#6, 12)
- Stéphane Paitreau—Color artist (#7, 10)
- Java Tartaglia—Color artist (#10–11)
- Marcio Menyz—Color artist (#18)
- Michael Garland—Color artist (#19–20)
- Daniel Acuña—Color artist (#20, 22–25)

- Chris O'Halloran—Color artist (#21–23)
- Laura Martin—Color artist (#25)

Lettering and Design

- Joe Sabino—Letterer (#1–25)

Editors

- Sarah Brunstad—Associate Editor (#1–25)
- Wil Moss—Editor (#1–25)

Appendix C: Contributors to *Wakanda: World of Black Panther* Omnibus (2022)

Writers

- Vita Ayala (*Shuri* #6–7, *Marvel's Voices*)
- Rembert Browne (*World of Wakanda* #6)
- Ta-Nehisi Coates (*Black Panther & The Crew* #1–6)
- Ta-Nehisi Coates and Yona Harvey (*Black Panther & The Crew* #2, 4, 6)
- Aaron Covington (*Long Live the King* #3–4)
- Roxane Gay (*World of Wakanda* #1–5)
- Yona Harvey (*World of Wakanda* "The People for the People" #1)
- Bryan Hill (*Killmonger* #1–5)
- Reginald Hudlin (*Black Panther Annual* #1)
- Daniel Kibblesmith (*Black Panther vs. Deadpool* #1–5)
- Don McGregor (*Black Panther Annual* #1)
- Evan Narcisse (*Rise of the Black Panther* #1–5, *The Last Annihilation: Wakanda*)
- Nnedi Okorafor (*Long Live the King* #1–2, 5–6; *Venomverse: War Stories*; *Shuri* #1–5, 8–10; *Amazing Spider-Man: Wakanda Forever*; *X-Men: Wakanda Forever*; *Avengers: Wakanda Forever*; *Marvel's Voices: Legacy*)
- Christopher Priest (*Black Panther Annual* #1, *Marvel Comics* #1000)

- Geoffrey Thorne (*King in Black: Black Panther*)
- Jim Zub (*Black Panther and the Agents of Wakanda #1–8*)

Plotters (*Credited with story plotting rather than full scripting*)

- Saint Bodhi (*Black Panther #23*)
- Bobby Sessions (*Black Panther #24*)
- Kaash Paige (*Black Panther #25*)

Appendix D: Checklist of Cover and Variant Artists for *Black Panther #1* (April 2016)

Standard Covers

- 1st Printing Regular Cover by Brian Stelfreeze and Laura Martin
- Variant Cover by Olivier Coipel
- Marvel U Variant Cover by Pasqual Ferry
- Connecting Variant A Cover by Sanford Greene
- Variant Cover by Dale Keown
- Marvel Collector Corps Variant Cover by Amos Maldonado
- Variant Cover by Alex Ross
- Variant Cover by Ryan Sook
- Black Panther 50th Anniversary Variant Cover by Felipe Smith
- Design Variant Cover by Brian Stelfreeze

Specialty Variants

- Negative space Variant Cover by John Tyler Christopher
- Middle East Film and Comic Con Dubai exclusive Variant Cover (Stan Lee and T'Challa) by Greg Horn
- Hip Hop Variant Cover by Brian Stelfreeze
- "Kitten" Variant Cover by Skottie Young (This is a "Young Variant," styled humorously, sometimes called "Little Marvel")
- KABAM Game/Disney Infinity Variant Cover (artist uncredited)

Retailer Exclusive Variants

- Newbury Comics Exclusive Variant Cover by Neal Adams
- Midtown Comics exclusive Variant Cover by Mark Brooks
- Bulletproof Comics and Games Exclusive Variant Cover by Gabriele Dell'Otto
- Bulletproof Comics and Games Exclusive B & W Variant Cover by Gabriele Dell'Otto
- StockX exclusive Variant Cover by Sanford Greene (Released February 2023)
- Comic Bug exclusive Variant Cover by Mike McKone
- Comic Book Legal Defense Fund (CBLDF) Exclusive Variant Cover by Todd Nauck
- Fried Pie exclusive Variant Cover by Larry Stroman

Reprint Covers

- 2nd Printing Regular Cover by Brian Stelfreeze (Released May 2016)
- 3rd Printing Regular Cover by Brian Stelfreeze (Released July 2016)

Appendix E: Checklist of Cover and Variant Artists for *Black Panther #1* (May 2018)

Standard Covers

- Regular Cover by Daniel Acuña
- 2nd Printing Cover by Daniel Acuña (Released June 2018)
- Variant Cover by Tom Beland
- Black & White Variant Cover by Tom Beland
- Variant Cover by Olivier Coipel
- Black & White Textless Sketch Variant Cover by Mike Deodato, Jr.
- Variant Cover by Mike Deodato, Jr.
- Variant Cover by Stanley "Artgerm" Lau
- Textless Variant Cover by Stanley "Artgerm" Lau
- Variant Cover by InHyuk Lee
- Variant Cover by Yasmine Putri

Specialty Variants

- Young Guns Variant Cover by Pepe Larraz
- Marvel Unlimited Venomized Variant Cover by Jamal Campbell

Archival Variants

- Black & White Remastered Variant Cover by Jack Kirby
- Remastered Variant Cover by Jack Kirby

Retailer Exclusive Variants

- Cape & Cowl Variant Cover by Jamal Campbell
- 2nd Printing Cape & Cowl Variant Cover by Jamal Campbell (Released June 2018)
- Sanctum Sanctorum Variant Cover by David Mack
- Newbury Comics Variant Cover by Olivier Vatine

Notes

Introduction

1 Ta-Nehisi Coates, interviewing Sana Amanat, "What If Captain America Were Muslim and Female / New York Ideas 2015," YouTube, May 21, 2015, https://www.youtube.com/watch?v=2Y1ihwPpIL4.

2 Tom Brevoort, "@tanehisicoates Heard That You Had an Interest in Writing Something for Marvel. Let's Talk! tbrevoort@marvel.com," Twitter, May 21, 2015.

3 I'm hardly the first and only one to use the term "representation struggles." An interchangeable phrase "struggle for representation" regularly emerged in discussions of film for quite some time.

4 For a discussion of the "one Black writer at a time" practice, see Howard Rambsy II and Kenton Rambsy's "How the *New York Times* Covers Black Writers," *Public Books*, October 12, 2022, https://www.publicbooks.org/how-the-new-york-times-covers-black-writers/.

5 Todd Steven Burroughs, "Black Panther, Black Writers, White Audience: Christopher Priest and/vs. Reginald Hudlin," *Fire!!!* 4, no. 2 (Fall 2018): 56, https://www.jstor.org/stable/10.5323/fire.4.2.0055.

6 Dwayne McDuffie, *Icon* #1 (May 1993).

7 I have been a witness: students enroll in my courses on comic book and diversity at much higher and faster rates than for my African American literature classes.

8 Yohana Desta, "Black Panther Is Officially a $1 Billion Hit," *Vanity Fair*, March 11, 2018, https://www.vanityfair.com/hollywood/2018/03/black-panther-box-office-billion-dollars-china-marvel?srsltid=AfmBOormqx8bO9fbSB-L0sXCNvtnF4GLkQKK83XNuNAoZdNubKug4nBo.

9 Karama Horne, "Riri, Rhodey and Re-skinning: How Marvel Is Misunderstanding Diversity," The Blerd Gurl, July 8, 2016, https://theblerdgurl.com/comics/riri-rhodey-re-skinning-marvel-misunderstanding-diversity/.

10 Joshua Rivera, "Ta-Nehisi Coates' Black Panther Comic Is a Dream Come True," *GQ*, September 23, 2015, https://www.gq.com/story/ta-nehisi-coates-black-panther-dream-come-true.

11 Tim Wu, *The Attention Merchants: The Epic Scramble to Get Inside Our Heads* (Knopf, 2016), 6.

12 Douglas Wolk, *All of the Marvels: A Journey to the Ends of the Biggest Story Ever Told* (Penguin Press, 2021); Wolf, *Reading Comics: How Graphic Novels Work and What They Mean* (Da Capo Press, 2007); Paul Young, *Frank Miller's Daredevil and the Ends of Heroism* (Rutgers University Press, 2016); Carolyn Cocca, *Superwomen: Gender, Power, and Representation* (Bloomsbury Academic, 2016); Sean Howe, *Marvel Comics: The Untold Story* (Harper, 2012).

13 Like countless scholars and literature professors, I benefited from numerous, wide-ranging informal conversations with several colleagues. My exchanges with literary scholar Elizabeth Cali, for instance, discussing Toni Morrison, Ta-Nehisi Coates, Colson Whitehead, and various Black artistic productions have persisted for more than a decade.

14 Emily J. Lordi, "Between the World and the Addressee: Epistolary Nonfiction by Ta-Nehisi Coates and His Peers," *CLA Journal* 60 no. 4 (2017): 434–47; James B Haile, III, "Ta-Nehisi Coates's Phenomenology of the Body," *The Journal of Speculative Philosophy* 31, no. 3 (2017): 493–503; Thabiti Lewis, "How Fresh and New Is the Case Coates Makes?" *African American Review* 49, no. 3 (2016): 192–96; Dana A. Williams, "Everybody's Protest Narrative: 'Between the World and Me' and the Limits of Genre," *African American Review* 49, no. 3 (Fall 2016): 179–83; Nicole Waller, "Marronage or Underground? The Black Geographies of Colson Whitehead's *The Underground Railroad* and Ta-Nehisi Coates's *The Water Dancer*," *MELUS: Multi-Ethnic Literature of the U.S.* 47, no. 1 (2022): 45–70.

15 NPR Staff, "Ta-Nehisi Coates Hopes 'Black Panther' Will Be Some Kid's 'Spider-Man,'" NPR, April 6, 2016, https://www.npr.org/sections/codeswitch/2016/04/06/473224606/a-reluctant-king-ta-nehisi-coates-takes-on-marvels-black-panther.

16 SYFY Wire, "The Making of Marvel Knights: Black Panther (Behind the Panel)." YouTube, May 15, 2019, https://www.youtube.com/watch?v=RAkoSLXiuQw.

17 Evan Narcisse, "Ta-Nehisi Coates Explains How He's Turning Black Panther into a Superhero Again," Gizmodo, September 14, 2016, https://gizmodo.com/ta-nehisi-coates-explains-how-hes-turning-black-panther-1786632598.

18 Narcisse, "Ta-Nehisi Coates Explains."

19 Shani O. Hilton, "The Black Experience Isn't Just About Men," *BuzzFeed*, July 10, 2015, https://www.buzzfeed.com/shani/between-the-world-and-she; Britni Danielle, "In Ta-Nehisi Coates' New Book, It's Clear All the Blacks Are Still Men," The Root, July 16, 2015, https://www.theroot.com/in-ta-nehisi-coates-new-book-it-s-clear-all-the-black-1790860550; Josie Duffy, "'Between the World and Me' Is for All of Us, Even If It Is Not About All of Us," Rewire News Group, July 15, 2015, https://rewirenewsgroup.com/2015/07/15/world-us-even-us/.

20 Quoted in Stauffer, Trodd, and Bernier, *Picturing Frederick Douglass* (Liveright Publishing Corporation, 2015), xi.

21 In 1987, six decades after the publication of Du Bois's questionnaire, Henry Louis Gates, Jr. questioned scholars about the representation of Black people. See Gates, "The Black Person in Art: How Should S/He Be Portrayed?" *Black American Literature Forum* (Spring–Summer 1987): 3–24.

22 Ezra Klein, "Ezra Klein Interviews Ta-Nehisi Coates and Nikole Hannah-Jones," *New York Times*, July 30, 2021, https://www.nytimes.com/2021/07/30/opinion/ezra-klein-podcast-ta-nehisi-coates-nikole-hannah-jones.html.

23 Jeffrey A. Brown, *Panthers, Hulks and Ironhearts: Marvel, Diversity, and the 21st Century Superhero* (New Brunswick, NJ: Rutgers University Press, 2021), 63.

24 Adilifu Nama, *Super Black: American Pop Culture and Black Superheroes* (Austin: University of Texas Press, 2011), 1–2.

25 Brown, *Panthers, Hulks and Ironhearts*, 61–62.

26 Carolyn Cocca, *Superwomen: Gender, Power, and Representation* (Bloomsbury, 2016), 3.

27 Osvaldo Oyola, "Between the World and Wakanda: Ta-Nehisi Coates and Brian Stelfreeze's 'Black Panther,'" *Los Angeles Review of Books*, December 27, 2016.

28 For more on attention as a highly valued commodity, see Tim Wu, *The Attention Merchants: The Epic Scramble to Get Inside Our Heads* (New York: Knopf, 2016); Chris Hayes, *The Sirens' Call: How Attention Became the World's Most Endangered Resource* (New York: Penguin Press, 2025).

29 For more on discussions of Black Aesthetic, see Hoyt Fuller's "Toward a Black Aesthetic" (1968); Larry Neal's "The Black Arts Movement;" and essays published in *The Black Aesthetic* (Doubleday, 1971), edited by Addison Gayle.

30 Alondra Nelson, "AfroFuturism: Past-Future Visions," *Color Lines* (Spring 2000): 35.

Chapter 1

1 Joseph Hughes, "Outrage Deferred: On the Lack of Black Writers in the Comic Book Industry," *Comics Alliance*, February 4, 2013, https://comicsalliance.com/black-writers-comic-book-industry/.

2 Hughes, "Outrage Deferred."

3 Heidi MacDonald, "Why Aren't There More Black Writers in the Comics Industry?" *The Beat*, February 5, 2013, https://www.comicsbeat.com/why-arent-there-more-black-writers-in-the-comics-industry/.

4 Jeffrey A. Brown, *Black Superheroes, Milestone Comics, and Their Fans* (Jackson: University Press of Mississippi, 2001), 58.

5 For more on the term, see Abby Ohlheiser, "Why 'Social Justice Warrior,' a Gamergate Insult, Is Now a Dictionary Entry," *The Washington Post*, October 7, 2015, https://www.washingtonpost.com/news/the-intersect/wp/2015/10/07/why-social-justice-warrior-a-gamergate-insult-is-now-a-dictionary-entry/.

6 Joseph Phillip Illidge, "The Color Barrier: A Message of Comics, Diversity, and Hope," *CBR*, February 6, 2014, https://www.cbr.com/the-color-barrier-a-message-of-comics-diversity-hope/.

7 William H. Evans, "About Us," *Black Nerd Problems*, 2015, https://blacknerdproblems.com/bnp/about-us/.

8 Aldo J. Regalado, *Bending Steel: Modernity and the American Superhero* (Jackson: University Press of Mississippi, 2015), 170.

9   Laura Hudson, "It's Time to Get Real About Racial Diversity in Comics," *Wired*, July 25, 2015, https://www.wired.com/2015/07/diversity-in-comics/.

10 Kamala Khan (Ms. Marvel) made a background cameo appearance in 2013; she made her first full appearance in February 2014.

11 Anna Silman and Abraham Riesman, "New Captain America Will Be Black, Marvel Announces on Colbert," *Vulture*, July 17, 2014, https://www.vulture.com/2014/07/new-captain-america-will-be-black.html.

12 Jess Denham, "Marvel Announces Black Captain America After Confirming New Female Thor," *The Independent*, July 17, 2014, https://www.the-independent.com/arts-entertainment/books/news/marvel-announces-black-captain-america-after-confirming-new-female-thor-9611345.html.

13 Graeme McMillan, "Giving Us a Female Thor and Black Captain America Isn't Enough," *Wired*, July 17, 2014, https://www.wired.com/2014/07/captain-america-announcement/.

14 Christopher R. Weingarten, "See Two New Marvel Comics Covers Paying Tribute to Run the Jewels," *Rolling Stone*, January 16, 2015, https://www.rollingstone.com/culture/culture-news/see-two-new-marvel-comics-covers-paying-tribute-to-run-the-jewels-45378/.

15 Evan Minsker, "Marvel Comics Pay Homage to Hip-Hop Albums with Variant Covers," *Pitchfork*, July 14, 2015, https://pitchfork.com/news/60386-marvel-comics-pay-homage-to-hip-hop-albums-with-variant-covers/.

16 Paul Thompson, "Marvel Mixes Hip-Hop with Comic Books to Make New Covers," *XXL*, July 14, 2015, https://www.xxlmag.com/marvel-mixes-hip-hop-with-comic-books-to-make-new-covers/.

17 Noah Berlatsky, "Marvel's Hip-Hop Tribute Embraces Black Metaphors but Excludes Black People," *The Guardian*, July 20, 2015, https://www.theguardian.com/music/2015/jul/20/marvel-hip-hop-tribute-classic-albums.

18 Noah Berlatsky, "I Should Apologize to Marvel Too, I Should Have Credited Them w/ Making an Effort to Address the Legacy of Hip Hop, There," Twitter, July 21, 2015.

19 Hudson, "It's Time to Get Real About Racial Diversity in Comics."

20 Joshua Rivera, "Marvel's New Hip-Hop Covers Highlight Comics' Big Diversity Problem," *Business Insider*, August 9, 2015, https://www.businessinsider.com/marvel-hip-hop-comics-controversy-2015-7.

21 J. A. Micheline, "The White Privilege, White Audacity, and White Priorities of STRANGE FRUIT #1," *Women Write About Comics*, July 8, 2015, https://womenwriteaboutcomics.com/2015/07/the-white-privilege-white-audacity-and-white-priorities-of-strange-fruit-1/.

22 David Brothers quoted in Evan Narcisse, "Marvel's Super-Hero Hip-Hop Covers Are Available for Free," *Kotaku*, February 4, 2016, https://kotaku.com/marvel-s-super-hero-hip-hop-covers-are-available-for-fr-1757200483.

23 Shaun Manning, "Seeley Reveals Why He Quit Marvel's Blade," *CBR*, September 20, 2016, https://www.cbr.com/seeley-reveals-why-he-quit-marvels-blade/.

24 Albert Ching, "Waid Responds to *Strange Fruit* Controversy: 'What I Say About This Is Not What's Important,'" *CBR*, July 20, 2015, https://www.cbr.com/

waid-responds-to-strange-fruit-controversy-what-i-say-about-this-is-not-whats-important/.

25 Brown, *Black Superheroes, Milestone Comics, and Their Fans*, 85.

26 J. A. Micheline, "Creating Responsibility: Comics Has a Race Problem," *Comics Alliance*, July 17, 2015, https://comicsalliance.com/creating-responsibly-comics-race-problem/.

27 Tom Brevoort, "@tanehisicoates Heard That You Had an Interest in Writing Something for Marvel. Let's Talk! tbrevoort@marvel.com," Twitter, May 21, 2015, https://twitter.com/TomBrevoort/status/601403701740359680?ref_src=twsrc%5Etfw.

28 "What If Captain America Were Muslim and Female / New York Ideas 2015," *AtlanticLIVE*, YouTube, May 21, 2015, https://www.youtube.com/watch?v=2Y1ihwPpIL4.

29 André M. Carrington, *Speculative Blackness: The Future of Race in Science Fiction* (Minneapolis: University of Minnesota Press, 2016), 200.

30 Ta-Nehisi Coates, "WalMart and the Civil War," *The Atlantic*, January/February 2010, https://www.theatlantic.com/magazine/archive/2010/01/walmart-and-the-civil-war/307826/.

31 Ta-Nehisi Coates, "'He Wears the Mask Just to Cover the Raw Flesh,'" *The Atlantic*, December 16, 2010, https://www.theatlantic.com/entertainment/archive/2010/12/he-wears-the-mask-just-to-cover-the-raw-flesh/68108/.

32 Ta-Nehisi Coates, "You Left Out the Part About…, " *The New York Times*, June 8, 2011, https://www.nytimes.com/2011/06/09/opinion/09coates.html.

33 Albert Ching, "Course-Correcting Diversity Problems, Bendis' Iron Man Expansion," *CBR*, July 31, 2015, https://www.cbr.com/course-correcting-diversity-problems-bendis-iron-man-expansion/.

34 Howard Rambsy II, "Coverage of Ta-Nehisi Coates and *Between the World and Me*," *Cultural Front*, June 26, 2015, https://www.culturalfront.org/2015/06/coverage-of-ta-nehisi-coates-and.html.

Chapter 2

1 Charles, "@richjohnston Can We Go Ahead & Call This 'Mystery' Solved?" Twitter, July 31, 2015.

2 Rich Johnston, "Is Ta-Nehisi Coates Writing a New Comic Book for Marvel?" *Bleeding Cool*, August 1, 2015, https://bleedingcool.com/comics/is-ta-nehisi-coates-writing-a-new-comic-book-for-marvel/.

3 Jeffrey A. Brown, *Black Superheroes, Milestone Comics, and Their Fans* (Jackson: University Press of Mississippi, 2001), 75.

4 Rich Johnston, "Yes, Ta-Nehisi Coates Is Writing a New Comic Book for Marvel," *Bleeding Cool*, September 22, 2015, http://bleedingcool.com/comics/yes-ta-nehisi-coates-is-writing-a-new-comic-book-for-marvel-black-panther-with-brian-stelfreeze-for-a-year/.

5 George Gene Gustines, "Ta-Nehisi Coates to Write Black Panther Comic for Marvel," *The New York Times*, November 17, 2017, https://www.nytimes.com/2017/11/17/books/marvel-entertainment-names-new-editor-in-chief.html.

6 Thanks to my undergraduate research assistant Al Smith for assisting me in identifying, working through, and organizing the massive news coverage on the Coates hire.

7 Abraham Josephine Riesman, "Ta-Nehisi Coates Writing Black Panther Is the Year's Biggest Comics News," *Vulture*, February 28, 2018, https://www.vulture.com/2015/09/ta-nehisi-coates-black-panther.html.

8 Lanre Bakare, "Ta-Nehisi Coates to Write Marvel's Black Panther Comic," *The Guardian*, September 22, 2015, https://www.theguardian.com/books/2015/sep/22/ta-nehisicoates-to-write-marvels-black-panther-comic.

9 Jason Concepcion, "Ta-Nehisi Coates Is Writing the 'Black Panther' Comic for Marvel," *Grantland*, September 23, 2015, https://grantland.com/hollywood-prospectus/ta-nehisi-coates-is-writing-the-black-panther-comic-for-marvel/.

10 Concepcion, "Ta-Nehisi Coates Is Writing the 'Black Panther' Comic for Marvel," *Grantland*, September 23, 2015, https://grantland.com/hollywood-prospectus/ta-nehisi-coates-is-writing-the-black-panther-comic-for-marvel/

11 Beth Driscoll and Claire Squires, *The Frankfurt Book Fair and Bestseller Business* (New York: Cambridge University Press, 2020), 12.

12 Tim Wu, *The Attention Merchants* (Knopf, 2016), 14, 18.

13 Driscoll and Squires, *The Frankfurt Book Fair and Bestseller Business*, 24.

14 Amy Brinker, "An Oral History of *Between the World and Me*," Penguin Random House, November 12, 2020, https://www.penguinrandomhouse.com/articles/an-oral-history-of-between-the-world-and-me/.

15 Brinker, "An Oral History of *Between the World and Me*."

16 Heather Schwedel, "There's Been a Run on Anti-Racist Books," *Slate*, June 1, 2020, https://slate.com/culture/2020/06/antiracist-books-sold-out-amazon-george-floyd-protests.html

17 Jocelyn McClurg, "Ta-Nehisi Coates Writes a Best Seller," *USA Today*, July 22, 2015, https://www.usatoday.com/story/life/books/2015/07/22/ta-nehisi-coates-between--world-and-me-harper-lee-el-james-usa-today-best-selling-books/30471757/.

18 Carlos Lozada, "The Radical Chic of Ta-Nehisi Coates," *Washington Post*, July 16, 2015, https://www.washingtonpost.com/news/book-party/wp/2015/07/16/the-radical-chic-of-ta-nehisi-coates/.

19 Jennifer Schuessler, "Ta-Nehisi Coates's 'Visceral' Take on Being Black in America," *The New York Times*, July 17, 2015, https://www.nytimes.com/2015/07/18/books/ta-nehisi-coatess-visceral-take-on-being-black-in-america.html.

20 David Betancourt, "Marvel Was Smart to Hire Coates to Write Black Panther. Here's Why," *Washington Post*, September 23, 2015, https://www.washingtonpost.com/news/comic-riffs/wp/2015/09/23/heres-why-marvel-comics-is-smart-to-hire-ta-nehisi-coates-to-write-black-panther/; Oliver Sava, "Marvel Wises Up, Hires Ta-Nehisi Coates to Write Black Panther Comic," *A. V. Club*, September 22,

2015, https://www.avclub.com/marvel-wises-up-hires-ta-nehisi-coates-to-write-black-1798284537; Joshua Rivera, "Ta-Nehisi Coates' Black Panther Comic Is a Dream Come True," *GQ*, September 23, 2015, https://www.gq.com/story/ta-nehisi-coates-black-panther-dream-come-true.

21 "Ending Radical and Wasteful Government DEI Programs and Preferencing," The White House, January 20, 2025, https://www.whitehouse.gov/presidential-actions/2025/01/ending-radical-and-wasteful-government-dei-programs-and-preferencing/.

22 McKinsey & Company, "What Is Diversity, Equity, and Inclusion?" *McKinsey & Company*, August 17, 2022, https://www.mckinsey.com/~/media/mckinsey/featured%20insights/mckinsey%20explainers/what%20is%20diversity%20equity%20and%20inclusion/what_is_diversity_equity_and_inclusion.pdf.

23 Gustines, "Ta-Nehisi Coates to Write Black Panther Comic for Marvel."

24 Joshua Lapin-Bertone, "Marvel vs. DC: The Key Differences and Distinctions Between the Two Superhero and Comics Titans," *Pop Verse*, April 1, 2024, https://www.thepopverse.com/marvel-dc-differences-comics-movies-tv.

25 Graeme McMillan, "Marvel Announces New 'Black Panther' Comic Book Series to Be Written by Ta-Nehisi Coates," *The Hollywood Reporter*, September 22, 2015, https://www.hollywoodreporter.com/movies/movie-news/ta-nehisi-coates-writing-black-826209/.

26 Evan Narcisse, "Ta-Nehisi Coates Will Write Marvel's New Black Panther Comic," *Kotaku*, September 22, 2015, https://kotaku.com/ta-nehisi-coates-will-write-marvels-new-black-panther-c-1732376928.

27 Rivera, "Ta-Nehisi Coates' Black Panther Comic Is a Dream Come True."

28 For one take on the problems with designating a single Black leader, see Norman Kelly, *The Head Negro in Charge Syndrome: The Dead End of Black Politics* (Nation Books, 2004).

29 Ta-Nehisi Coates, "The Black Journalist and the Racial Mountain," *The Atlantic*, June 2, 2016, https://www.theatlantic.com/politics/archive/2016/06/black-journalist-and-the-racist-mountain/484808/; Ta-Nehisi Coates, "How Racism Invented Race in America," *The Atlantic*, June 23, 2014, https://www.theatlantic.com/politics/archive/2014/06/the-case-for-reparations-a-narrative-bibliography/372000/.

30 Alex Abad-Santos, "Ta-Nehisi Coates Will Be Writing Marvel's Black Panther Comic Book," *Vox*, September 22, 2015, https://www.vox.com/2015/9/22/9373185/coates-black-panther.

31 Rob Salkowitz, "Ta-Nehisi Coates Will Write Marvel's Black Panther," *Forbes*, September 22, 2015, https://www.forbes.com/sites/robsalkowitz/2015/09/22/ta-nehisi-coates-will-write-marvels-black-panther/.

32 Joseph Illidge, "Between Wakanda and Us—Ta-Nehisi Coates' 'Black Panther' and the Uncertain Future," *CBR*, September 23, 2015, https://www.cbr.com/between-wakanda-and-us-ta-nehisi-coates-black-panther-the-uncertain-future/.

33 Arturo Garcia, "Ta-Nehisi Coates's Black Panther Is a Hopeful First Step for Diversity at Marvel," *The Guardian*, September 23, 2015, https://www.theguardian.com/books/2015/sep/23/ta-nehisi-coates-black-panther-marvel-diversity.

34 Scott Woods, "Ta-Nehisi Coates and the Blackest Black Panther Ever," *Black Nerd Problems*, September 23, 2015, https://blacknerdproblems.com/ta-nehisi-coates-and-the-blackest-black-panther-ever/.

35 Betancourt, "Marvel Was Smart to Hire Coates to Write Black Panther"; Yanan Wang, "Ta-Nehisi Coates, 'Black Panther' and Superhero Diversity," *The Washington Post*, September 23, 2015, https://www.washingtonpost.com/news/morning-mix/wp/2015/09/23/ta-nehisi-coates-black-panther-and-superhero-diversity/; Rivera, "Ta-Nehisi Coates' Black Panther Comic Is a Dream Come True"; Hugh Armitage, "Marvel Gets It Right by Hiring African American Journalist Ta-Nehisi Coates to Write Black Panther Comic," *Digital Spy*, September 23, 2015, https://www.digitalspy.com/comics/a670028/marvel-gets-it-right-by-hiring-african-american-journalist-ta-nehisi-coates-to-write-black-panther-comic/; Illidge, "Between Wakanda and Us—Ta-Nehisi Coates' 'Black Panther' and the Uncertain Future."

36 Armitage, "Marvel Gets It Right."

37 "Ta-Nehisi Coates to Write Black Panther, but Mainstream Comic Books Still Struggle with Diversity," *LAist*, September 24, 2015, https://laist.com/shows/the-frame/ta-nehisi-coates-to-write-black-panther-but-mainstream-comic-books-still-struggle-with-diversity.

38 Oliver Sava, "Marvel Wises Up, Hires Ta-Nehisi Coates to Write Black Panther Comic," *A. V. Club*, September 22, 2015, https://www.avclub.com/marvel-wises-up-hires-ta-nehisi-coates-to-write-black-1798284537.

39 Milton Griepp, "World According to Griepp: Why Is It Called the Comics 'Direct Market'?" *ICv2*, March 22, 2023, https://icv2.com/articles/columns/view/53638/world-according-griepp-why-is-it-called-comics-direct-market.

40 *Comic Book Roundup* serves as one place to peruse reviews of individual comic book issues.

Chapter 3

1 Stephen Gerding, "C2E2: Marvel's 'Black Panther' #1 Tops 300K in Sales," *CBR*, March 18, 2016, https://www.cbr.com/c2e2-marvels-black-panther-1-tops-300k-in-sales/.

2 Robert Ito, "Ta-Nehisi Coates Helps a New Panther Leave Its Print," *The New York Times*, March 31, 2016, https://www.nytimes.com/2016/04/03/movies/ta-nehisi-coates-helps-a-new-panther-leave-its-print.html.

3 For a roundup of more than seventy-five articles about Whitehead's novel, see Howard Rambsy II, "The Coverage of Colson Whitehead's *The Underground Railroad*," *Cultural Front*, August 3, 2016, https://www.culturalfront.org/search?q=underground+railroad.

4 Alex Abad-Santos, "Black Panther by Ta-Nehisi Coates and Brian Stelfreeze Is Brilliant, Political, and Human," *Vox*, April 6, 2016, https://www.vox.com/2016/4/5/11362636/black-panther-tanehisi-coates-review.

5 Toussaint Egan, "Advance: Black Panther #1 by Ta-Nehisi Coates and Brian Stelfreeze," *Paste Magazine*, April 4, 2016, https://www.pastemagazine.com/comics/black-panther/advance-review-black-panther-1-by-ta-nehisi-coates.

6 Jesse Schedeen, "Black Panther #1 Review," *IGN,* April 7, 2016, https://www.ign.com/articles/2016/04/04/black-panther-1-review.

7 Robert Reed, "Best Shots Advance Review: BLACK PANTHER #1" *Newsrama*, April 4, 2016.

8 Eric Diaz, "Review: Marvel's Black Panther #1 Is Full of Potential," *Nerdist*, April 4, 2016, https://nerdist.com/article/review-marvels-black-panther-1-is-full-of-potential/.

9 Troy Powell, "Black Panther #1," *Graphic Policy*, April 11, 2016, https://graphicpolicy.com/2016/04/11/review-black-panther1/.

10 Douglas Ernst, "Black Panther #1: Ta-Nehisi Coates Debut a Mixed Bag for Marvel Fans," *Douglas Ernst Blog*, April 21, 2016, https://douglasernst.blog/2016/04/21/black-panther-1-ta-nehisi-coates-debut-a-mixed-bag-for-marvel-fans/.

11 Brett Schenker, "Black Panther #1," *Graphic Policy*, April 7, 2016, https://graphicpolicy.com/2016/04/07/review-black-panther-1/.

12 Elizabeth Méndez Berry and Chi-hui Yang, "The Dominance of the White Male Critic," *The New York Times*, July 5, 2019, https://www.nytimes.com/2019/07/05/opinion/sunday/we-need-more-critics-of-color.html.

13 David Betancourt, "Ta-Nehisi Coates's New Black Panther Comic Provides a Debut Fit for a King," *The Washington Post*, April 6, 2016, https://www.washingtonpost.com/news/comic-riffs/wp/2016/04/06/ta-nehisi-coatess-new-black-panther-comic-provides-a-debut-fit-for-a-king/.

14 William Evans, "*Black Panther* #1 Review," *Black Nerd Problems*, April 6, 2016, https://blacknerdproblems.com/black-panther-1-review/.

15 J. A. Micheline, "Ta-Nehisi Coates on 'Black Panther' and Creating a Comic That Reflects the Black Experience," *Vice*, April 5, 2016, https://www.vice.com/en/article/ta-nehisi-coates-talks-about-black-panther-and-writing-from-a-black-experience/.

16 Evan Narcisse, "Ta-Nehisi Coates Is Trying to Do Right by Marvel Comics' First Black Superhero," *Kotaku*, April 7, 2016, https://kotaku.com/marvel-s-super-hero-hip-hop-covers-are-available-for-fr-1757200483; Evan Narcisse, "Spoiler Space: More from Ta-Nehisi Coates on Black Panther," *Kotaku*, April 6, 2016, https://kotaku.com/spoiler-space-more-from-ta-nehisi-coates-on-black-pant-1769472432.

17 Narcisse, "Spoiler Space: More from Ta-Nehisi Coates on Black Panther."

18 Jason Johnson, "How io9's Evan Narcisse Went from Writing About Comics to Writing Rise of the Black Panther," *The Root*, January 17, 2018, https://www.theroot.com/how-io9-s-evan-narcisse-went-from-writing-about-comics-1821912630.

19 Joshua Rivera, "Black Panther, Marvel's First Black Superhero, Is Now the Star of the Year's Most Important Comic," *GQ*, April 12, 2016, https://www.gq.com/story/black-panther-ta-nehisi-coates.

20 Rich Johnston, "Black Panther #1 and Empress #1 Sell Out, Go to Second Print," *Bleeding Cool*, April 8, 2016, https://bleedingcool.com/comics/black-panther-1-and-empress-1-sell-out-go-to-second-print/.

21 Eliana Dockterman, "Marvel's Editor on What You Need to Know About Ta-Nehisi Coates' Black Panther," *Time*, April 6, 2016, https://time.com/4281426/ta-nehisi-coates-black-panther-marvel/.

22 Two of those variants include the second and third printings for *Black Panther* #1. For list, see appendix D. For visual examples, visit https://blackpanther.siue.edu.

23 The variant was on sale for that price in May 2024. Rachiday8, "2016 Marvel Comic Black Panther #1 Horn Variant Signed Stan Lee Chadwick Boseman," *eBay*.

24 "StockX Partners with Marvel to Release Exclusive Black Panther Comic," *StockX*, February 1, 2023, https://stockx.com/about/stockx-partners-with-marvel-to-release-exclusive-black-panther-comic/.

25 Schedeen, "Black Panther #1 Review."

26 Betancourt, "Ta-Nehisi Coates's New Black Panther Comic Provides a Debut Fit for a King."

27 Abad-Santos, "Black Panther by Ta-Nehisi Coates and Brian Stelfreeze."

28 Mark Yarm, "Ta-Nehisi Coates Fights the Power—Literally—With Black Panther," *Wired*, April 6, 2016, https://www.wired.com/2016/04/ta-nehisi-coates-black-panther-comics/.

29 Sean Bartley, "Black Panther #1," *Comics Verse*, April 7, 2016, http://comicsverse.com/black-panther-1-review-wakanda-fire/.

30 David F. Walker, "Marvel Is Making a Reasonable Decision Given the Sales," Twitter, August 28, 2016, https://x.com/DavidWalker1201/status/769764816172953600.

31 David Betancourt, "What Marvel Canceling Nighthawk Means for Superheroes of Color," *The Washington Post*, September 8, 2016, https://www.washingtonpost.com/news/comic-riffs/wp/2016/09/08/what-marvel-canceling-nighthawk-means-for-superheroes-of-color/.

32 Joseph Illidge, "Nighthawk's Fatal Battle Against a Civil War and a Rebirth," *CBR*, August 29, 2016, https://www.cbr.com/nighthawks-fatal-battle-against-a-civil-war-and-a-rebirth/.

33 George Gene Gustines, "Marvel's World of Wakanda Will Spotlight Women, on the Page and Behind It," *The New York Times*, July 22, 2016, https://www.nytimes.com/2016/07/23/books/black-panther-marvel-comics-roxane-gay-ta-nehisi-coates-wakanda.html.

34 Graeme McMillan, "Ta-Nehisi Coates Spins Out Third 'Black Panther' Comic Book for Marvel," *The Hollywood Reporter*, January 20, 2017, https://www.hollywoodreporter.com/movies/movie-news/ta-nehisi-coates-spins-third-black-panther-comic-book-marvel-966598/.

35 Jeet Heer, "Superhero Comics Have a Race Problem. Can Ta-Nehisi Coates Fix It?" *The New Republic*, September 22, 2015, https://newrepublic.com/article/122897/superhero-comics-have-race-problem-can-ta-nehisi-coates-fix-it.

36 Rich Johnston, "The Top Ten Bestselling Comics of 2016—In the Direct Market," *Bleeding Cool*, December 11, 2016, https://bleedingcool.com/comics/2016s-top-ten-comics-by-sales-in-the-direct-market/.

37 Brian Cronin, "Number Ones: The Most Important #1 Issues (2010–Today)," *CBR*, November 19, 2016, https://www.cbr.com/15-most-important-1-issues-of-the-current-decade-2010-now/.

38 According to the figures from Diamond Comic Distributors, *Black Panther* #1 was ranked twenty-nine on the list of one hundred best-selling comic books. See "The 2010s' Top 100 Best-Selling Comics," Previews World, January 13, 2020, https://previewsworld.com/Article/238869-Exclusive-The-2010s-Top-100-Best-Selling-Comics.

Chapter 4

1 Manning Marable, *Malcolm X: A Life of Reinvention*, (New York: Viking, 2011), 127–28.

2 Adilifu Nama, *Super Black: American Pop Culture and Black Superheroes* (Austin: University of Texas, 2011), 43.

3 Mark Yarm, "Ta-Nehisi Coates Fights the Power—Literally—With Black Panther," *Wired*, April 6, 2016, https://www.wired.com/2016/04/ta-nehisi-coates-black-panther-comics/.

4 Ta-Nehisi Coates, "The Return of the Black Panther," *The Atlantic*, April 2016, https://www.theatlantic.com/magazine/archive/2016/04/the-return-of-the-black-panther/471516/, 51.

5 Ta-Nehisi Coates et al., *Black Panther* 2 (May 2016).

6 Ta-Nehisi Coates et al., *Black Panther* 3 (June 2016).

7 Ta-Nehisi Coates et al., *Black Panther* 2 (May 2016).

8 Ta-Nehisi Coates et al., *Black Panther* 4 (July 2016).

9 "Ta-Nehisi Coates' Acceptance Speech for the 2015 National Book Award for Non-Fiction," National Book Foundation, November 18, 2015.

10 Ta-Nehisi Coates et al., *Black Panther* 4 (July 2016).

11 Ta-Nehisi Coates et al., *Black Panther* 2 (May 2016).

12 Ta-Nehisi Coates et al., *Black Panther* 6 (September 2016).

13 Du Bois, "Strivings of the Negro People," *The Atlantic*, August 1897, https://www.theatlantic.com/magazine/archive/1897/08/strivings-of-the-negro-people/305446/.

14 Rebecca Wanzo, "And All Our Past Decades Have Seen Revolutions: The Long Decolonization of Black Panther," *The Black Scholar*, February 19, 2018, https://www.theblackscholar.org/past-decades-seen-revolutions-long-decolonization-black-panther-rebecca-wanzo/.

15 Ta-Nehisi Coates et al., *Black Panther* 10 (January 2017).

16 Ta-Nehisi Coates et al., *Black Panther* 10 (January 2017).

17 Ta-Nehisi Coates et al., *Black Panther* 9 (December 2016).

18 Ta-Nehisi Coates et al., *Black Panther* 10 (January 2017).

19 Ta-Nehisi Coates et al., *Black Panther* 11 (February 2017).

20 Ta-Nehisi Coates et al., *Black Panther* 11 (February 2017).

21 Robert Reed, "Civil War Gives Way to War of Ideas in BLACK PANTHER #12," *Newsarama*, March 22, 2017.

22 Evan Narcisse, "'The Miracle Is Wakanda': Ta-Nehisi Coates Says Goodbye to Black Panther," *Polygon*, May 26, 2021, https://www.polygon.com/interviews/22454722/black-panther-comics-ending-ta-nehisi-coates-interview/.

23 Reed, "Civil War Gives Way to War."

24 Ta-Nehisi Coates et al., *Black Panther* 12 (March 2017).

25 Oz Longworth, "Black Panther #4 Review," *Black Nerd Problems*, July 28, 2016, https://blacknerdproblems.com/black-panther-4-review/.

26 Christian Holub, "Black Panther: A Nation Under Our Feet, Book Two: EW Review," *Entertainment Weekly,* January 31, 2017, https://ew.com/books/2017/01/31/black-panther-nation-under-our-feet-book-two-ew-review/.

27 See, for instance, Frederick Douglas's *The Narrative of the Life of Frederick Douglass* (1845); Richard Wright's *Native Son* (1940); *Black Boy* (1945); and *The Outsider* (1953); Ralph Ellison's *Invisible Man* (1952); James Baldwin's *Go Tell It On the Mountain* (1953); Ishmael Reed's *Flight to Canada* (1976); Charles Johnson's *Middle Passage* (1990); Paul Beatty's *The White Boy Shuffle* (1996) and *The Sellout* (2015); Colson Whitehead's *John Henry Days* (2001).

28 See Cornelius Eady's *Brutal Imagination* (2001), Tyehimba Jess's *Leadbelly* (2005); Adrian Matejka's *The Big Smoke* (2013).

29 See Ta-Nehisi Coates, "My President Was Black," *The Atlantic*, January/February 2017, https://www.theatlantic.com/magazine/archive/2017/01/my-president-was-black/508793/; Coates, "Fear of a Black President," *The Atlantic*, September 2012, https://www.theatlantic.com/magazine/archive/2012/09/fear-of-a-black-president/309064/; Coates, "The Legacy of Malcolm X," *The Atlantic*, May 2011, https://www.theatlantic.com/magazine/archive/2011/05/the-legacy-of-malcolm-x/308438/; Coates, "The Mask of Doom," *The New Yorker*, September 14, 2009, https://www.newyorker.com/magazine/2009/09/21/the-mask-of-doom; Coates, "'This Is How We Lost to the White Man': The Audacity of Bill Cosby's Black Conservatism," *The Atlantic*, May 2008, https://www.theatlantic.com/magazine/archive/2008/05/-this-is-how-we-lost-to-the-white-man/306774/.

Chapter 5

1 George Gene Gustines, "Marvel's World of Wakanda Will Spotlight Women, on the Page and Behind It," *The New York Times,* July 22, 2016, https://www.nytimes.com/2016/07/23/books/black-panther-marvel-comics-roxane-gay-ta-nehisi-coates-wakanda.html.

2 Christian Holub, "Roxane Gay Will Write a 'Black Panther' Spin-Off Comic About the Women of Wakanda," *Entertainment Weekly,* July 22, 2016, https://ew.com/article/2016/07/22/roxane-gay-black-panther/.

3 Gustines, "Marvel's World of Wakanda Will Spotlight Women."

4   *The Atlantic*, "Marvel's New Black Panther Comic | Q&A with Author Ta-Nehisi Coates," YouTube, August 9, 2016, https://www.youtube.com/watch?v=CRJ4URjtgxU.

5   Joshua Yehl, "Kelly Sue DeConnick Talks Captain Marvel, Pretty Deadly, and the Sexy Lamp Test," *IGN*, June 20, 2013, https://www.ign.com/articles/2013/06/20/kelly-sue-deconnick-talks-captain-marvel-pretty-deadly-and-the-sexy-lamp-test.

6   Carolyn Cocca, *Superwomen: Gender, Power, and Representation* (Bloomsbury, 2016), 13–15.

7   Ta-Nehisi Coates, "The Feminists of Wakanda," *The Atlantic*, April 8, 2016, https://www.theatlantic.com/culture/archive/2016/04/the-feminists-of-wakanda/624392/.

8   Rich Johnston, "Priest Credits Joe Quesada and Jimmy Palmiotti for Dora Milaje," *Bleeding Cool*, October 6, 2018, https://bleedingcool.com/comics/joe-quesada-christopher-priest-marvel-knights-cup-o-joe-nycc-201/.

9   Christopher Priest, *Black Panther* #1 (November 1998).

10   Ta-Nehisi Coates, *Black Panther* Vol. 6, #1 (April 2016).

11   Ta-Nehisi Coates, *Black Panther* Vol. 6, #1 (April 2016).

12   L. E. H. Light, "Black Panther #1: The Dora Milaje Come Center Stage."

13   Ta-Nehisi Coates, *Black Panther* Vol. 6, #1 (April 2016).

14   Jonathan Maberry, *Doomwar* #5 (June 2010).

15   "Marvel's New Black Panther Comic | Q&A."

16   Ta-Nehisi Coates, *Black Panther* Vol. 6, #4 (July 2016).

17   Ta-Nehisi Coates, *Black Panther* Vol. 6, #4 (July 2016).

18   Ta-Nehisi Coates, *Black Panther* Vol. 6, #9 (December 2016).

19   Ta-Nehisi Coates, *Black Panther* Vol. 6, #10 (January 2017).

20   Audre Lorde, "The Master's Tools Will Never Dismantle the Master's House," *Sister Outsider* (Penguin, 2020), 110–13.

21   June Jordan, "Poem About My Rights," *Directed by Desire: The Collected Poems of June Jordan* (Copper Canyon Press, 2012), 309–12.

22   Ta-Nehisi Coates, *Black Panther* Vol. 6, #6 (September 2016).

23   Frederick Douglass, *Narrative of the Life of Frederick Douglass*, 1845 rpt. (Barnes & Noble Classics, 2003).

24   Ta-Nehisi Coates, *Black Panther* Vol. 6, #3 (June 2016).

25   Amiri Baraka, *Digging: The Afro-American Soul of American Classical Music* (University of California Press, 2009), 6.

26   Ta-Nehisi Coates, *Black Panther* Vol. 6, #3 (June 2016).

27   Ta-Nehisi Coates, *Black Panther* Vol. 6, #3 (June 2016).

28   Ta-Nehisi Coates, *Black Panther* Vol. 6, #6 (September 2016).

29   Ta-Nehisi Coates, *Black Panther* Vol. 6, #3 (June 2016).

30   Ta-Nehisi Coates, *Black Panther* Vol. 6, #8 (November 2016).

31   The Plane of Wakandan memory scenes appear in Ta-Nehisi Coates, *Black Panther* Vol. 6, nos. 2, 3, 5, 6, 7, and 8.

32 Ta-Nehisi Coates, *Black Panther* Vol. 6, #10 (January 2017).

33 Ta-Nehisi Coates, *Black Panther* Vol. 6, #10 (January 2017).

34 Shani O. Hilton, "The Black Experience Isn't Just About Men," *BuzzFeed*, July 10, 2015, https://www.buzzfeed.com/shani/between-the-world-and-she; Britni Danielle, "In Ta-Nehisi Coates' New Book, It's Clear All the Blacks Are Still Men," *The Root*, July 16, 2015, https://www.theroot.com/in-ta-nehisi-coates-new-book-it-s-clear-all-the-black-1790860550; Josie Duffy, "'Between the World and Me' Is for All of Us, Even if It Is Not About All of Us," Rewire News Group, July 15, 2015, https://rewirenewsgroup.com/2015/07/15/world-us-even-us/.

35 During a podcast discussion, Coates and Chris Jackson discussed taking multiple steps to ensure that women are represented in thoughtful ways in Coates's novel *The Water Dancer*. "#360: Ta-Nehisi Coates and Chris Jackson," *Longform Podcast*, September 18, 2019.

36 "Marvel's New Black Panther Comic | Q&A."

Chapter 6

1 Evan Narcisse, "Ta-Nehisi Coates Is Trying to Do Right by Marvel Comics' First Black Superhero," *Kotaku*, April 7, 2016, https://kotaku.com/marvel-s-super-hero-hip-hop-covers-are-available-for-fr-1757200483.

2 Evan Narcisse, "Spoiler Space: More from Ta-Nehisi Coates on Black Panther," *Kotaku*, April 6, 2016, https://kotaku.com/spoiler-space-more-from-ta-nehisi-coates-on-black-pant-1769472432.

3 Ta-Nehisi Coates, "Building the World of Wakanda," *The Atlantic*, April 22, 2016, https://www.theatlantic.com/culture/archive/2016/04/the-world-of-wakanda/624241/.

4 Coates, "Building the World of Wakanda."

5 Ta-Nehisi Coates, *Black Panther* Vol. 6, #4 (July 2016).

6 Narcisse, "Spoiler Space: More from Ta-Nehisi Coates."

7 Narcisse, "Spoiler Space: More from Ta-Nehisi Coates."

8 Evan Narcisse, *Rise of the Black Panther* Vol. 1, #1 (January 2018).

9 Don McGregor, *Jungle Action* Vol. 2, #6 (June 1973).

10 Simon Stevens, "Like So Many (Wildly Varying) Writers on Africa, Adichie Gets the Acacia Tree Sunset Treatment," Twitter, May 7, 2014, https://x.com/simonmstevens/status/464049317926686720.

11 Marta Bausells, "Book Cover Clichés: Have You Spotted Recurrent Designs?" *The Guardian*, June 12, 2014, https://www.theguardian.com/books/booksblog/2014/jun/12/book-cover-cliches-have-you-spotted-recurrent-designs.

12 Elliot Ross, "The Dangers of a Single Book Cover," *Africa Is a Country*, May 7, 2014, https://africasacountry.com/2014/05/the-dangers-of-a-single-book-cover-the-acacia-tree-meme-and-african-literature.

13 Quoted in Michael Silverberg, "The Reason Every Book About Africa Has the Same Cover—And It's Not Pretty," *Quartz*, May 12, 2014, https://qz.com/207527/the-reason-every-book-about-africa-has-the-same-cover-and-its-not-pretty.

14 Ta-Nehisi Coates, *Black Panther* Vol. 6, #1 (April 2016).

15 Ta-Nehisi Coates, *Black Panther* Vol. 6, #2 (May 2016).

16 Quoted in Jenn Fujikawa, "The Architectural Inspirations Behind Wakanda in Marvel Studios' 'Black Panther,'" *Marvel*, February 9, 2018, https://www.marvel.com/articles/movies/the-architectural-inspirations-behind-wakanda-in-marvel-studios-black-panther.

17 Kelle Long, "How the Black Panther Production Designer Rooted the World's Most Advanced Nation in African Culture," *Motion Pictures Association,* February 14, 2018, https://www.motionpictures.org/2018/02/black-panther-production-designer-rooted-worlds-advanced-nation-african-culture/; Sala Elise Patterson, "2018 Rouse Visiting Artist Hannah Beachler on Her History-Making Oscar Nomination," Harvard Graduate School of Design, February 22, 2019, https://www.gsd.harvard.edu/2019/02/2018-rouse-visiting-artist-hannah-beachler-on-her-history-making-oscar-nomination/.

18 Sam Keeper, "Starkitecture: Should We Be Worried About Black Panther's Concept Art?" *Storming the Ivory Tower*, February 28, 2017, https://www.stormingtheivorytower.com/2017/02/starkitecture-should-we-be-worried.html.

19 Evan Narcisse, *Black Panther: Wakanda Atlas* (New York: DK/Penguin Random House, 2022), 6.

20 John Keene, "Ta-Nehisi Coates Re-imagines the Black Panther Comics," *Frieze*, June 1, 2016, https://www.frieze.com/article/books-48.

21 Oz Longworth, "Black Panther #10 Review," *Black Nerd Problems*, January 25, 2017, https://blacknerdproblems.com/black-panther-10-review/.

22 I am indebted to my younger brother, Kenton Rambsy, a specialist on Edward P. Jones's fiction, for sharing maps and numerous city landmark references related to Washington, DC, as they appear in Jones's short stories. See Kenton Rambsy, "Edward P. Jones, a Black Storytelling Demographer," *Journal of the Short Story in English* (Spring 2024): 81–97, https://journals.openedition.org/jsse/4337?lang=en; Kenton Rambsy, *The Geographies of African American Short Fiction* (University of Mississippi, 2022), especially chapter 5, "Up South: Geo-Tagging DC and Eward P. Jones's Homegrown Characters"; Kenton Rambsy, "Edward P. Jones—The Neighborhood Preservationist," *Fire!!!* 5, no. 2 (Spring 2020): 40–52, https://www.jstor.org/stable/10.5323/48573837.

23 Peter Vujakovic, "World Weary?" *The Cartographic Journal* 56, no. 2 (2019): 97–100, https://www.tandfonline.com/doi/full/10.1080/00087041.2019.1624004; Reuben Rose-Redwood et al., "Decolonizing the Map: Recentering Indigenous Mappings," *Cartographica* 55, no. 3 (2020): 151–62, https://utppublishing.com/doi/full/10.3138/cart.53.3.intro.

24 Trudier Harris, *The Scary Mason-Dixon Line: African American Writers and the South* (Baton Rogue: LSU Press, 2013); Paola A. Nardi, "'They Lived There Because They

Were Poor and Black': Spatial Injustice in Toni Morrison's *The Bluest Eye*," *Journal of African American Studies* 26 (November 4, 2022): 401–12, https://link.springer.com/article/10.1007/s12111-022-09593-3; Huiying Liang, "'Keep Chaos Out, Order In': Grid and Architectural Space in Colson Whitehead's *Zone One*," *The Explicator* 82, no. 4 (2024): 217–22, https://www.researchgate.net/publication/382482303_Keep_Chaos_Out_Order_In_Grid_and_Architectural_Space_in_Colson_Whitehead's_Zone_One.

25 Ta-Nehisi Coates, *Black Panther* Vol. 6, #5 (August 2016).

26 Ta-Nehisi Coates, *Black Panther* Vol. 6, #6 (September 2016).

27 Jonathan Hickman, *Fantastic Four* #607 and #608. Jonathan Hickman, *New Avengers* #18.

28 Jonathan Hickman, *Fantastic Four* #608.

29 Ian Cardona, "What Is the Djalia? Black Panther's Mystical Realm, Explained," *Comic Book Resources*, October 18, 2017, https://www.cbr.com/black-panther-djalia-explained/.

30 Joshua Rivera, "The New Black Panther Trailer Is a Hell of a Way to Start Your Week," *GQ*, October 16, 2018, https://www.gq.com/story/black-panther-trailer-2.

31 Nnedi Okorafor, *Shuri*, #9 and #10.

32 Eve Ewing, *Black Panther* Vol. 9, #6 (November 2023); Cheryl Lynn Eaton, *Black Panther: Blood Hunt* #1 (May 2024).

33 Joseph Illidge, "Marvel's Black Panther, Wakandan Colors and the Forgotten Warrior," *Comic Book Resources*, April 11, 2016, https://www.cbr.com/marvels-black-panther-wakandan-colors-and-the-forgotten-warrior/.

34 Ta-Nehisi Coates, *Black Panther* #4 (July 2016).

35 "Black Panther Interior by Laura Martin—Marvel Quickdraw," YouTube, May 4, 2017, https://www.youtube.com/watch?v=MgncgjMunBA.

36 Ta-Nehisi Coates, *Black Panther* Vol. 6, #4 (July 2016).

37 Ta-Nehisi Coates, *Black Panther* Vol. 6, #2 (May 2016) and #4 (July 2014).

38 Ta-Nehisi Coates, *Black Panther* Vol. 6, #4 (July 2014) and #9 (December 2016).

39 Ta-Nehisi Coates, *Black Panther* Vol. 6, #5 (August 2016).

40 Ta-Nehisi Coates, *Black Panther* Vol. 6, #11 (February 2017).

41 Ta-Nehisi Coates, *Black Panther* Vol. 6, #12 (March 2017).

Chapter 7

1 Eliana Dockterman, "Ta-Nehisi Coates Is Expanding the Black Panther Universe with *The Crew*," *Time*, January 20, 2017, https://time.com/4639911/ta-nehisi-coates-is-expanding-the-black-panther-universe-with-the-crew/.

2 Pauly D, "Everything You Want to Know About Black Panther," *Pop Culture Uncovered*, May 5, 2016, https://popcultureuncovered.com/2016/05/05/everything-you-want-to-know-about-black-panther/.

3 Ta-Nehisi Coates, *Black Panther* Vol. 6, #6, #7, and #8 (2016).

4 Jelani Cobb, "Creating 'Luke Cage,' the First Woke Black-Superhero Show," *The New Yorker*, October 5, 2016, https://www.newyorker.com/culture/culture-desk/creating-luke-cage-the-first-woke-black-superhero-show.

5 Joanna Robinson, "Luke Cage and the Year Marvel Finally Reckoned with Its Black Audience," *Vanity Fair*, September 29, 2016, https://www.vanityfair.com/hollywood/2016/09/luke-cage-mike-colter-black-panther-netflix-marvel-black-voices.

6 See Julian C. Chambliss et al., *Assembling the Marvel Cinematic Universe: Essays on the Social, Cultural and Geopolitical Domains* (Jefferson, NC: McFarland, 2018).

7 Nigel Mitchell, "'Black Panther' Director Ryan Coogler Says Marvel's Current Comics Influencing His Film," *Comic Book Resources*, July 25, 2016, https://www.cbr.com/black-panther-director-ryan-coogler-says-marvels-current-comics-influencing-his-film/.

8 Tara Betts, "The Luke Cage Syllabus: A Breakdown of All the Black Literature Featured in Netflix's *Luke Cage*," *Black Nerd Problems*, October 4, 2016, https://blacknerdproblems.com/the-luke-cage-syllabus-a-breakdown-of-all-the-black-literature-featured-in-netflixs-luke-cage/; Matthew Teutsch, "Luke Cage and the African American Literary Tradition," *Black Perspectives*, November 1, 2016, https://www.aaihs.org/luke-cage-and-the-african-american-literary-tradition/.

9 Sarah Nicolas, "The Books of Marvel's Luke Cage," *Book Riot*, October 4, 2016, https://bookriot.com/the-books-of-marvels-luke-cage/.

10 Daniel Fienberg, "Marvel's Luke Cage': TV Review," *The Hollywood Reporter*, September 27, 2016, https://www.hollywoodreporter.com/tv/tv-reviews/marvels-luke-cage-review-932977/.

11 Sarah Nicole Prickett and Jody Rosen, "Sarah Jessica Parker and Ta-Nehisi Coates, on New Literary Paths," *New York Times*, October 5, 2016, https://www.nytimes.com/2016/10/05/t-magazine/entertainment/sarah-jessica-parker-sjp-hogarth-tanehisi-coates-black-panther.html.

12 Chip Zdarsky, *Howard the Duck* #10 (August 2016).

13 Victoria M. Massie, "You Need to Read Sonia Sotomayor's Devastating, Ta-Nehisi Coates-Citing Supreme Court Dissent," *Vox*, June 20, 2016, https://www.vox.com/2016/6/20/11976560/sonia-sotomayor-dissent-supreme-court.

14 Saturday Night Live, "The Bubble—SNL," YouTube, November 20, 2016, https://www.youtube.com/watch?v=vKOb-kmOgpI.

15 Ta-Nehisi Coates, "The Black Journalist and the Racial Mountain," *The Atlantic*, June 2, 2016, https://www.theatlantic.com/politics/archive/2016/06/black-journalist-and-the-racist-mountain/484808/.

16 See *Black American Literature Forum*, Special issue on Henry Dumas (Summer 1988), https://www.jstor.org/stable/i346164.

17 Ta-Nehisi Coates, "Wakanda and the Black Aesthetic," *The Atlantic*, June 29, 2016, https://www.theatlantic.com/culture/archive/2016/06/wakanda-and-the-black-aesthetic/623664/.

18 Jonathan W. Gray, "A Conflicted Man: An Interview with Ta-Nehisi Coates About Black Panther," *The New Republic*, April 4, 2016, https://newrepublic.com/article/132355/conflicted-man-interview-ta-nehisi-coates-black-panther.

19 Coates, "Wakanda and the Black Aesthetic."

20 Ta-Nehisi Coates, *Between the World and Me* (Spiegel & Grau, 2015).

21 Amiri Baraka, "Dope," *The Amiri Baraka Reader*, edited by William J. Harris (Thunder's Mouth Press, 1991), 263–66. For a reading by the author, see Amiri Baraka, "Dope," YouTube, October 2, 2009, https://www.youtube.com/watch?v=qJ89IZDBDR4; Baraka, "Digging Max," *Digging: The Afro-American Soul of American Classical Music* (University of California Press, 2009), 217–18.

22 Aaron McGruder, *A Right to Be Hostile: The Boondocks Treasury* (Three Rivers Press, 2003). For more on McGruder's cultural cataloging, see Rambsy, *Bad Men: Creative Touchstones of Black Writers* (Charlottesville: University of Virginia Press, 2020), especially chapter 4: "The Sagas of Huey and Riley Freeman," 105–32.

23 Ta-Nehisi Coates, "Conceptualizing the Black Panther," *The Atlantic*, December 2, 2016, https://www.theatlantic.com/culture/archive/2015/12/conceptualizing-the-black-panther/625627/.

24 Borys Kit, "Ta-Nehisi Coates to Narrate 'Black Panther' Marvel Recaps (Exclusive Video)," *The Hollywood Reporter*, May 3, 2016, https://www.hollywoodreporter.com/movies/movie-news/ta-nehisi-coates-narrate-black-889698/.

25 Alex Abad-Santos, "The 7 Best New Comics of 2016," *Vox*, December 21, 2016, https://www.vox.com/culture/2016/12/21/13919580/best-new-comics-2016.

26 Chancellor Agard and Christian Holub, "The Best Comic Books of 2016," *Entertainment Weekly*, December 20, 2016, https://ew.com/gallery/best-comic-books-2016/; Gavia Baker-Whitelaw, "The 9 Best Comics We Read in 2016," *The Daily Dot*, December 25, 2016, https://www.dailydot.com/unclick/best-superhero-sci-fi-comics-2016/.

27 See appendix A, B, and C.

28 Evan Narcisse, "Spoiler Space: More from Ta-Nehisi Coates on Black Panther," *Kotaku*, April 6, 2016, https://kotaku.com/spoiler-space-more-from-ta-nehisi-coates-on-black-pant-1769472432.

29 Jason Johnson, "How io9's Evan Narcisse Went from Writing About Comics to Writing Rise of the Black Panther," *The Root*, January 10, 2018, https://www.theroot.com/how-io9-s-evan-narcisse-went-from-writing-about-comics-1821912630.

30 Eve Ewing, "Flying While Black: Two Creators on Inventing (and Reinventing) Black Superheroes," *The New York Times*, April 23, 2021, https://www.nytimes.com/2021/04/23/arts/black-superheroes-comic-books.html.

31 Karama Horne, "Riri, Rhodey and Re-skinning: How Marvel Is Misunderstanding Diversity," *The Blerd Gurl*, July 8, 2016, https://theblerdgurl.com/comics/riri-rhodey-re-skinning-marvel-misunderstanding-diversity/.

32 Horne, "Riri, Rhodey and Re-skinning."

33 Karama Horne, "Indie Comics Spotlight: Alitha Martinez Has Been Here Before," *Syfy*, February 15, 2018, https://web.archive.org/web/20180318010236/https://

www.syfy.com/syfywire/indie-comics-spotlight-alitha-martinez-has-been-here-before.

34 Kerry James Marshall, "Marvel's *Black Panther*," *Art Forum*, September 1, 2016, https://www.artforum.com/columns/marvels-black-panther-230462/.

Chapter 8

1 Milton Griepp, "Marvel's David Gabriel on the 2016 Market Shift," *ICv2*, March 31, 2017, https://icv2.com/articles/news/view/37152/marvels-david-gabriel-2016-market-shift.

2 Griepp, "Marvel's David Gabriel on the 2016 Market Shift."

3 Tim Adams, "Marvel Exec Clarifies Comments That 'People Didn't Want Any More Diversity,'" *CBR*, April 1, 2017, https://www.cbr.com/marvel-sales-diversity/.

4 Marykate Jasper, "Marvel VP Said Sales Slumped Because 'People Didn't Want Any More Diversity,'" *The Mary Sue*, April 1, 2017, https://www.themarysue.com/marvel-vp-no-more-diversity/.

5 Alex Abad-Santos, "The Outrage over Marvel's Alleged Diversity Blaming, Explained," *Vox*, April 8, 2017, https://www.vox.com/culture/2017/4/4/15169572/marvel-diversity-outrage-gabriel.

6 Dan Gearino, *Comic Shop: The Retail Mavericks Who Gave Us a New Geek Culture* (Swallow Press, 2017).

7 Abad-Santos, "The Outrage over Marvel's Alleged Diversity Blaming, Explained."

8 Alex Brown, "Let's Talk About Marvel Comics, the 'Diversity Doesn't Sell' Myth, and What Diversity Really Means," *Reactor*, April 5, 2017, https://reactormag.com/lets-talk-about-marvel-comics-the-diversity-doesnt-sell-myth-and-what-diversity-really-means/.

9 Jessica Lachenal, "Roxane Gay Confirms World of Wakanda's Disappointing Cancellation," *The Mary Sue*, June 13, 2017, https://www.themarysue.com/world-of-wakanda-cancelled/.

10 Alex Abad-Santos, "Marvel Canceled Roxane Gay and Ta-Nehisi Coates's Black Panther Comics. The Problem Goes Beyond Marvel," *Vox*, June 16, 2017, https://www.vox.com/culture/2017/6/16/15804600/marvel-cancel-roxane-gay-ta-nehisi-coates-comic.

11 Ta-Nehisi Coates, *Black Panther* #13 (April 2017).

12 See, for example Octavia Butler's *Kindred* (1979), Toni Morrison's *Song of Solomon* (1977), Colson Whitehead's *The Underground Railroad* (2016).

13 Ta-Nehisi Coates, *Black Panther* #167 (November 2017).

14 Courtney Thorsson, "*The Chaneysville Incident* and the Research Narrative in Contemporary African American Literature," *Studies in the Novel* 55, no. 1 (Spring 2023): 17, 29, https://www.researchgate.net/publication/369750386_The_Chaneysville_Incident_and_the_Research_Narrative_in_Contemporary_African_American_Literature.

15 Ta-Nehisi Coates, *Black Panther* #14 (May 2017).

16 Ta-Nehisi Coates, *Black Panther* #15 (June 2017).

17 Ta-Nehisi Coates, *Black Panther* #172 (April 2018).

18 Ta-Nehisi Coates, *Black Panther* #17 (August 2017).

19 Ta-Nehisi Coates, *Black Panther* #170 (February 2018).

20 Ta-Nehisi Coates, *Black Panther* #17 (August 2017).

21 Dawn Fallik, "Ta-Nehisi Coates, Jen Bartel to Partner on New Comic Book," *The Inquirer*, October 11, 2017, https://www.inquirer.com/philly/entertainment/geek/exclusive-ta-nehisi-coates-jen-bartel-to-partner-on-new-comic-book-20171011.html.

22 Rich Johnston, "Storm Gets a Series from Ta-Nehisi Coates and Jen Bartel for Marvel Comics."

23 CBR Staff, "Storm Series from Coates and Bartel Not Currently in the Works," *Bleeding Cool News*, October 13, 2017, https://bleedingcool.com/comics/storm-gets-series-ta-nehisi-coates-jen-bartel-marvel-comics/.

24 Ta-Nehisi Coates, *Black Panther* #16 (July 2017).

25 Osvaldo Oyola, "Between the World and Wakanda: Ta-Nehisi Coates and Brian Stelfreeze's 'Black Panther,'" *Los Angeles Review of Books*, December 27, 2016, https://lareviewofbooks.org/article/between-the-world-and-wakanda-ta-nehisi-coates-and-brian-stelfreezes-black-panther/.

26 *The Atlantic*, "Marvel's New Black Panther Comic | Q&A with Author Ta-Nehisi Coates," YouTube, August 9, 2016, https://www.youtube.com/watch?v=CRJ4URjtgxU.

27 Robert Reed, "Black Panther #169."

Chapter 9

1 Andrea Ayres, "Q&A with World of Wakanda's Roxane Gay—SDCC '17," *The Beat*, July 22, 2017, https://www.comicsbeat.com/qa-with-world-of-wakandas-roxane-gay-sdcc-17/.

2 Salamishah Tillet, "'Black Panther' Brings Hope, Hype and Pride," *The New York Times*, February 9, 2018, https://www.nytimes.com/2018/02/09/movies/black-panther-african-american-fans.html.

3 Anthony D'Alessandro, "'Black Panther: Wakanda Forever' Claws Way to No. 5 in *Deadline's* 2022 Most Valuable Blockbuster Tournament," *Deadline*, April 7, 2023, https://deadline.com/2023/04/black-panther-wakanda-forever-box-office-profits-1235320190/.

4 Terence McSweeney, *Black Panther: Interrogating a Cultural Phenomenon* (University Press of Mississippi, 2021), 4.

5 Lynn Stuart Parramore, "Why Does a White CIA Agent Play the Hero to Killmonger's Villain in 'Black Panther'?" *NBC News*, March 11, 2018, https://www.nbcnews.com/think/opinion/why-does-white-cia-agent-play-hero-killmonger-s-villain-ncna855401.

6   Susan Williams, *White Malice: The CIA and the Covert Recolonization of Africa* (Public Affairs, 2021).

7   Christopher Lebron, "*Black Panther* Is Not the Movie We Deserve," *Boston Review*, February 17, 2018, https://www.bostonreview.net/articles/christopher-lebron-black-panther/.

8   Christopher Orr, "Black Panther Is More than a Superhero Movie," *The Atlantic*, February 16, 2018, https://www.theatlantic.com/entertainment/archive/2018/02/black-panther-review/553508/.

9   Wesley Morris and Jenna Wortham, "Still Processing: We Sink Our Claws into 'Black Panther' with Ta-Nehisi Coates," *The New York Times*, March 16, 2018, https://www.nytimes.com/2018/03/16/podcasts/still-processing-we-sink-our-claws-into-black-panther-with-ta-nehisi-coates.html.

10   Lebron, "*Black Panther* Is Not the Movie We Deserve."

11   Ramin Setoodeh, "Chadwick Boseman and Ryan Coogler on How 'Black Panther' Makes History," *Variety*, February 5, 2018, https://variety.com/2018/film/features/black-panther-chadwick-boseman-ryan-coogler-interview-1202686402/.

12   "The Apollo and *The Atlantic* Present *Black Panther* in Conversation: Featuring Chadwick Boseman and Ta-Nehisi Coates," February 23, 2018, https://www.theatlantic.com/press-releases/archive/2018/02/the-apollo-and-the-atlantic-present-black-panther-in-conversation-featuring-chadwick-boseman-and-ta-nehisi-coates/554147/.

13   Ta-Nehisi Coates, "Why I'm Writing *Captain America*," *The Atlantic*, February 28, 2018, https://www.nytimes.com/2011/06/09/opinion/09coates.html.

14   Joseph Hughes, "Outrage Deferred: On the Lack of Black Writers in the Comic Book Industry," *Comics Alliance*, February 4, 2013, https://comicsalliance.com/black-writers-comic-book-industry/; Joseph Phillip Illidge, "The Color Barrier: A Message of Comics, Diversity and Hope," *CBR*, February 6, 2014, https://www.cbr.com/the-color-barrier-a-message-of-comics-diversity-hope/.

15   Coates, "Why I'm Writing *Captain America*."

16   Abraham Josephine Riesman, "Ta-Nehisi Coates Will Write Captain America for Marvel Comics," *Vulture*, February 28, 2018, https://www.vulture.com/2015/09/ta-nehisi-coates-black-panther.html.

17   Graeme McMillan, "Ta-Nehisi Coates Writing Captain America Comic Book Series," *The Hollywood Reporter*, February 28, 2018, https://www.hollywoodreporter.com/movies/movie-news/ta-nehisi-coates-writing-captain-america-comic-book-series-1089302/.

18   Jonah Engel Bromwich, "Ta-Nehisi Coates Will Write the Captain America Comic," *The New York Times*, February 28, 2018, https://www.nytimes.com/2018/02/28/books/ta-nehisi-coates-captain-america.html.

19   Susana Polo, "Ta-Nehisi Coates to Write Captain America, Starting on July 4," *Polygon*, February 28, 2018, https://www.polygon.com/comics/2018/2/28/17062320/ta-nehisi-coates-to-write-captain-america-starting-on-july-4/.

20   Coates, "Why I'm Writing *Captain America*."

21 George Gene Gustines, "Marvel Entertainment Names New Editor in Chief," *The New York Times*, November 17, 2017, https://www.nytimes.com/2017/11/17/books/marvel-entertainment-names-new-editor-in-chief.html.

22 Eliana Dockterman, "Behind Marvel's Decision to Create These Controversial Female Superheroes," *Time*, August 28, 2015, https://time.com/4014894/marvel-female-superheroes-thor-ms-marvel/.

23 David Walker, "Marvel Has Been Very Supportive…" Twitter, https://x.com/DavidWalker1201/status/769574503965863936.

24 Coates, "Why I'm Writing *Captain America*."

25 Claire Grossman, Stephanie Young, and Juliana Spahr, "Who Gets to Be a Writer?" *Public Books*, April 15, 2021; Grossman, Spahr, and Young, "Literature's Vexed Democratization," *American Literary History* 33, no. 2 (Summer 2021): 298–319, https://muse.jhu.edu/pub/8/article/797935; Spahr and Young, "On Poets and Prizes," *ASAP Journal*, November 11, 2020, https://asapjournal.com/feature/on-poets-and-prizes-juliana-spahr-and-stephanie-young/; Spahr and Young, "The Program Era and the Mainly White Room," *Los Angeles Review of Books,* September 20, 2015, https://lareviewofbooks.org/article/the-program-era-and-the-mainly-white-room/.

26 Spahr and Young, "On Poets and Prizes."

27 Coates, "Why I'm Writing *Captain America*."

28 Coates, "Why I'm Writing *Captain America*."

29 Ta-Nehisi Coates, "Dwayne McDuffie, the Icon," *The Atlantic*, February 24, 2011, https://www.theatlantic.com/entertainment/archive/2011/02/dwayne-mcduffie-the-icon/71652/.

30 Coates, "Why I'm Writing *Captain America*."

31 "Top 500 Comics—July 2018," *ICv2*, August 13, 2018, https://icv2.com/articles/news/view/41125/top-500-comics-july-2018.

32 John Jackson Miller, "2018 Comic Book Sales to Comics Shops," *Comichron*, May 30, 2018, https://www.comichron.com/monthlycomicssales/2018/2018-05.html.

33 In May 2018, Marvel rebooted its numbering for several titles, including *Black Panther* #1.

34 David Betancourt, "Ta-Nehisi Coates Writes a 'Captain America' Filled with Star-Spangled Doubt," *The Washington Post*, July 4, 2018, https://www.washingtonpost.com/news/comic-riffs/wp/2018/07/04/ta-nehisi-coates-writes-a-captain-america-filled-with-star-spangled-doubt/.

35 Brett Schenker, "Review: Captain America #1," *Graphic Policy*, July 4, 2018, https://graphicpolicy.com/2018/07/04/review-captain-america-1-2/.

36 Justin Partridge, "CAPTAIN AMERICA #1 'a Triumph for One of Marvel's A-Listers,'" https://www.newsarama.com/40652-best-shots-review-captain-america-1.html.

37 Jesse Schedeen, "Marvel's Captain America Relaunch Shows Promise (Captain America #1 Review)," *IGN*, July 4, 2018, https://www.ign.com/articles/2018/07/04/marvels-captain-america-relaunch-shows-promise-captain-america-1-review.

38   Keith Reid-Cleveland, "Captain America #1 Review," *Black Nerd Problems*, July 5, 2018, https://blacknerdproblems.com/captain-america-1-review/.

39   Gavia Baker-Whitelaw, "'Captain America #1' Offers a Grim View of America in 2018," *Daily Dot*, July 4, 2018, https://www.dailydot.com/news/captain-america-1-2018-review/.

40   Coates, "Why I'm Writing *Captain America*."

41   Kwame Opam, "Captain America No. 1, by Ta-Nehisi Coates, Annotated," *The New York Times*, July 4, 2018, https://www.nytimes.com/2018/07/04/books/captain-america-ta-nehisi-coates-annotated.html.

42   Quoted in Danielle Taylor-Guthrie (Ed.), *Conversations with Toni Morrison* (University Press of Mississippi, 1994), 67.

43   Susana Polo, "Marvel Comics Announces Line-Wide Relaunch 'Fresh Start,'" *Polygon*, February 20, 2018, https://www.polygon.com/comics/2018/2/20/17031924/marvel-fresh-start-relaunch-announcement/.

44   Robot Overlord, "[Solicitations] Marvel Comics for May 2018," *Major Spoilers*, February 22, 2018, https://majorspoilers.com/2018/02/22/solicitations-marvel-comics-may-2018/.

45   Charles Nicholas Raymond, "Marvel's Latest Relaunch Sends Black Panther into Space," *Screen Rant*, February 21, 2018, https://screenrant.com/black-panther-marvel-comics-relaunch-space/.

Chapter 10

1   "#BlackPantherApollo: Chadwick Boseman, Lupita Nyong'o and Ta-Nehisi Coates," Apollo Theater. *Facebook*, March 2, 2018, https://www.facebook.com/ApolloTheater/videos/blackpantherapollo-chadwick-boseman-lupita-nyongo-and-ta-nehisi-coates/10155079109361050/.

2   Andy Beta, "10 Things We Learned at Ta-Nehisi Coates' 'Black Panther' Cast Talk," *Rolling Stone*, February 28, 2018, https://www.rollingstone.com/tv-movies/tv-movie-news/10-things-we-learned-at-ta-nehisi-coates-black-panther-cast-talk-204025/; Jake Nevins, "Ta-Nehisi Coates to Write Marvel's New Captain America Comics," *The Guardian*, February 28, 2018, https://www.theguardian.com/books/2018/feb/28/ta-nehisi-coates-to-write-marvels-new-captain-america-comics.

3   Steven Thrasher, "There Is Much to Celebrate–and Much to Question–About Marvel's Black Panther," *Esquire*, February 20, 2018, https://www.esquire.com/entertainment/movies/a18241993/black-panther-review-politics-killmonger/.

4   Andy Beta, "10 Things We Learned at Ta-Nehisi Coates' 'Black Panther' Cast Talk."

5   Nevins, "Ta-Nehisi Coates to Write Marvel's New Captain America Comics."

6   Josh Sykes, "Review—Black Panther #16 (Marvel Comics)," *Word of the Nerd*, September 27, 2019, https://web.archive.org/web/20200928140946/https://wordofthenerdonline.com/review-black-panther-16-marvel-comics/; Charles Martin, "Black Panther #22 Review," *Comics: The Gathering*, March 25, 2020, http://www.comicsthegathering.com/review/charles-martin/13847/black-panther-22-review;

David Brooke, "'Black Panther Book 9: The Intergalactic Empire of Wakanda,' Review," *AIPT Comics*, July 7, 2021, https://aiptcomics.com/2021/07/07/black-panther-book-9-the-intergalactic-empire-of-wakanda-review/; Matthew Peterson, "Black Panther #25 Review," *Major Spoilers*, June 1, 2021, https://majorspoilers.com/2021/12/28/black-panther-2-review-2/; Oz Longworth, "Black Panther #25 Review," *Black Nerd Problems*, May 28, 2021, https://blacknerdproblems.com/black-panther-25-review/.

7   Kieran Shiach, "Marvel Legacy: Jason Aaron Explains THAT Black Panther Revelation," *Comic Book Resources*, September 27, 2017, https://www.cbr.com/marvel-legacy-jason-aaron-explains-that-black-panther-revelation/.

8   Jonathan Hickman, *New Avengers* #1 (January 2013).

9   Jonathan Hickman, *Secret Wars* #9 (January 2016).

10   Jason Aaron, *Marvel Legacy* #1 (September 2017).

11   Ta-Nehisi Coates, *Black Panther* #1 (May 2018).

12   Frederick Douglass, *Narrative of the Life of Frederick Douglass*, 1845 rpt. (Barnes & Noble Classics, 2003), 64.

13   Deron Generally, "Black Panther #1 Review," *The Super Powered Fancast*, May 23, 2018, https://www.superpoweredfancast.com/black-panther-1-review/.

14   Logan Dalton, "Review: Black Panther #1," *Graphic Policy*, May 27, 2018, https://graphicpolicy.com/2018/05/27/review-black-panther-1-4/.

15   Charles Martin, "Black Panther #1 Review," *Comics: The Gathering*, May 23, 2018, http://www.comicsthegathering.com/review/charles-martin/11624/black-panther-1-review.

16   John Jackson Miller, "May 2018 Comic Book Sales to Comics Shops," *Comichron*, January 2019, https://www.comichron.com/monthlycomicssales/2018.html.

17   Miller, "2018 Comic Book Sales to Comics Shops."

18   Anthony Composto, "Black Panther Meets Star Wars in 'The Intergalactic Empire of Wakanda,'" *Monkeys Fighting Robots*, January 20, 2019, https://monkeysfightingrobots.co/black-panther-meets-star-wars-in-the-intergalactic-empire-of-wakanda/.

19   Ta-Nehisi Coates, *Black Panther* #2 (2018).

20   Matthew Peterson, "Black Panther #2 Review," *Major Spoilers*, July 3, 2018, https://majorspoilers.com/2021/06/01/black-panther-25-review/.

21   Robert Reed, "Best Shots Review: Black Panther #2's Acuna 'Gives the Book an Epic Quality,'" July 2, 2018.

22   Adam Bradley, "The Black Nerds Redefining the Culture," *The New York Times*, March 24, 2021, https://www.nytimes.com/2021/03/24/t-magazine/black-nerds-culture.html.

23   Nisi Shawl, "A Crash Course in the History of Black Science Fiction," *Nisi Shawl*, December 1, 2018, http://www.nisishawl.com/CCHBSF.html.

24   Ta-Nehisi Coates, *Black Panther* #7 (December 2018).

25 Daniel Stein, "Ta-Nehisi Coates's *Black Panther* and Afrodiasporic Archives," *Amerikastudien / American Studies* 67, no. 2 (2022): 135–36, https://amst.winter-verlag.de/article/amst/2022/2/5

26 Ta-Nehisi Coates, "We Have Received Provocation Enough," *The Atlantic*, August 11, 2010, https://www.theatlantic.com/national/archive/2010/08/we-have-received-provocation-enough/61276/.

27 Ta-Nehisi Coates, "The Case for Reparations," *The Atlantic*, June 2014, https://www.theatlantic.com/magazine/archive/2014/06/the-case-for-reparations/361631/

28 Ta-Nehisi Coates, "Of Plunder and the Killing Fields," *Literary Hub*, July 16, 2015, https://lithub.com/ta-nehisi-coates-of-plunder-and-the-killing-fields/; Coates, "The Plunder of Black Life Was Drilled into This Country in Its Infancy," *Truthout*, August 19, 2015, https://truthout.org/articles/ta-nehisi-coates-the-plunder-of-black-life-was-drilled-into-this-country-in-its-infancy/.

29 Ta-Nehisi Coates, "The First White President," *The Atlantic*, October 2017, https://www.theatlantic.com/magazine/archive/2017/10/the-first-white-president-ta-nehisi-coates/537909/.

30 Ta-Nehisi Coates, *Black Panther* #1 (May 2018).

31 Ta-Nehisi Coates, *Black Panther* #6 (November 2018).

32 Ta-Nehisi Coates, *Black Panther* #16 (September 25, 2019).

33 Ta-Nehisi Coates, *Black Panther* #19 (December 18, 2019); Coates, *Black Panther* #20 (January 2020).

34 Trevor Richardson, "Black Panther #1 (2018) Review," *AIPT*, May 23, 2018, https://aiptcomics.com/2018/05/23/black-panther-1-2018-review/.

35 Ta-Nehisi Coates, *Black Panther* #8 (January 2019).

36 Matthew Peterson, "Black Panther #25 Review," *Major Spoilers*, June 1, 2021, https://majorspoilers.com/2021/12/28/black-panther-2-review-2/.

37 Evan Narcisse, "'The Miracle Is Wakanda': Ta-Nehisi Coates Says Goodbye to Black Panther," *Polygon*, May 26, 2021, https://www.polygon.com/interviews/22454722/black-panther-comics-ending-ta-nehisi-coates-interview/.

38 Ta-Nehisi Coates, *Black Panther* #5 (October 2018).

39 Chase Magnett, "Black Panther #19," *ComicBook.com*, December 18, 2019, https://comicbook.com/comics/news/new-comic-reviews-dc-marvel-image-302578/#:~:text=BLACK%20PANTHER%20%2319,%E2%80%94%20Chase%20Magnett.

40 Ethan Alexander, "Chadwick Boseman: Ta-Nehisi Coates Honors the Actor in This Week's Marvel Comics," *Comic Book Resources*, October 1, 2020, https://www.cbr.com/chadwick-boseman-ta-nehisi-coates-tribute-marvel-comics/.

41 Ta-Nehisi Coates, *Black Panther* #24 (March 2021); Coates, *Black Panther* #25 (May 2021).

Conclusion

1 Trey Mangum, "Ta-Nehisi Coates to Write Upcoming Superman Film from DC and Warner Bros," *Blavity*, February 26, 2021, https://blavity.com/entertainment/ta-nehisi-coates-superman-dc-warner-bros-film.

2 Chancellor Agard, "Ta-Nehisi Coates Tapped to Write New Superman Movie Produced by J.J. Abrams," *Entertainment Weekly,* February 26, 2021, https://ew.com/movies/ta-nehisi-coates-write-superman-movie/; Petrana Radulovic, "Superman Movie Reboot in Works with Ta-Nehisi Coates, J.J. Abrams," *Polygon*, February 26, 2021, https://www.polygon.com/movies/2021/2/26/22303271/superman-movie-reboot-ta-nehisi-coates-jj-abrams/; Matt Singer, "A New 'Superman' Is Coming from J.J. Abrams and Ta-Nehisi Coates," *ScreenCrush*, February 26, 2021, https://screencrush.com/superman-film-j-j-abrams-ta-nehisi-coates/.

3 Joanna Robinson, "Why Ta-Nahesi [*sic*] Coates Is Such a Strong Choice for Superman," *Vanity Fair*, February 26, 2021, https://www.vanityfair.com/hollywood/2021/02/superman-ta-nehisi-coates-jj-abrams.

4 Borys Kit and Aaron Couch, "Ta-Nehisi Coates to Write New Superman Movie for Warner Bros," *The Hollywood Reporter*, February 26, 2021, https://www.hollywoodreporter.com/movies/movie-news/ta-nehisi-coates-to-write-new-superman-movie-for-warner-bros-4139376/.

5 Justin Carter, "Why Ta-Nehisi Coates' Possible Black Superman Is So Exciting [And, Honestly, Expected]," *Syfy*, March 4, 2021, https://www.syfy.com/syfy-wire/black-superman-movie-ta-nehisi-coates; Eric Switzer, "The DCEU's Black Superman Movie Should Follow the Comics and Make Him the President," *The Gamer*, March 1, 2021, https://www.thegamer.com/black-superman-president-calvin-ellis-dceu-bad-robot-movie/.

6 Rich Johnston, "Warner Bros Black Superman Movie Sees DC Comics eBay Sales Explodes," *Bleeding Cool*, December 11, 2016, https://bleedingcool.com/comics/2016s-top-ten-comics-by-sales-in-the-direct-market/.

7 Evan Narcisse, "Spoiler Space: More from Ta-Nehisi Coates on Black Panther," *Kotaku*, April 6, 2016, https://kotaku.com/spoiler-space-more-from-ta-nehisi-coates-on-black-pant-1769472432.

8 Evan Narcisse, "'The Miracle Is Wakanda': Ta-Nehisi Coates Says Goodbye to Black Panther," *Polygon*, May 26, 2021, https://www.polygon.com/interviews/22454722/black-panther-comics-ending-ta-nehisi-coates-interview/.

9 Narcisse, "'The Miracle Is Wakanda.'"

10 Robert Wood, "Black Panther Writer Criticizes Marvel's Treatment of Comic Creators," *Screen Rant*, May 27, 2021, https://screenrant.com/ta-nehisi-coates-black-panther-criticize-marvel-disney/.

11 Charles Pulliam-Moore, "Black Panther Writer Ta-Nehisi Coates Wants Better for Creators Bringing These Stories to Life," *Gizmodo*, May 28, 2021, https://gizmodo.com/black-panther-writer-ta-nehisi-coates-wants-better-for-1846994018.

12 JB Augustine, "Captain America Writer Ed Brubaker and More Say DC and Marvel Still Not Paying Creators Royalties for Movies Based on Their Work," *Bounding into Comics*, August 19, 2021, https://boundingintocomics.com/comic-books/captain-america-writer-ed-brubaker-and-more-say-dc-and-marvel-still-not-paying-creators-royalties-for-movies-based-on-their-work/.

13 Evan Narcisse, "Introduction," *Wakanda: World of Black Panther Omnibus* (Marvel Entertainment, 2022), 4.

14 Robert Iger, *The Ride of a Lifetime: Lessons Learned from 15 Years as CEO of the Walt Disney Company* (Random House, 2019), 169.

15 Aurelien Breeden, "France Gave Teenagers $350 for Culture. They're Buying Comic Books," *The New York Times*, July 28, 2021, https://www.nytimes.com/2021/07/28/arts/france-culture-pass.html.

16 Howard Rambsy II, "The Coverage of Colson Whitehead's The Underground Railroad," *Cultural Front*, August 3, 2016, https://www.culturalfront.org/search?q=underground+railroad.

17 Joseph Hughes, "Outrage Deferred: On the Lack of Black Writers in the Comic Book Industry," *Comics Alliance*, February 4, 2013, https://comicsalliance.com/black-writers-comic-book-industry/; Heidi MacDonald, "Why Aren"t There More Black Writers in the Comics Industry?," The Beat, February 5, 2013, https://www.comicsbeat.com/why-arent-there-more-black-writers-in-the-comics-industry/; Joseph Phillip Illidge, "The Color Barrier: A Message of Comics, Diversity and Hope," *CBR*, February 6, 2014, https://www.cbr.com/the-color-barrier-a-message-of-comics-diversity-hope/; J. A. Micheline, "The White Privilege, White Audacity, and White Priorities of STRANGE FRUIT #1," *Women Write About Comics*, July 8, 2015, https://womenwriteaboutcomics.com/2015/07/the-white-privilege-white-audacity-and-white-priorities-of-strange-fruit-1/.

18 Narcisse, "Spoiler Space."

19 Narcisse, "'The Miracle Is Wakanda.'"

20 Ta-Nehisi Coates, *Black Panther* #1 (May 2018).

Bibliography

"The 2010s' Top 100 Best-Selling Comics." Previews World, January 13, 2020. https://previewsworld.com/Article/238869-Exclusive-The-2010s-Top-100-Best-Selling-Comics.

Aaron, Jason. *Marvel Legacy* #1. Marvel Comics, September 27, 2017.

Abad-Santos, Alex. "The 7 Best New Comics of 2016." *Vox*, December 21, 2016. https://www.vox.com/culture/2016/12/21/13919580/best-new-comics-2016.

Abad-Santos, Alex. "Black Panther by Ta-Nehisi Coates and Brian Stelfreeze Is Brilliant, Political, and Human." *Vox*, April 6, 2016. https://www.vox.com/2016/4/5/11362636/black-panther-tanehisi-coates-review.

Abad-Santos, Alex. "Marvel Canceled Roxane Gay and Ta-Nehisi Coates's *Black Panther* Comics. The Problem Goes Beyond Marvel." *Vox*, June 16, 2017. https://www.vox.com/culture/2017/6/16/15804600/marvel-cancel-roxane-gay-ta-nehisi-coates-comic.

Abad-Santos, Alex. "The Outrage over Marvel's Alleged Diversity Blaming, Explained." *Vox*, April 8, 2017. https://www.vox.com/culture/2017/4/4/15169572/marvel-diversity-outrage-gabriel.

Abad-Santos, Alex. "Ta-Nehisi Coates Will Be Writing Marvel's Black Panther Comic Book." *Vox*, September 22, 2015. https://www.vox.com/2015/9/22/9373185/coates-black-panther.

Adams, Tim. "Marvel Exec Clarifies Comments That 'People Didn't Want Any More Diversity.'" *CBR*, April 1, 2017. https://www.cbr.com/marvel-sales-diversity/.

Agard, Chancellor, and Christian Holub. "The Best Comic Books of 2016." *Entertainment Weekly*, December 20, 2016. https://ew.com/gallery/best-comic-books-2016/.

Agard, Chancellor, and Christian Holub. "Ta-Nehisi Coates Tapped to Write New Superman Movie Produced by J.J. Abrams." *Entertainment Weekly*, February 26, 2021. https://ew.com/movies/ta-nehisi-coates-write-superman-movie/.

Alexander, Ethan. "Chadwick Boseman: Ta-Nehisi Coates Honors the Actor in This Week's Marvel Comics." *Comic Book Resources*, October 1, 2020. https://www.cbr.com/chadwick-boseman-ta-nehisi-coates-tribute-marvel-comics/.

"The Apollo and *The Atlantic* Present Black Panther in Conversation: Featuring Chadwick Boseman and Ta-Nehisi Coates." February 23, 2018. https://www.theatlantic.com/press-releases/archive/2018/02/the-apollo-and-the-atlantic-present-black-panther-in-conversation-featuring-chadwick-boseman-and-ta-nehisi-coates/554147/.

Armitage, Hugh. "Marvel Gets It Right by Hiring African American Journalist Ta-Nehisi Coates to Write Black Panther Comic." *Digital Spy*, September 23, 2015. https://www.digitalspy.com/comics/a670028/marvel-gets-it-right-by-hiring-african-american-journalist-ta-nehisi-coates-to-write-black-panther-comic/.

The Atlantic. "Marvel's New *Black Panther* Comic | Q&A with Author Ta-Nehisi Coates." YouTube, August 9, 2016. https://www.youtube.com/watch?v=CRJ4URjtgxU.

Augustine, JB. "Captain America Writer Ed Brubaker and More Say DC and Marvel Still Not Paying Creators Royalties for Movies Based on Their Work." *Bounding into Comics*, August 19, 2021. https://boundingintocomics.com/comic-books/captain-america-writer-ed-brubaker-and-more-say-dc-and-marvel-still-not-paying-creators-royalties-for-movies-based-on-their-work/.

Ayres, Andrea. "Q&A with *World of Wakanda*'s Roxane Gay—SDCC '17." *The Beat*, July 22, 2017. https://www.comicsbeat.com/qa-with-world-of-wakandas-roxane-gay-sdcc-17/.

Bakare, Lanre. "Ta-Nehisi Coates to Write Marvel's Black Panther Comic." *The Guardian*, September 22, 2015. https://www.theguardian.com/books/2015/sep/22/ta-nehisi-coates-to-write-marvels-black-panther-comic.

Baker-Whitelaw, Gavia. "The 9 Best Comics We Read in 2016." *The Daily Dot*, December 25, 2016. https://www.dailydot.com/unclick/best-superhero-sci-fi-comics-2016/.

Baker-Whitelaw, Gavia. "'Captain America #1' Offers a Grim View of America in 2018." *Daily Dot*, July 4, 2018. https://www.dailydot.com/news/captain-america-1-2018-review/.

Baraka, Amiri. "Digging Max." *Digging: The Afro-American Soul of American Classical Music*. Berkeley: University of California Press, 2009, 217–18.

Baraka, Amiri. "Dope". *The Amiri Baraka Reader*, ed. by William J. Harris, 263–66. Thunder's Mouth Press, 1991.

Baraka, Amiri. "Dope." YouTube, October 2, 2009. https://www.youtube.com/watch?v=qJ89lZDBDR4.

Bartley, Sean. "Black Panther #1." *Comics Verse*, April 7, 2016. http://comicsverse.com/black-panther-1-review-wakanda-fire/.

Bausells, Marta. "Book Cover Clichés: Have You Spotted Recurrent Designs?" *The Guardian*, June 12, 2014. https://www.theguardian.com/books/booksblog/2014/jun/12/book-cover-cliches-have-you-spotted-recurrent-designs.

Bausells, Marta. "Dope." *The LeRoi Jones/Amiri Baraka Reader*, ed. by William J. Harris. New York: Thunder's Mouth Press, 1991, 263–66.

Berlatsky, Noah. "I Should Apologize to Marvel Too, I Should Have Credited Them w/ Making an Effort to Address the Legacy of Hip Hop, There." Twitter, July 21, 2015. https://twitter.com/nberlat/status/623547833262542850.

Berlatsky, Noah. "Marvel's Hip-Hop Tribute Embraces Black Metaphors but Excludes Black People." *The Guardian*, July 20, 2015. https://www.theguardian.com/music/2015/jul/20/marvel-hip-hop-tribute-classic-albums.

Berry, Elizabeth Méndez, and Chi-hui Yang, "The Dominance of the White Male Critic." *The New York Times*, July 5, 2019. https://www.nytimes.com/2019/07/05/opinion/sunday/we-need-more-critics-of-color.html.

Beta, Andy. "10 Things We Learned at Ta-Nehisi Coates' 'Black Panther' Cast Talk." *Rolling Stone*, February 28, 2018. https://www.rollingstone.com/tv-movies/tv-movie-news/10-things-we-learned-at-ta-nehisi-coates-black-panther-cast-talk-204025/.

Betancourt, David. "Marvel Was Smart to Hire Coates to Write Black Panther. Here's Why." *The Washington Post*, September 23, 2015. https://www.washingtonpost.

com/news/comic-riffs/wp/2015/09/23/heres-why-marvel-comics-is-smart-to-hire-ta-nehisi-coates-to-write-black-panther/.

Betancourt, David. "Ta-Nehisi Coates's New Black Panther Comic Provides a Debut Fit for a King." *The Washington Post*, April 6, 2016. https://www.washingtonpost.com/news/comic-riffs/wp/2016/04/06/ta-nehisi-coatess-new-black-panther-comic-provides-a-debut-fit-for-a-king/.

Betancourt, David. "Ta-Nehisi Coates Writes a 'Captain America' Filled with Star-Spangled Doubt." *The Washington Post*, July 4, 2018. https://www.washingtonpost.com/news/comic-riffs/wp/2018/07/04/ta-nehisi-coates-writes-a-captain-america-filled-with-star-spangled-doubt/.

Betancourt, David. "What Marvel Canceling Nighthawk Means for Superheroes of Color." *The Washington Post*, September 8, 2016. https://www.washingtonpost.com/news/comic-riffs/wp/2016/09/08/what-marvel-canceling-nighthawk-means-for-superheroes-of-color/.

Betts, Tara. "The Luke Cage Syllabus: A Breakdown of All the Black Literature Featured in Netflix's Luke Cage." *Black Nerd Problems*, October 4, 2016. https://blacknerdproblems.com/the-luke-cage-syllabus-a-breakdown-of-all-the-black-literature-featured-in-netflixs-luke-cage/.

Black American Literature Forum. Special issue on Henry Dumas (Summer 1988), https://www.jstor.org/stable/i346164.

"Black Panther Interior by Laura Martin—Marvel Quickdraw." YouTube, May 4, 2017. https://www.youtube.com/watch?v=MgncgjMunBA.

"#BlackPantherApollo: Chadwick Boseman, Lupita Nyong'o and Ta-Nehisi Coates." Apollo Theater. Facebook, March 2, 2018. https://www.facebook.com/ApolloTheater/videos/blackpantherapollo-chadwick-boseman-lupita-nyongo-and-ta-nehisi-coates/10155079109361050/.

Bradley, Adam. "The Black Nerds Redefining the Culture." *The New York Times*, March 24, 2021. https://www.nytimes.com/2021/03/24/t-magazine/black-nerds-culture.html.

Breeden, Aurelien. "France Gave Teenagers $350 for Culture. They're Buying Comic Books." *The New York Times*, July 28, 2021. https://www.nytimes.com/2021/07/28/arts/france-culture-pass.html.

Brevoort, Tom. "@tanehisicoates Heard That You Had an Interest in Writing Something for Marvel. Let's Talk! tbrevoort@marvel.com." Twitter, May 21, 2015. https://twitter.com/TomBrevoort/status/601403701740359680?ref_src=twsrc%5Etfw.

Brinker, Amy. "An Oral History of *Between the World and Me*." Penguin Random House, November 12, 2020. https://www.penguinrandomhouse.com/articles/an-oral-history-of-between-the-world-and-me/.

Bromwich, Jonah Engel. "Ta-Nehisi Coates Will Write the Captain America Comic." *The New York Times*, February 28, 2018. https://www.nytimes.com/2018/02/28/books/ta-nehisi-coates-captain-america.html.

Brooke, David. "'Black Panther Book 9: The Intergalactic Empire of Wakanda,' Review." *AIPT Comics*, July 7, 2021. https://aiptcomics.com/2021/07/07/black-panther-book-9-the-intergalactic-empire-of-wakanda-review/.

Brown, Alex. "Let's Talk About Marvel Comics, the 'Diversity Doesn't Sell' Myth, and What Diversity Really Means." *Reactor*, April 5, 2017. https://reactormag.com/lets-talk-about-marvel-comics-the-diversity-doesnt-sell-myth-and-what-diversity-really-means/.

Brown, Jeffrey A. *Black Superheroes, Milestone Comics, and Their Fans*. Jackson: University Press of Mississippi, 2001.

Brown, Jeffrey A. *Panthers, Hulks and Ironhearts: Marvel, Diversity, and the 21st Century Superhero*. New Brunswick, NJ: Rutgers University Press, 2021.

Burroughs, Todd Steven. "Black Panther, Black Writers, White Audience: Christopher Priest and/vs. Reginald Hudlin." *Fire!!!* 4, no. 2. (Fall 2018): 55–93. https://www.jstor.org/stable/10.5323/fire.4.2.0055.

Cardona, Ian. "What Is the Djalia? Black Panther's Mystical Realm, Explained." *Comic Book Resources*, October 18, 2017. https://www.cbr.com/black-panther-djalia-explained/.

Carrington, André M. *Speculative Blackness: The Future of Race in Science Fiction*. Minneapolis: University of Minnesota Press, 2016.

Carter, Justin. "Why Ta-Nehisi Coates' Possible Black Superman Is So Exciting [And, Honestly, Expected]." *Syfy*, March 4, 2021. https://www.syfy.com/syfy-wire/black-superman-movie-ta-nehisi-coates.

CBR Staff. "Storm Series from Coates and Bartel Not Currently in the Works." *CBR*, June 5, 2018. https://www.cbr.com/storm-coates-bartel-no-plans/.

Chambliss, Julian C., William L. Svitavsky, and Daniel Fandino Eds., *Assembling the Marvel Cinematic Universe: Essays on the Social, Cultural and Geopolitical Domains*. Jefferson, NC: McFarland, 2018.

Charles. "@richjohnston Can We Go Ahead & Call This 'Mystery' Solved?" Twitter, July 31, 2015. https://twitter.com/ChuckSydnor/status/627249617927671808.

Ching, Albert. "Course-Correcting Diversity Problems, Bendis' Iron Man Expansion." *CBR*, July 31, 2015. https://www.cbr.com/course-correcting-diversity-problems-bendis-iron-man-expansion/.

Ching, Albert. "Waid Responds to *Strange Fruit* Controversy: 'What I Say About This Is Not What's Important.'" *CBR*, July 20, 2015. https://www.cbr.com/waid-responds-to-strange-fruit-controversy-what-i-say-about-this-is-not-whats-important/.

Coates, Ta-Nehisi. *The Beautiful Struggle: A Father, Two Sons, and an Unlikely Road to Manhood*. New York: Spiegel & Grau, 2008.

Coates, Ta-Nehisi. *Between the World and Me*. Spiegel & Grau, 2015.

Coates, Ta-Nehisi. "The Black Journalist and the Racial Mountain." *The Atlantic*, June 2, 2016. https://www.theatlantic.com/politics/archive/2016/06/black-journalist-and-the-racist-mountain/484808/.

Coates, Ta-Nehisi. "Building the World of Wakanda." *The Atlantic*, April 22, 2016. https://www.theatlantic.com/culture/archive/2016/04/the-world-of-wakanda/624241/.

Coates, Ta-Nehisi. "The Case for Reparations." *The Atlantic*, June 2014. https://www.theatlantic.com/magazine/archive/2014/06/the-case-for-reparations/361631/.

Coates, Ta-Nehisi. "Conceptualizing the Black Panther." *The Atlantic*, December 2, 2016. https://www.theatlantic.com/culture/archive/2015/12/conceptualizing-the-black-panther/625627/.

Coates, Ta-Nehisi. "Dwayne McDuffie, the Icon." *The Atlantic*, February 24, 2011. https://www.theatlantic.com/entertainment/archive/2011/02/dwayne-mcduffie-the-icon/71652/.

Coates, Ta-Nehisi. "Fear of a Black President." *The Atlantic*, May 2012. https://www.theatlantic.com/magazine/archive/2012/09/fear-of-a-black-president/309064/.

Coates, Ta-Nehisi. "The Feminists of Wakanda." *The Atlantic*, April 8, 2016. https://www.theatlantic.com/culture/archive/2016/04/the-feminists-of-wakanda/624392/.

Coates, Ta-Nehisi. "The First White President." *The Atlantic*, October 2017. https://www.theatlantic.com/magazine/archive/2017/10/the-first-white-president-ta-nehisi-coates/537909/.

Coates, Ta-Nehisi. "He Wears the Mask Just to Cover the Raw Flesh." *The Atlantic*, December 16, 2010. https://www.theatlantic.com/entertainment/archive/2010/12/he-wears-the-mask-just-to-cover-the-raw-flesh/68108/.

Coates, Ta-Nehisi. "How Racism Invented Race in America." *The Atlantic*, June 23, 2014. https://www.theatlantic.com/politics/archive/2014/06/the-case-for-reparations-a-narrative-bibliography/372000/.

Coates, Ta-Nehisi. "The Legacy of Malcolm X." *The Atlantic*, May 2011. https://www.theatlantic.com/magazine/archive/2011/05/the-legacy-of-malcolm-x/308438/.

Coates, Ta-Nehisi. "The Mask of Doom." *The New Yorker*, September 14, 2009. https://www.newyorker.com/magazine/2009/09/21/the-mask-of-doom.

Coates, Ta-Nehisi. "My President Was Black." *The Atlantic*, January/February 2017. https://www.theatlantic.com/magazine/archive/2017/01/my-president-was-black/508793/.

Coates, Ta-Nehisi. "Of Plunder and the Killing Fields." *Literary Hub*, July 16, 2015. https://lithub.com/ta-nehisi-coates-of-plunder-and-the-killing-fields/.

Coates, Ta-Nehisi. "The Plunder of Black Life Was Drilled into This Country in Its Infancy." *Truthout*, August 19, 2015.

Coates, Ta-Nehisi. "The Return of the Black Panther." *The Atlantic*, April 2016. https://www.theatlantic.com/magazine/archive/2016/04/the-return-of-the-black-panther/471516/.

Coates, Ta-Nehisi. "'This Is How We Lost to the White Man': The Audacity of Bill Cosby's Black Conservatism." *The Atlantic*, May 2008. https://www.theatlantic.com/magazine/archive/2008/05/-this-is-how-we-lost-to-the-white-man/306774/.

Coates, Ta-Nehisi. "Wakanda and the Black Aesthetic." *The Atlantic*, June 29, 2016. https://www.theatlantic.com/culture/archive/2016/06/wakanda-and-the-black-aesthetic/623664/.

Coates, Ta-Nehisi. "WalMart and the Civil War." *The Atlantic*, January/February 2010. https://www.theatlantic.com/magazine/archive/2010/01/walmart-and-the-civil-war/307826/.

Coates, Ta-Nehisi. *The Water Dancer*. New York: One World, 2019.

Coates, Ta-Nehisi. "'We Have Received Provocation Enough.'" *The Atlantic*, August 11, 2010. https://www.theatlantic.com/national/archive/2010/08/we-have-received-provocation-enough/61276/.

Coates, Ta-Nehisi. *We Were Eight Years in Power: An American Tragedy*. New York: One World, 2017.

Coates, Ta-Nehisi. "What If Captain America Were Muslim and Female / New York Ideas 2015." Interview with Sana Amanat. YouTube, May 21, 2015. https://www.youtube.com/watch?v=2Y1ihwPplL4.

Coates, Ta-Nehisi. "Why I'm Writing *Captain America*." *The Atlantic*, February 28, 2018. https://www.nytimes.com/2011/06/09/opinion/09coates.html.

Coates, Ta-Nehisi. "You Left Out the Part About... " *The New York Times*, June 8, 2011. https://www.nytimes.com/2011/06/09/opinion/09coates.html.

Coates, Ta-Nehisi and Brian Stelfreeze. *Black Panther Vol. 1: A Nation Under Our Feet*. New York: Marvel Universe, 2017.

Coates, Ta-Nehisi and Chris Sprouse. *Black Panther Vol. 2: Avengers of the New World*. New York: Marvel Universe, 2018.

Coates, Ta-Nehisi, Chris Sprouse, and Brian Stelfreeze. *Black Panther Vol. 3: The Intergalactic Empire of Wakanda*. New York: Marvel Universe, 2020.

Coates, Ta-Nehisi, Wilfredo Torres, and Chris Sprouse. *Black Panther Vol. 4: The Intergalactic Empire of Wakanda*. New York: Marvel Universe, 2022.

Cobb, Jelani. "Creating 'Luke Cage,' the First Woke Black-Superhero Show." *The New Yorker*, October 5, 2016. https://www.newyorker.com/culture/culture-desk/creating-luke-cage-the-first-woke-black-superhero-show.

Cocca, Carolyn. *Superwomen: Gender, Power, and Representation*. Bloomsbury, 2016.

Composto, Anthony. "Black Panther Meets Star Wars in 'The Intergalactic Empire of Wakanda'." *Monkeys Fighting Robots*, January 20, 2019. https://monkeysfightingrobots.co/black-panther-meets-star-wars-in-the-intergalactic-empire-of-wakanda/.

Concepcion, Jason. "Ta-Nehisi Coates Is Writing the 'Black Panther' Comic for Marvel." *Grantland*, September 23, 2015. https://grantland.com/hollywood-prospectus/ta-nehisi-coates-is-writing-the-black-panther-comic-for-marvel/.

Cronin, Brian. "Number Ones: The Most Important #1 Issues 2010–Today." *CBR*, November 19, 2016. https://www.cbr.com/15-most-important-1-issues-of-the-current-decade-2010-now/.

D, Pauly. "Everything You Want to Know About Black Panther." *Pop Culture Uncovered*, May 5, 2016. https://popcultureuncovered.com/2016/05/05/everything-you-want-to-know-about-black-panther/.

D'Alessandro, Anthony. "'Black Panther: Wakanda Forever' Claws Way to No. 5 in *Deadline*'s 2022 Most Valuable Blockbuster Tournament." *Deadline*, April 7, 2023. https://deadline.com/2023/04/black-panther-wakanda-forever-box-office-profits-1235320190/.

Dalton, Logan. "Review: *Black Panther* #1." *Graphic Policy*, May 27, 2018. https://graphicpolicy.com/2018/05/27/review-black-panther-1-4/.

Danielle, Britni. "In Ta-Nehisi Coates' New Book, It's Clear All the Blacks Are Still Men." *The Root*, July 16, 2015, https://www.theroot.com/in-ta-nehisi-coates-new-book-it-s-clear-all-the-black-1790860550.

Denham, Jess. "Marvel Announces Black Captain America After Confirming New Female Thor." *The Independent*, July 17, 2014. https://www.the-independent.com/arts-entertainment/books/news/marvel-announces-black-captain-america-after-confirming-new-female-thor-9611345.html.

Desta, Yohana. "Black Panther Is Officially a $1 Billion Hit." *Vanity Fair*, March 11, 2018. https://www.vanityfair.com/hollywood/2018/03/black-panther-box-office-billion-dollars-china-marvel.

Diaz, Eric. "Marvel's Black Panther #1 Is Full of Potential." *Nerdist*, April 4, 2016. https://nerdist.com/article/review-marvels-black-panther-1-is-full-of-potential/.

Dockterman, Eliana. "Behind Marvel's Decision to Create These Controversial Female Superheroes." *TIME*, August 28, 2015. https://time.com/4014894/marvel-female-superheroes-thor-ms-marvel/.

Dockterman, Eliana. "Marvel's Editor on What You Need to Know About Ta-Nehisi Coates' Black Panther." *TIME*, April 6, 2016. https://time.com/4281426/ta-nehisi-coates-black-panther-marvel/.

Dockterman, Eliana. "Ta-Nehisi Coates Is Expanding the Black Panther Universe with The Crew." *TIME*, January 20, 2017. https://time.com/4639911/ta-nehisi-coates-is-expanding-the-black-panther-universe-with-the-crew/.

Douglass, Frederick. *Narrative of the Life of Frederick Douglass, an American Slave*. 1845 rpt. Barnes & Noble Classics, 2003.

Driscoll, Beth, and Claire Squires. *The Frankfurt Book Fair and Bestseller Business*. Cambridge University Press, 2020.

Du Bois, W. E. B. "The Negro in Art: How Shall He Be Portrayed?" *The Crisis* 32, no. 6 (October 1926): 219–20, 232.

Du Bois, W. E. B. "Strivings of the Negro People." *The Atlantic*, August 1897. https://www.theatlantic.com/magazine/archive/1897/08/strivings-of-the-negro-people/305446/.

Duffy, Josie. "'Between the World and Me' Is for All of Us, Even If It Is Not About All of Us." Rewire News Group, July 15, 2015. https://rewirenewsgroup.com/2015/07/15/world-us-even-us/.

Eaton, Cheryl Lynn. *Black Panther: Blood Hunt* #1. Marvel Comics, May 29, 2024.

Egan, Toussaint. "Black Panther #1 by Ta-Nehisi Coates & Brian Stelfreeze." *Paste Magazine*, April 4, 2016. https://www.pastemagazine.com/comics/black-panther/advance-review-black-panther-1-by-ta-nehisi-coates.

"Ending Radical and Wasteful Government DEI Programs and Preferencing." The White House, January 20, 2025. https://www.whitehouse.gov/presidential-actions/2025/01/ending-radical-and-wasteful-government-dei-programs-and-preferencing/.

Ernst, Douglas. "Black Panther #1: Ta-Nehisi Coates Debut a Mixed Bag for Marvel Fans." *Douglas Ernst Blog*, April 21, 2016. https://douglasernst.blog/2016/04/21/black-panther-1-ta-nehisi-coates-debut-a-mixed-bag-for-marvel-fans/.

Evans, William H. "About Us." *Black Nerd Problems*, 2015. https://blacknerdproblems.com/bnp/about-us/.

Evans, William H. "Black Panther #1 Review." *Black Nerd Problems*, April 6, 2016. https://blacknerdproblems.com/black-panther-1-review/.

Ewing, Eve. "Flying While Black: Two Creators on Inventing (and Reinventing) Black Superheroes." *The New York Times*, April 23, 2021. https://www.nytimes.com/2021/04/23/arts/black-superheroes-comic-books.html.

Ewing, Eve, Mark Chater, and Chris Allen. *Black Panther Vol. 2: Reign at Dusk*. New York: Marvel Universe, 2024.

Fallik, Dawn. "Ta-Nehisi Coates, Jen Bartel to Partner on New Comic Book." *The Inquirer*, October 11, 2017. https://www.inquirer.com/philly/entertainment/geek/exclusive-ta-nehisi-coates-jen-bartel-to-partner-on-new-comic-book-20171011.html.

Fienberg, Daniel. "Marvel's 'Luke Cage': TV Review." *The Hollywood Reporter*, September 27, 2016. https://www.hollywoodreporter.com/tv/tv-reviews/marvels-luke-cage-review-932977/.

Fujikawa, Jenn. "The Architectural Inspirations Behind Wakanda in Marvel Studios' 'Black Panther.'" *Marvel*, February 9, 2018. https://www.marvel.com/articles/movies/the-architectural-inspirations-behind-wakanda-in-marvel-studios-black-panther.

Fuller, Hoyt. "Toward a Black Aesthetic (1968)." *Within the Circle: An Anthology of African American Literary Criticism from the Harlem Renaissance to the Present*, ed. by Angelyn Mitchell. Durham, NC: Duke University Press, 1994, 199–206.

Garcia, Arturo. "Ta-Nehisi Coates's Black Panther Is a Hopeful First Step for Diversity at Marvel." *The Guardian*, September 23, 2015. https://www.theguardian.com/books/2015/sep/23/ta-nehisi-coates-black-panther-marvel-diversity.

Gayle, Addison, Jr., Ed. *The Black Aesthetic*. New York: Doubleday, 1971.

Gearino, Dan. *Comic Shop: The Retail Mavericks Who Gave Us a New Geek Culture*. Athens, OH: Swallow Press, 2017.

Generally, Deron. "*Black Panther* #1 Review." *The Super Powered Fancast*, May 23, 2018. https://www.superpoweredfancast.com/black-panther-1-review/.

Gerding, Stephen. "C2E2: Marvel's 'Black Panther' #1 Tops 300K in Sales." *CBR*, March 18, 2016. https://www.cbr.com/c2e2-marvels-black-panther-1-tops-300k-in-sales/.

Gray, Jonathan W. "A Conflicted Man: An Interview with Ta-Nehisi Coates About Black Panther." *The New Republic*, April 4, 2016. https://newrepublic.com/article/132355/conflicted-man-interview-ta-nehisi-coates-black-panther.

Griepp, Milton. "Marvel's David Gabriel on the 2016 Market Shift." *ICv2*, March 31, 2017. https://icv2.com/articles/news/view/37152/marvels-david-gabriel-2016-market-shift.

Griepp, Milton. "World According to Griepp: Why Is It Called the Comics 'Direct Market?'" *ICv2*, March 22, 2023. https://icv2.com/articles/columns/view/53638/world-according-griepp-why-is-it-called-comics-direct-market.

Grossman, Claire, Stephanie Young, and Juliana Spahr. "Literature's Vexed Democratization." *American Literary History* 33, no. 2 (Summer 2021): 298–319. https://muse.jhu.edu/pub/8/article/797935.

Grossman, Claire, Stephanie Young, and Juliana Spahr. "Who Gets to Be a Writer?" *Public Books*, April 15, 2021. https://www.publicbooks.org/who-gets-to-be-a-writer/.

Gustines, George Gene. "Marvel Entertainment Names New Editor in Chief." *The New York Times*, November 17, 2017. https://www.nytimes.com/2017/11/17/books/marvel-entertainment-names-new-editor-in-chief.html.

Gustines, George Gene. "Marvel's World of Wakanda Will Spotlight Women, on the Page and Behind It." *The New York Times*, July 22, 2016. https://www.nytimes.com/2016/07/23/books/black-panther-marvel-comics-roxane-gay-ta-nehisi-coates-wakanda.html.

Gustines, George Gene. "Ta-Nehisi Coates to Write Black Panther Comic for Marvel." *The New York Times*, September 22, 2015. https://www.nytimes.com/2015/09/23/books/ta-nehisi-coates-to-write-black-panther-comic-for-marvel.html.

Hahn, Steven. *A Nation Under Our Feet: Black Political Struggles in the Rural South from Slavery to the Great Migration*. Cambridge, MA: Harvard University Press, 2003.

Harris, Trudier. *The Scary Mason-Dixon Line: African American Writers and the South*. Baton Rogue: LSU Press, 2013.

Hayes, Chris. *The Sirens' Call: How Attention Became the World's Most Endangered Resource*. New York: Penguin Press, 2025.

Heer, Jeet. "Superhero Comics Have a Race Problem. Can Ta-Nehisi Coates Fix It?" *The New Republic*, September 22, 2015. https://newrepublic.com/article/122897/superhero-comics-have-race-problem-can-ta-nehisi-coates-fix-it.

Hickman, Jonathan. *Fantastic Four* #607. Marvel Comics, June 13, 2012.

Hickman, Jonathan. *Fantastic Four* #608. Marvel Comics, July 18, 2012.

Hickman, Jonathan. *New Avengers* #1. Marvel Comics, January 2, 2013.

Hickman, Jonathan. *New Avengers* #18. Marvel Comics, May 14, 2014.

Hickman, Jonathan. *Secret Wars* #9. Marvel Comics, January 13, 2016.

Hilton, Shani O. "The Black Experience Isn't Just About Men." *BuzzFeed*, July 10, 2015, https://www.buzzfeed.com/shani/between-the-world-and-she.

Holub, Christian. "Black Panther: A Nation Under Our Feet, Book Two: EW Review." *Entertainment Weekly*, January 31, 2017. https://ew.com/books/2017/01/31/black-panther-nation-under-our-feet-book-two-ew-review/..

Holub, Christian. "Roxanne Gay Will Write a 'Black Panther' Spin-Off Comic About the Women of Wakanda." *Entertainment Weekly*. https://ew.com/article/2016/07/22/roxane-gay-black-panther/.

Horne, Karama. "Indie Comics Spotlight: Alitha Martinez Has Been Here Before." *Syfy*, February 15, 2018. https://web.archive.org/web/20180318010236/https://www.syfy.com/syfywire/indie-comics-spotlight-alitha-martinez-has-been-here-before.

Horne, Karama. "Riri, Rhodey and Re-skinning: How Marvel Is Misunderstanding Diversity." The Blerd Gurl, July 8, 2016. https://theblerdgurl.com/comics/riri-rhodey-re-skinning-marvel-misunderstanding-diversity/.

Howard, Sheena C., Ronald L. Jackson II. *Black Comics: Politics of Race and Representation*. New York: Bloomsbury Academic, 2013.

Hudson, Laura. "It's Time to Get Real About Racial Diversity in Comics." *Wired*, July 25, 2015. https://www.wired.com/2015/07/diversity-in-comics/.

Hughes, Joseph. "Outrage Deferred: On the Lack of Black Writers in the Comic Book Industry." *Comics Alliance*, February 4, 2013. https://comicsalliance.com/black-writers-comic-book-industry/.

Iger, Robert. *The Ride of a Lifetime: Lessons Learned from 15 Years as CEO of the Walt Disney Company*. New York: Random House, 2019.

Illidge, Joseph Phillip. "Between Wakanda and Us - Ta-Nehisi Coates' 'Black Panther' & the Uncertain Future." *CBR*, September 23, 2015. https://www.cbr.com/between-wakanda-and-us-ta-nehisi-coates-black-panther-the-uncertain-future/.

Illidge, Joseph Phillip. "The Color Barrier: A Message of Comics, Diversity and Hope." *CBR*, February, 6. 2014. https://www.cbr.com/the-color-barrier-a-message-of-comics-diversity-hope/.

Illidge, Joseph Phillip. "Marvel's Black Panther, Wakandan Colors and the Forgotten Warrior." *Comic Book Resources*, April 11, 2016. https://www.cbr.com/marvels-black-panther-wakandan-colors-and-the-forgotten-warrior/.

Illidge, Joseph Phillip. "Nighthawk's Fatal Battle Against a Civil War and a Rebirth." *CBR*, August 29, 2016. https://www.cbr.com/nighthawks-fatal-battle-against-a-civil-war-and-a-rebirth/.

Ito, Robert. "Ta-Nehisi Coates Helps a New Panther Leave Its Print." *The New York Times*, March 31, 2016. https://www.nytimes.com/2016/04/03/movies/ta-nehisi-coates-helps-a-new-panther-leave-its-print.html.

Jackson, Tim. *Pioneering Cartoonists of Color*. Jackson: University Press of Mississippi, 2016.

Jasper, Marykate. "Marvel VP Said Sales Slumped Because 'People Didn't Want Any More Diversity.'" *The Mary Sue*, April 1, 2017. https://www.themarysue.com/marvel-vp-no-more-diversity/.

Johnson, Jason. "How io9's Evan Narcisse Went from Writing About Comics to Writing Rise of the Black Panther." *The Root*, January 10, 2018. https://www.theroot.com/how-io9-s-evan-narcisse-went-from-writing-about-comics-1821912630.

Johnston, Rich. "Black Panther #1 and Empress #1 Sell Out, Go to Second Print." *Bleeding Cool*, April 8, 2016. https://bleedingcool.com/comics/black-panther-1-and-empress-1-sell-out-go-to-second-print/.

Johnston, Rich. "Is Ta-Nehisi Coates Writing a New Comic Book for Marvel?" *Bleeding Cool*, August 1, 2015. https://bleedingcool.com/comics/is-ta-nehisi-coates-writing-a-new-comic-book-for-marvel/.

Johnston, Rich. "Priest Credits Joe Quesada and Jimmy Palmiotti for Dora Milaje." *Bleeding Cool*, October 6, 2018. https://bleedingcool.com/comics/joe-quesada-christopher-priest-marvel-knights-cup-o-joe-nycc-201/.

Johnston, Rich. "Storm Gets a Series from Ta-Nehisi Coates and Jen Bartel for Marvel Comics." *Bleeding Cool News*, October 13, 2017. https://bleedingcool.com/comics/storm-gets-series-ta-nehisi-coates-jen-bartel-marvel-comics/.

Johnston, Rich. "The Top Ten Bestselling Comics of 2016—In The Direct Market." *Bleeding Cool*, December 11, 2016. https://bleedingcool.com/comics/2016s-top-ten-comics-by-sales-in-the-direct-market/.

Johnston, Rich. "Warner Bros. Black Superman Movie Sees DC Comics eBay Sales Explode." *Bleeding Cool News*, February 28, 2021. https://bleedingcool.com/comics/warner-bros-black-superman-movie-sees-dc-comics-ebay-sales-explodes/.

Johnston, Rich. "Yes, Ta-Nehisi Coates Is Writing a New Comic Book for Marvel." *Bleeding Cool*, September 22, 2015. http://bleedingcool.com/comics/yes-ta-nehisi-coates-is-writing-a-new-comic-book-for-marvel-black-panther-with-brian-stelfreeze-for-a-year/.

Jordan, June. "Poem About My Rights." *Directed by Desire: The Collected Poems of June Jordan*. Copper Canyon Press, 2012, 309–12.

Keene, John. "Ta-Nehisi Coates Re-imagines the Black Panther Comics." *Frieze*, June 1, 2016. https://www.frieze.com/article/books-48.

Keeper, Sam. "Starkitecture: Should We Be Worried About Black Panther's Concept Art?" *Storming the Ivory Tower*, February 28, 2017. https://www.stormingtheivorytower.com/2017/02/starkitecture-should-we-be-worried.html.

Kit, Borys. "Ta-Nehisi Coates to Narrate 'Black Panther' Marvel Recaps (Exclusive Video)." *The Hollywood Reporter*, May 3, 2016. https://www.hollywoodreporter.com/movies/movie-news/ta-nehisi-coates-narrate-black-889698/.

Kit, Borys, and Aaron Couch. "Ta-Nehisi Coates to Write New Superman Movie for Warner Bros." *The Hollywood Reporter*, February 26, 2021. https://www.hollywoodreporter.com/movies/movie-news/ta-nehisi-coates-to-write-new-superman-movie-for-warner-bros-4139376/.

Klein, Ezra. "Ezra Klein Interviews Ta-Nehisi Coates and Nikole Hannah-Jones." *The New York Times*, July 30, 2021. https://www.nytimes.com/2021/07/30/opinion/ezra-klein-podcast-ta-nehisi-coates-nikole-hannah-jones.html.

Lachenal, Jessica. "Roxane Gay Confirms *World of Wakanda*'s Disappointing Cancellation." *The Mary Sue*, June 13, 2017. https://www.themarysue.com/world-of-wakanda-cancelled/.

Lapin-Bertone, Joshua. "Marvel vs. DC: The Key Differences and Distinctions Between the Two Superhero and Comics Titans." *Pop Verse*, April 1, 2024. https://www.thepopverse.com/marvel-dc-differences-comics-movies-tv.

Lebron, Christopher. "Black Panther Is Not the Movie We Deserve." *Boston Review*, February 17, 2018. https://www.bostonreview.net/articles/christopher-lebron-black-panther/.

Liang, Huiying, "'Keep Chaos Out, Order In': Grid and Architectural Space in Colson Whitehead's *Zone One*." *The Explicator* 82, no. 4 (2024): 217–22. https://www.

researchgate.net/publication/382482303_Keep_Chaos_Out_Order_In_Grid_and_ Architectural_Space_in_Colson_Whitehead's_Zone_One.

Light, L. E. H. "Black Panther #1: The Dora Milaje Come Center Stage." *Black Nerd Problems*, April 7, 2016. https://blacknerdproblems.com/black-panther-1-the-dora-milaje-come-center-stage/.

Long, Kelle. "How the Black Panther Production Designer Rooted the World's Most Advanced Nation in African Culture." *Motion Pictures*, February 14, 2018. https://www.motionpictures.org/2018/02/black-panther-production-designer-rooted-worlds-advanced-nation-african-culture/.

Longworth, Oz. "Black Panther #4 Review." *Black Nerd Problems*, July 28, 2016. https://blacknerdproblems.com/black-panther-4-review/.

Longworth, Oz. "Black Panther #10 Review." *Black Nerd Problems*, January 25, 2017. https://blacknerdproblems.com/black-panther-10-review/.

Longworth, Oz. "Black Panther #25 Review." *Black Nerd Problems*, May 28, 2021. https://blacknerdproblems.com/black-panther-25-review/.

Lorde, Audre. "The Master's Tools Will Never Dismantle the Master's House." *Sister Outsider*. New York: Penguin, 2020, 110–13.

Lorde, Audre. *Zami: A New Spelling of My Name*. New York: Penguin, 1982.

Lozada, Carlos. "The Radical Chic of Ta-Nehisi Coates." *The Washington Post*, July 16, 2015. https://www.washingtonpost.com/news/book-party/wp/2015/07/16/the-radical-chic-of-ta-nehisi-coates/.

Maberry, Jonathan. *Doomwar #5*. Marvel Comics, June 30, 2010.

MacDonald, Heidi. "Why Aren't There More Black Writers in the Comics Industry?" *Comics Beat*, February 5, 2013. https://www.comicsbeat.com/why-arent-there-more-black-writers-in-the-comics-industry/.

Magnett, Chase. "*Black Panther #19*." *ComicBook.com*, December 18, 2019. https://comicbook.com/comics/news/new-comic-reviews-dc-marvel-image-302578/~:text=BLACK%20PANTHER%20%2319,%E2%80%94%20Chase%20 Magnett.

Mangum, Trey. "Ta-Nehisi Coates to Write Upcoming Superman Film from DC and Warner Bros." *Blavity*, February 26, 2021. https://blavity.com/entertainment/ta-nehisi-coates-superman-dc-warner-bros-film.

Manning, Shaun. "Seeley Reveals Why He Quit Marvel's Blade." *CBR*, September 20, 2016. https://www.cbr.com/seeley-reveals-why-he-quit-marvels-blade/.

Marable, Manning. *Malcolm X: A Life of Reinvention*. New York: Viking, 2011.

Marshall, Kerry James. "Marvel's Black Panther." *Art Forum*, September 1, 2016. https://www.artforum.com/columns/marvels-black-panther-230462/.

Martin, Charles. "*Black Panther #1 Review*." *Comics: The Gathering*, May 23, 2018. http://www.comicsthegathering.com/review/charles-martin/11624/black-panther-1-review.

Martin, Charles. "Black Panther #22 Review." *Comics: The Gathering*, March 25, 2020. http://www.comicsthegathering.com/review/charles-martin/13847/black-panther-22-review.

Massie, Victoria M. "You Need to Read Sonia Sotomayor's Devastating, Ta-Nehisi Coates-Citing Supreme Court Dissent." *Vox*, June 20, 2016. https://www.vox.com/2016/6/20/11976560/sonia-sotomayor-dissent-supreme-court.

McClurg, Jocelyn. "Ta-Nehisi Coates Writes a Best Seller." *USA Today*, July 22, 2015. https://www.usatoday.com/story/life/books/2015/07/22/ta-nehisi-coates-between--world-and-me-harper-lee-el-james-usa-today-best-selling-books/30471757/.

McDuffie, Dwayne. *Icon* #1. DC Comics, May 1993.

McGregor, Don. *Jungle Action* Vol. 2, #6. Marvel Comics, June 26, 1973.

McGruder, Aaron. *A Right to Be Hostile: The Boondocks Treasury*. Three Rivers Press, 2003.

McKinsey & Company. "What Is Diversity, Equity, and Inclusion?" *McKinsey & Company*, August 17, 2022. https://www.mckinsey.com/~/media/mckinsey/featured%20 insights/mckinsey%20explainers/what%20is%20diversity%20equity%20and%20 inclusion/what_is_diversity_equity_and_inclusion.pdf.

McMillan, Graeme. "Giving Us a Female Thor and Black Captain America Isn't Enough." *Wired*, July 17, 2014. https://www.wired.com/2014/07/captain-america-announcement/.

McMillan, Graeme. "Marvel Announces New 'Black Panther' Comic Book Series to Be Written by Ta-Nehisi Coates." *The Hollywood Reporter*, September 22, 2015. https://www.hollywoodreporter.com/movies/movie-news/ta-nehisi-coates-writing-black-826209/.

McMillan, Graeme. "Ta-Nehisi Coates Spins Out Third 'Black Panther' Comic Book for Marvel." *The Hollywood Reporter*, January 20, 2017. https://www.hollywoodreporter.com/movies/movie-news/ta-nehisi-coates-spins-third-black-panther-comic-book-marvel-966598/.

McMillan, Graeme. "Ta-Nehisi Coates Writing Captain America Comic Book Series." *The Hollywood Reporter*, February 28, 2018. https://www.hollywoodreporter.com/movies/movie-news/ta-nehisi-coates-writing-captain-america-comic-book-series-1089302/.

McSweeney, Terence. *Black Panther: Interrogating a Cultural Phenomenon*. University Press of Mississippi, 2021.

Micheline, J. A. "Creating Responsibility: Comics Has a Race Problem." *Comics Alliance*, July 17, 2015. https://comicsalliance.com/creating-responsibly-comics-race-problem/.

Micheline, J. A. "Ta-Nehisi Coates on 'Black Panther' and Creating a Comic That Reflects the Black Experience." *Vice*, April 5, 2016. https://www.vice.com/en/article/ta-nehisi-coates-talks-about-black-panther-and-writing-from-a-black-experience/.

Micheline, J. A. "The White Privilege, White Audacity, and White Priorities of Strange Fruit #1." *Women Write About Comics*, July 8, 2015. https://womenwriteaboutcomics.com/2015/07/the-white-privilege-white-audacity-and-white-priorities-of-strange-fruit-1/.

Miller, John Jackson. "2018 Comic Book Sales to Comics Shops." *Comichron*, January 2019. https://www.comichron.com/monthlycomicssales/2018.html.

Miller, John Jackson. "May 2018 Comic Book Sales to Comics Shops." *Comichron*, May 30, 2018. https://www.comichron.com/monthlycomicssales/2018/2018-05.html.

Minsker, Evan. "Marvel Comics Pay Homage to Hip-Hop Albums with Variant Covers." *Pitchfork*, July 14, 2014. https://pitchfork.com/news/60386-marvel-comics-pay-homage-to-hip-hop-albums-with-variant-covers/.

Mitchell, Nigel. "'Black Panther' Director Ryan Coogler Says Marvel's Current Comics Influencing His Film." *Comic Book Resources*, July 25, 2016. https://www.cbr.com/black-panther-director-ryan-coogler-says-marvels-current-comics-influencing-his-film/.

Morris, Wesley, and Jenna Wortham. "Still Processing: We Sink Our Claws into 'Black Panther' with Ta-Nehisi Coates." *The New York Times*, March 16, 2018. https://www.nytimes.com/2018/03/16/podcasts/still-processing-we-sink-our-claws-into-black-panther-with-ta-nehisi-coates.html.

Nama, Adilifu. *Super Black: American Pop Culture and Black Superheroes*. Austin: University of Texas Press, 2011.

Narcisse, Evan. *Black Panther: Wakanda Atlas*. New York: DK/Penguin Random House, 2022.

Narcisse, Evan. Introduction. *Wakanda: World of Black Panther Omnibus*. New York: Marvel Entertainment, 2022.

Narcisse, Evan. "Marvel's Super-Hero Hip-Hop Covers Are Available for Free." *Kotaku*, February 4, 2016. https://kotaku.com/marvel-s-super-hero-hip-hop-covers-are-available-for-fr-1757200483.

Narcisse, Evan. "'The Miracle Is Wakanda': Ta-Nehisi Coates Says Goodbye to *Black Panther*." *Polygon*, May 26, 2021. https://www.polygon.com/interviews/22454722/black-panther-comics-ending-ta-nehisi-coates-interview/.

Narcisse, Evan. *Rise of the Black Panther* Vol. 1, #1. Marvel Comics, January 3, 2018.

Narcisse, Evan. "Spoiler Space: More from Ta-Nehisi Coates on Black Panther." *Kotaku*, April 6, 2016. https://kotaku.com/spoiler-space-more-from-ta-nehisi-coates-on-black-pant-1769472432.

Narcisse, Evan. "Ta-Nehisi Coates Explains How He's Turning Black Panther into a Superhero Again." *Gizmodo*, September 14, 2016. https://gizmodo.com/ta-nehisi-coates-explains-how-hes-turning-black-panther-1786632598.

Narcisse, Evan. "Ta-Nehisi Coates Is Trying to Do Right by Marvel Comics' First Black Superhero." *Kotaku*, April 7, 2016. https://kotaku.com/marvel-s-super-hero-hip-hop-covers-are-available-for-fr-1757200483.

Narcisse, Evan. "Ta-Nehisi Coates Will Write Marvel's New Black Panther Comic." *Kotaku*, September 22, 2015. https://kotaku.com/ta-nehisi-coates-will-write-marvels-new-black-panther-c-1732376928.

Nardi, Paola A. "'They Lived There Because They Were Poor and Black': Spatial Injustice in Toni Morrison's *The Bluest Eye*." *Journal of African American Studies* 26 (2022): 401–12. https://link.springer.com/article/10.1007/s12111-022-09593-3.

Neal, Larry. "The Black Arts Movement (1968)." *Within the Circle: An Anthology of African American Literary Criticism from the Harlem Renaissance to the Present*, ed. Angelyn Mitchell. Durham, NC: Duke University Press, 1994, 184–98.

Neal, Mark Anthony. *Looking for Leroy: Illegible Black Masculinities*. New York: New York University Press, 2013.

Nelson, Alondra. "Afrofuturism: Past-Future Visions." *Color Lines* 3, no. 1 (Spring 2000.): 34–37.

Nevins, Jake. "Ta-Nehisi Coates to Write Marvel's New Captain America Comics." *The Guardian*, February 28, 2018. https://www.theguardian.com/books/2018/feb/28/ta-nehisi-coates-to-write-marvels-new-captain-america-comics.

Nicolas, Sarah. "The Books of Marvel's Luke Cage." *Book Riot*, October 4, 2016. https://bookriot.com/the-books-of-marvels-luke-cage/.

NPR Staff. "Ta-Nehisi Coates Hopes 'Black Panther' Will Be Some Kid's 'Spider-Man.'" *NPR Code Switch*, April 6, 2016. https://www.npr.org/sections/codeswitch/2016/04/06/473224606/a-reluctant-king-ta-nehisi-coates-takes-on-marvels-black-panther.

Ohlheiser, Abby. "Why 'Social Justice Warrior,' a Gamergate Insult, Is Now a Dictionary Entry." *The Washington Post*, October 7, 2015. https://www.washingtonpost.com/news/the-intersect/wp/2015/10/07/why-social-justice-warrior-a-gamergate-insult-is-now-a-dictionary-entry/.

Okorafor, Nnedi. *Shuri* #9. Marvel Comics, June 19, 2019.

Okorafor, Nnedi. *Shuri* #10. Marvel Comics, July 24, 2019.

Opam, Kwame. "Captain America No. 1, by Ta-Nehisi Coates, Annotated." *The New York Times*, July 4, 2018. https://www.nytimes.com/2018/07/04/books/captain-america-ta-nehisi-coates-annotated.html.

Orr, Christopher. "Black Panther Is More than a Superhero Movie." *The Atlantic*, February 16, 2018. https://www.theatlantic.com/entertainment/archive/2018/02/black-panther-review/553508/.

Oyola, Osvaldo. "Between the World and Wakanda: Ta-Nehisi Coates and Brian Stelfreeze's 'Black Panther.'" *Los Angeles Review of Books*, December 27, 2016. https://lareviewofbooks.org/article/between-the-world-and-wakanda-ta-nehisi-coates-and-brian-stelfreezes-black-panther/.

Parramore, Lynn Stuart. "Why Does a White CIA Agent Play the Hero to Killmonger's Villain in *Black Panther*?" *NBC News*, March 11, 2018. https://www.nbcnews.com/think/opinion/why-does-white-cia-agent-play-hero-killmonger-s-villain-ncna855401.

Partridge, Justin. "CAPTAIN AMERICA #1 'a Triumph for One of Marvel's A-Listers.'" *Newsarama*, July 3, 2018. https://www.newsarama.com/40652-best-shots-review-captain-america-1.html.

Patterson, Sala Elise. "2018 Rouse Visiting Artist Hannah Beachler on Her History-Making Oscar Nomination." *Harvard Graduate School of Design*, February 22, 2019. https://www.gsd.harvard.edu/2019/02/2018-rouse-visiting-artist-hannah-beachler-on-her-history-making-oscar-nomination/.

Peterson, Matthew. "*Black Panther* #2 Review." *Major Spoilers*, July 3, 2018. https://majorspoilers.com/2021/06/01/black-panther-25-review/.

Peterson, Matthew. "*Black Panther* #25 Review." *Major Spoilers*, June 1, 2021. https://majorspoilers.com/2021/12/28/black-panther-2-review-2/.

Polo, Susana. "Marvel Comics Announces Line-Wide Relaunch 'Fresh Start.'" *Polygon*, February 20, 2018. https://www.polygon.com/comics/2018/2/20/17031924/marvel-fresh-start-relaunch-announcement/.

Polo, Susana. "Ta-Nehisi Coates to Write Captain America, Starting on July 4." *Polygon*, February 28, 2018. https://www.polygon.com/comics/2018/2/28/17062320/ta-nehisi-coates-to-write-captain-america-starting-on-july-4/.

Powell, Troy. "Black Panther #1." *Graphic Policy*, April 11, 2016. https://graphicpolicy.com/2016/04/11/review-black-panther1/.

Prickett, Sarah Nicole, and Jody Rosen. "Sarah Jessica Parker and Ta-Nehisi Coates, on New Literary Paths." *The New York Times*, October 5, 2016. https://www.nytimes.com/2016/10/05/t-magazine/entertainment/sarah-jessica-parker-sjp-hogarth-tanehisi-coates-black-panther.html.

Priest, Christopher. *Black Panther* #1. Marvel Comics, November 1, 1998.

Pulliam-Moore, Charles. "Black Panther Writer Ta-Nehisi Coates Wants Better for Creators Bringing These Stories to Life." *Gizmodo*, May 28, 2021. https://gizmodo.com/black-panther-writer-ta-nehisi-coates-wants-better-for-1846994018.

Radulovic, Petrana. "Superman Movie Reboot in Works with Ta-Nehisi Coates, J.J. Abrams." *Polygon*, February 26, 2021. https://www.polygon.com/movies/2021/2/26/22303271/superman-movie-reboot-ta-nehisi-coates-jj-abrams/.

Rambsy, Howard II. *Bad Men: Creative Touchstones of Black Writers*. Charlottesville: University of Virginia Press, 2020.

Rambsy, Howard II. "The Coverage of Colson Whitehead's *The Underground Railroad*." *Cultural Front*, August 3, 2016. https://www.culturalfront.org/search?q=underground+railroad.

Rambsy, Howard II. "Coverage of Ta-Nehisi Coates and *Between the World and Me*." *Cultural Front*, June 26, 2015. https://www.culturalfront.org/search?q=coverage+of+ta-nehisi+coates+and+between+the+world+and+me.

Rambsy, Howard II, and Kenton Rambsy. "How the *New York Times* Covers Black Writers." *Public Books*, October 12, 2022. https://www.publicbooks.org/how-the-new-york-times-covers-black-writers/.

Rambsy, Kenton. "Edward P. Jones, a Black Storytelling Demographer." *Journal of the Short Story in English* (Spring 2024): 81–97. https://journals.openedition.org/jsse/4337?lang=en.

Rambsy, Kenton. "Edward P. Jones—The Neighborhood Preservationist." *Fire!!!* 5, no. 2 (Spring 2020): 40–52. https://www.jstor.org/stable/10.5323/48573837.

Rambsy, Kenton. *The Geographies of African American Short Fiction*. University Press of Mississippi, 2022.

Raymond, Charles Nicholas. "Marvel's Latest Relaunch Sends Black Panther into Space." *Screen Rant*, February 21, 2018. https://screenrant.com/black-panther-marvel-comics-relaunch-space/.

Reed, Robert. "Best Shots Advance Review: BLACK PANTHER #1." *Newsarama*, April 4, 2016.

Reed, Robert. "Best Shots Review: *Black Panther* #2's Acuna 'Gives the Book an Epic Quality'." *Newsarama*, July 2, 2018.

Reed, Robert. "*Black Panther* #169." *Newsarama*, January 29, 2018.

Reed, Robert. "Civil War Gives Way to War of Ideas in Black Panther #12." *Newsrama*, March 22, 2017.

Regalado, Aldo J. *Bending Steel: Modernity and the American Superhero*. Jackson: University Press of Mississippi, 2015.

Reid-Cleveland, Keith. "Captain America #1 Review." *Black Nerd Problems*, July 5, 2018. https://blacknerdproblems.com/captain-america-1-review/.

Richardson, Trevor. "*Black Panther* #1 (2018) Review." *AIPT*, May 23, 2018. https://aiptcomics.com/2018/05/23/black-panther-1-2018-review/.

Riesman, Abraham Josephine. "Ta-Nehisi Coates Will Write *Captain America* for Marvel Comics." *Vulture*, February 28, 2018. https://www.vulture.com/2015/09/ta-nehisi-coates-black-panther.html.

Riesman, Abraham Josephine. "Ta-Nehisi Coates Writing Black Panther Is the Year's Biggest Comics News." *Vulture*, September 22, 2015. https://www.vulture.com/2015/09/ta-nehisi-coates-black-panther.html.

Rivera, Joshua. "Black Panther, Marvel's First Black Superhero, Is Now the Star of the Year's Most Important Comic." *GQ*, April 12, 2016. https://www.gq.com/story/black-panther-ta-nehisi-coates.

Rivera, Joshua. "Marvel's New Hip-Hop Covers Highlight Comics' Big Diversity Problem." *Business Insider*, August 9, 2015. https://www.businessinsider.com/marvel-hip-hop-comics-controversy-2015-7.

Rivera, Joshua. "The New Black Panther Trailer Is a Hell of a Way to Start Your Week." *GQ*, October 16, 2018. https://www.gq.com/story/black-panther-trailer-2.

Rivera, Joshua. "Ta-Nehisi Coates' Black Panther Comic Is a Dream Come True." *GQ*, September 23, 2015. https://www.gq.com/story/ta-nehisi-coates-black-panther-dream-come-true.

Robinson, Joanna. "Luke Cage and the Year Marvel Finally Reckoned with Its Black Audience." *Vanity Fair*, September 29, 2016. https://www.vanityfair.com/hollywood/2016/09/luke-cage-mike-colter-black-panther-netflix-marvel-black-voices.

Robinson, Joanna. "Why Ta-Nahesi [*sic*] Coates Is Such a Strong Choice for Superman." *Vanity Fair*, February 26, 2021. https://www.vanityfair.com/hollywood/2021/02/superman-ta-nehisi-coates-jj-abrams.

Robot Overlord. "[Solicitations] Marvel Comics for May 2018." *Major Spoilers*, February 22, 2018. https://majorspoilers.com/2018/02/22/solicitations-marvel-comics-may-2018/.

Rose-Redwood, Reuben, Natchee Blu Barnd, Annita Hetoevėhotohke'e Lucchesi, Sharon Dias, and Wil Patrick. "Decolonizing the Map: Recentering Indigenous Mappings." *Cartographica* 55, no. 3, (2020): 151–62. https://utppublishing.com/doi/full/10.3138/cart.53.3.intro.

Ross, Elliot. "The Dangers of a Single Book Cover." *Africa Is a Country*, May 7, 2014. https://africasacountry.com/2014/05/the-dangers-of-a-single-book-cover-the-acacia-tree-meme-and-african-literature.

Salkowitz, Rob. "Ta-Nehisi Coates Will Write Marvel's Black Panther." *Forbes*, September 22, 2015. https://www.forbes.com/sites/robsalkowitz/2015/09/22/ta-nehisi-coates-will-write-marvels-black-panther/.

Saturday Night Live. "The Bubble—SNL." YouTube, November 20, 2016. https://www.youtube.com/watch?v=vKOb-kmOgpI.

Sava, Oliver. "Marvel Wises Up, Hires Ta-Nehisi Coates to Write Black Panther Comic." *A. V. Club*, September 22, 2015. https://www.avclub.com/marvel-wises-up-hires-ta-nehisi-coates-to-write-black-179828453.

Schedeen, Jesse. "Black Panther #1 Review." *IGN*, April 7, 2016. https://www.ign.com/articles/2016/04/04/black-panther-1-review.

Schedeen, Jesse. "Marvel's Captain America Relaunch Shows Promise (Captain America #1 Review)." *IGN*, July 4, 2018. https://www.ign.com/articles/2018/07/04/marvels-captain-america-relaunch-shows-promise-captain-america-1-review.

Schenker, Brett. "Black Panther #1." *Graphic Policy*, April 7, 2016. https://graphicpolicy.com/2016/04/07/review-black-panther-1/.

Schenker, Brett. "Review: Captain America #1." *Graphic Policy*, July 4, 2018. https://graphicpolicy.com/2018/07/04/review-captain-america-1-2/.

Schuessler, Jennifer. "Ta-Nehisi Coates's 'Visceral' Take on Being Black in America." *The New York Times*, July 17, 2015. https://www.nytimes.com/2015/07/18/books/ta-nehisi-coatess-visceral-take-on-being-black-in-america.html.

Schwedel, Heather. "There's Been a Run on Anti-Racist Books." *Slate*, June 1, 2020. https://slate.com/culture/2020/06/antiracist-books-sold-out-amazon-george-floyd-protests.html.

Setoodeh, Ramin. "Chadwick Boseman and Ryan Coogler on How *Black Panther* Makes History." *Variety*, February 5, 2018. https://variety.com/2018/film/features/black-panther-chadwick-boseman-ryan-coogler-interview-1202686402/.

Shawl, Nisi. "A Crash Course in the History of Black Science Fiction." *Nisi Shawl*, December 1, 2018. http://www.nisishawl.com/CCHBSF.html.

Shiach, Kieran. "Marvel Legacy: Jason Aaron Explains THAT Black Panther Revelation." *Comic Book Resources*, September 27, 2017. https://www.cbr.com/marvel-legacy-jason-aaron-explains-that-black-panther-revelation/.

Silman, Anna, and Abraham Riesman. "New Captain America Will Be Black, Marvel Announces on Colbert." *Vulture*, July 17, 2014. https://www.vulture.com/2014/07/new-captain-america-will-be-black.html.

Silverberg, Michael. "The Reason Every Book About Africa Has the Same Cover—And It's Not Pretty." *Quartz*, May 12, 2014. https://qz.com/207527/the-reason-every-book-about-africa-has-the-same-cover-and-its-not-pretty.

Singer, Matt. "A New 'Superman' Is Coming from J.J. Abrams and Ta-Nehisi Coates." *ScreenCrush*, February 26, 2021. https://screencrush.com/superman-film-j-j-abrams-ta-nehisi-coates/.

Spahr and Young. "On Poets and Prizes." *ASAP Journal*, November 11, 2020.

Spahr and Young. "The Program Era and the Mainly White Room." *Los Angeles Review of Books*, September 20, 2015. https://asapjournal.com/feature/on-poets-and-prizes-juliana-spahr-and-stephanie-young/.

Stauffer, John, Zoe Trodd, and Celeste-Marie Bernier. *Picturing Frederick Douglass: An Illustrated Biography of the Nineteenth Century's Most Photographed American*. New York: Liveright Publishing Corporation, 2015.

Stein, Daniel. "Ta-Nehisi Coates's *Black Panther* and Afrodiasporic Archives." *Amerikastudien / American Studies* 67, no. 2 (2022): 135–6. https://amst.winter-verlag.de/article/amst/2022/2/5.

Stevens, Simon. "Like so Many (Wildly Varying) Writers on Africa, Adichie Gets the Acacia Tree Sunset Treatment …" Twitter, May 7, 2014. https://x.com/simonmstevens/status/464049317926686720.

"StockX Partners with Marvel to Release Exclusive Black Panther Comic." *StockX*, February 1, 2023. https://stockx.com/about/stockx-partners-with-marvel-to-release-exclusive-black-panther-comic/.

Switzer, Eric. "The DCEU's Black Superman Movie Should Follow the Comics and Make Him the President." *The Gamer*, March 1, 2021. https://www.thegamer.com/black-superman-president-calvin-ellis-dceu-bad-robot-movie/.

SYFY Wire. "The Making of Marvel Knights: Black Panther (Behind The Panel)." YouTube, May 15, 2019. https://www.youtube.com/watch?v=RAkoSLXiuQw.

Sykes, Josh. "Review—Black Panther #16 (Marvel Comics)." *Word of the Nerd*, September 27, 2019. https://web.archive.org/web/20200928140946/https://wordofthenerdonline.com/review-black-panther-16-marvel-comics/.

"Ta-Nehisi Coates to Write Black Panther, but Mainstream Comic Books Still Struggle with Diversity." *LAist*, September 24, 2015. https://laist.com/shows/the-frame/ta-nehisi-coates-to-write-black-panther-but-mainstream-comic-books-still-struggle-with-diversity.

"Ta-Nehisi Coates to Write Black Panther Comic for Marvel." *The New York Times*, September 22, 2015.

Taylor-Guthrie, Danielle, Ed. *Conversations with Toni Morrison*. Jackson: University Press of Mississippi, 1994.

Teutsch, Matthew. "Luke Cage and the African American Literary Tradition." *Black Perspectives*, November 1, 2016. https://www.aaihs.org/luke-cage-and-the-african-american-literary-tradition/.

Thompson, Paul. "Marvel Mixes Hip-Hop with Comic Books to Make New Covers." *XXL*, July 14, 2015. https://www.xxlmag.com/marvel-mixes-hip-hop-with-comic-books-to-make-new-covers/.

Thorsson, Courtney. "*The Chaneysville Incident* and the Research Narrative in Contemporary African American Literature." *Studies in the Novel* 55 no. 1 (Spring 2023): 17–36. https://www.researchgate.net/publication/369750386_The_Chaneysville_Incident_and_the_Research_Narrative_in_Contemporary_African_American_Literature.

Thrasher, Steven. "There Is Much to Celebrate–and Much to Question–About Marvel's Black Panther." *Esquire*, February 20, 2018. https://www.esquire.com/entertainment/movies/a18241993/black-panther-review-politics-killmonger/.

Tillet, Salamishah. "'Black Panther' Brings Hope, Hype and Pride." *The New York Times*, February 9, 2018. https://www.nytimes.com/2018/02/09/movies/black-panther-african-american-fans.html.

"Top 500 Comics—July 2018." *ICv2*, August 13, 2018. https://icv2.com/articles/news/view/41125/top-500-comics-july-2018.

Vujakovic, Peter. "World Weary?" *The Cartographic Journal* 56, no. 2 (2019): 97–100. https://www.tandfonline.com/doi/full/10.1080/00087041.2019.1624004.

Walker, David. "Marvel Has Been Very Supportive… " Twitter, August 27, 2016. https://x.com/DavidWalker1201/status/769574503965863936.

Walker, David. "Marvel Is Making a Reasonable Decision Given the Sales." Twitter, August 28, 2016. https://x.com/DavidWalker1201/status/769764816172953600.

Wang, Yanan. "Ta-Nehisi Coates, 'Black Panther' and Superhero Diversity." *The Washington Post*, September 23, 2015. https://www.washingtonpost.com/news/morning-mix/wp/2015/09/23/ta-nehisi-coates-black-panther-and-superhero-diversity/.

Wanzo, Rebecca. "And All Our Past Decades Have Seen Revolutions: The Long Decolonization of Black Panther." *The Black Scholar*, February 19, 2018. https://www.theblackscholar.org/past-decades-seen-revolutions-long-decolonization-black-panther-rebecca-wanzo/.

Wanzo, Rebecca. *The Content of Our Caricature: African American Comic Art and Political Belonging*. New York: New York University Press, 2020.

Weingarten, Christopher R. "See Two New Marvel Comics Covers Paying Tribute to Run the Jewels." *Rolling Stone*, January 16, 2015. https://www.rollingstone.com/culture/culture-news/see-two-new-marvel-comics-covers-paying-tribute-to-run-the-jewels-45378/.

Whitted, Qiana. *EC Comics: Race, Shock, and Social Protest*. New Brunswick, NJ: Rutgers University Press, 2019.

Williams, Susan. *White Malice: The CIA and the Covert Recolonization of Africa*. New York: PublicAffairs, 2021.

Wood, Robert. "Black Panther Writer Criticizes Marvel's Treatment of Comic Creators." *Screen Rant*, May 27, 2021. https://screenrant.com/ta-nehisi-coates-black-panther-criticize-marvel-disney/.

Woods, Scott. "Ta-Nehisi Coates and the Blackest Black Panther Ever." *Black Nerd Problems*, September 23, 2015. https://blacknerdproblems.com/ta-nehisi-coates-and-the-blackest-black-panther-ever/.

Wu, Tim. *The Attention Merchants: The Epic Scramble to Get Inside Our Heads*. New York: Knopf, 2016.

Yarm, Mark. "Ta-Nehisi Coates Fights the Power—Literally—with Black Panther." *Wired*, April 6, 2016. https://www.wired.com/2016/04/ta-nehisi-coates-black-panther-comics/.

Yehl, Joshua. "Kelly Sue DeConnick Talks Captain Marvel, Pretty Deadly, and the Sexy Lamp Test." *IGN*, June 20, 2013. https://www.ign.com/articles/2013/06/20/kelly-sue-deconnick-talks-captain-marvel-pretty-deadly-and-the-sexy-lamp-test.

Zdarsky, Chip. *Howard the Duck* #10. Marvel Comics, August 31, 2016.

Index